D1605243

*Don Troiani's*

# REGIMENTS & UNIFORMS

## OF THE CIVIL WAR

*Art by Don Troiani*

*Text by Earl J. Coates,
Michael J. McAfee, and Don Troiani*

*With an introduction by Leslie D. Jensen*

STACKPOLE
BOOKS

Published by
STACKPOLE BOOKS
5067 Ritter Road
Mechanicsburg, PA 17055
www.stackpolebooks.com



Printed in China

10 9 8 7 6 5 4 3 2 1

FIRST EDITION



For free information on the artwork and limited edition prints of Don Troiani, contact:
Historical Art Prints
P.O. Box 660
Southbury, CT 06488
203-262-6680
*www.historicalartprints.com*

**Library of Congress Cataloging-in-Publication Data**

Troiani, Don.
Don Troiani's regiments and uniforms of the Civil War / art by Don Troiani ; text by Earl J. Coates, Michael J. McAfee, and Don Troiani ; with an introduction by Leslie D. Jensen.— 1st ed.
p. cm.
Includes bibliographical references (p. ) and index.
ISBN 0-8117-0520-X
1. United States. Army—History—Civil War, 1861–1865—Pictorial works. 2. Confederate States of America. Army—Pictorial works. 3. Soldiers—United States—History—19th century—Pictorial works. 4. Soldiers—Confederate States of America—History—Pictorial works. 5. United States. Army—Uniforms—Pictorial works. 6. Confederate States of America. Army—Uniforms—Pictorial works. 7. United States—History—Civil War, 1861–1865—Regimental histories. 8. United States—History—Civil War, 1861–1865. Art and the war. I. Title: Regiments and uniforms of the Civil War. II. Coates, Earl J. III. McAfee, Michael J. IV. Title.

E491 .T76 2002
973.7'42—dc21

2002018906

*To my enchanting wife, Donna,*
*who cheerfully countenances my nonsense on a daily basis*

# CONTENTS

# AUTHOR'S NOTE

THE SUBJECT OF CIVIL WAR UNIFORMS COULD not be comprehensively covered in a hundred volumes such as this. During the course of the war more than a thousand regiments composed of many more thousands of companies existed, sometimes each with their own distinctive clothing. Confounding the situation further, units often changed their uniforms or components of dress during their term of service. In *Don Troiani's Regiments and Uniforms of the Civil War,* the authors and I have attempted to fabricate a broad overview of interesting regiments and artifacts that represent the main theaters of the war, both early and late. Rather then omitting intriguing units where the available information was sparse at best, we employed some very educated conjecture to fill in the gaps. It is our hope that in the future more specific information will come to light and clarify some of these gray areas.

My longtime friends, Earl J. Coates and Michael J. McAfee, represent the pinnacle of their fields in research, and working with them has always been an enjoyable and enriching experience. Contributing authors Tom Arliskis and David M. Sullivan, also leaders in their areas of study, presented fresh information and ideas. Working with primary source materials, period photography, and original artifacts gave us the opportunity to explore the dress of many units from a multidimensional perspective. Equally important was the wise counsel offered by some of the great Civil War collectors and students of material culture: James C. Frasca, John Henry Kurtz, Paul Loane, Dean Nelson, Michael O'Donnell, John Ockerbloom, among many others. Their decades of practical hands-on experience provided a knowledge that cannot be "book learned."

Posing fully dressed models for all the studies in the book also opened the vista of seeing what some of this stuff really looked like on the soldier. Reading about it is one thing; seeing it is quite another. One of the most challenging problems as an artist was the quest for nearly a hundred individuals to pose for the figure studies in my attempt to impart to each a special character all his own!

As the main topic is uniforms, we have not explored firearms or edged weapons as they are exhaustively covered by many other books. We have touched on accoutrements but not in anything approaching complete coverage, selecting mostly items that augmented illustrated uniforms.

In researching the figure studies, the authors consulted every available source. Despite our more than a hundred years of combined study, we recognize that there's a good chance that another interesting nugget of new or conflicting data, perhaps from an unpublished account or collection, could surface after this book's publication. But that is the way of historical research and, indeed, one of the facets that makes it both frustrating and fascinating. To those who are disappointed that a favorite regiment has been left out, please forgive me, I'll try to get to it in the future!

Don Troiani
Southbury, Connecticut

# ACKNOWLEDGMENTS

I OWE A DEBT OF GRATITUDE TO MY DISTINGUISHED friends Earl J. Coates and Michael J. McAfee, two of the greatest gurus on the subject of Civil War uniforms, who graciously tolerated my ceaseless questions and, as always, shared the fruits of their lifetime research with me. They are genuinely "national treasures."

Particular thanks to contributing authors Tom Arliskis, who provided important primary information on Western units, and David Sullivan, renowned authority on Civil War marines.

Special credit to renowned Civil War author-photographer Michael O'Donnell, for taking many of the fine color photos of artifacts for this book, and to Tracy Studios of Southbury, Connecticut.

The following individuals and institutions also contributed to the creation of this book: Gil Barrett, Bruce Bazelon, Carl Borick, Robert Braun, William Brayton, Maj. William Brown, William L. Brown III, Christopher Bryant, Rene Chartrand, Charles Childs, Dr. Michael Cunningham, Ray Darida, William Erquitt, Dr. David Evans, Robin Feret, James C. Frasca, Joseph Fulginiti, Fred Gaede, Randy Hackenburg, Holly Hageman, Charles Harris, Gary Hendershott, Bruce Hermann, Steven Hill, Robert Hodge, Mark Jaeger, Les Jensen, James L. Kochan, Michael Kramer, Robert K. Krick, John Henry Kurtz, John P. Langellier, William Lazenby, Claude Levet, Paul C. Loane, Howard M. Madaus, Bob McDonald, Edward McGee, Steven McKinney, Michael P. Musick, Col. J. Craig Nannos, Dean Nelson, Donna O'Brien, John Ockerbloom, Stephen Osmun, Larry Page, Ron Palm, Andrew Pells, Nicholas Picerno, Brian Pohanka, Cricket Pohanka, Kenneth Powers, Shannon Pritchard, Pat Ricci, Steven Rogers, Nancy Dearing Rossbacher, A. H. Seibel, Jr., Mark Sherman, Sam Small, Wes Small, James R. H. Spears, David Sullivan, Steve Sylvia, Brendan Synonmon, William Synonmon, Donald Tharpe, Mike Thorson, Warren Tice, Ken Turner, William A. Turner, Cole Unson, James Vance, Michael Vice, Gary Wilkensen, Don Williams, and Michael J. Winey.

The Booth Museum of Western Art, Cartersville, Georgia; Confederate Memorial Hall, New Orleans; Charleston Museum, Charleston, South Carolina; Connecticut Historical Society; Connecticut State Library; New York State Collection; Pamplin Historical Park and the National Museum of the Civil War Soldier; Middlesex County Historical Society; the Company of Military Historians; the Nelsonian Institute; *North South Trader* magazine; The Horse Soldier; The Union Drummer Boy; and the West Point Museum, United States Military Academy.

# INTRODUCTION

FOR MANY, THE AMERICAN CIVIL WAR REMAINS THE most important and the most fascinating of all the conflicts of the American past. It has been said to be the defining moment of our history; before which we were different groups of people living and competing in the same territory; after which we were one nation. The war came at a time, in the mid-nineteenth century, when there was a singular confluence of old and new. It was the last of the old Napoleonic-style wars, perhaps the last war where the old romantic values, the code of the gentleman, and the selflessness of true nobility held sway, and at the same time a modern slaughter of talent and youth and hope that only led onward to the mud of 1918 and the horror of World War II. It was a war of the musket and the ironclad warship, the horse and the railroad, the rope tension drum and the telegraph. Today, we may tend to look back on the veterans of that war with a particular admiration and a particular familiarity, for the nineteenth century was a literate age that has left us with a bounty of letters, journals, diaries, and reminiscences. It is possible, or at least we may believe it is possible, to get close to these men, to get to know them, to even view them as friends and comrades. And, perhaps most humbling, to realize that it would be very hard indeed for us, in our selfish, materialistic age, to match them in integrity, honesty, and simply as good, solid human beings.

Of particular fascination to many are the uniforms of that war. In part because this was the last of the romantic wars, some men went to battle in outlandish Zouave uniforms, smart chasseur costume, or old-fashioned claw-hammer coats. Many wore plain frock coats in blue or gray while still others fought in simple homespun. Some of those uniforms were well documented at the time and may even survive today; others are known imperfectly through partial descriptions, foggy photographs, or poor drawings. Reconstructing the variety of dress worn by the troops, and understanding how and why it looked as it did, is what is behind the quest of the uniform researcher. Understanding the uniform, in turn, tells much about the soldiers' attitudes, their esprit de corps, and the overall effectiveness of their government's efforts to keep them clothed. In the end, uniform studies is as much about systems, policies, procurement, and transportation as it is about sartorial elegance or the lack of it.

The study of uniforms has, naturally enough, always had a pictorial side to it. Throughout the centuries in the old world, artists depicted soldiers at war and at peace, at work and at rest. Whether the subject was a Roman centurion, a medieval knight, or a Napoleonic foot soldier, these depictions have generally been colorful, and sometimes extremely accurate. At the same time, there have been many that left a good deal to be desired in terms of both artistic skill and authenticity. In the early days, the best artists generally worked for well-heeled patrons or even kings and princes, and they depicted their soldiers as their patrons desired. Thus, distortions were sometimes deliberate. Others, often printmakers trying to create a market, depicted fighting men with a naïveté that revealed their lack of familiarity with their subject. In either case, in Europe a strong tradition developed of producing prints and paintings of military events and individual soldiers.

In this country, such a tradition did not begin to develop until recently. Until the Civil War, military paintings and drawings were limited to the portraits of Trumbull, Peale, and a few others, a small group of heroic paintings, primarily of the American Revolution and mainly by Trumbull, and a few small groups of uniform prints, many printed as pictorial sheet music covers. The rise of the pictorial newspaper in the 1850s created a medium for woodcuts, but military subjects in these sources still tended to be few and far between and, of course, in black and white. Once the Civil War began, the artists who worked for these newspapers produced a wide variety of images. Unfortunately, often the conversion from the artist's sketch to the woodcut seriously distorted the original image. The actual eyewitness sketches, though far better than the woodcuts, are far less common, and many were hasty field sketches with a minimum of detail.

The Civil War came at the time when photography had developed the capability of producing multiple photographs of the same subject through negatives. Issued primarily in the carte de visite format, these small card photographs were produced in the hundreds of thousands and a great many of them showed soldiers as they prepared to march off to war. Once the war began in earnest, a few professional photographers such as the men of the Brady firm, and successors such as Alexander Gardner brought their cameras into the field to depict the troops in camp, and occasionally in the aftermath of battle. Because of the difficulty of capturing action with the slow cameras of the period, there are only a couple of surviving actual battle photographs, and these are naval scenes taken at a great distance during the siege of Charleston. The photography of the war has given us a great volume of images, but they are in black and white, the overwhelming majority are Northern, and they are all carefully posed. Although the Union soldier was well documented in many cases, he certainly wasn't in all. Many units were never photographed in the field. While the Federal, in general, was commonly photographed, his Confederate counterpart is much more rarely seen. Rarest of all are field photographs of Confederates. Of all the thousands of images taken during the war, probably less than fifty were taken outdoors in field conditions, and of these, the vast majority were done in the opening weeks of the war. We know the typical Confederate of the mid- to late-war period only through a tiny number of photographs of prisoners and dead bodies.

Once the war was over, there seems to have been little interest in depicting its events on canvas. Some illustrators, such as wartime veterans William Ludwell Sheppard and Allan C. Redwood, depicted Southern scenes in pen and ink for various magazines, while a number of artists, mostly non-veterans, pooled their talents for the great *Battles and Leaders of the Civil War* series in the late 1880s. Although a few monumental paintings, including those of Rothermel and Walker, and eventually the great cycloramas of Philippoteaux and others were created, their number was not great and they sometimes suffered in their accurate depiction of uniforms and equipment. The chromolithographs of Louis Prang and Company, produced in the 1880s, were some of the very few images that had widespread distribution, were in color, and depicted the soldier of the Civil War with some accuracy. Thus, unlike Europe, where a great tradition of battle paintings and prints resulted in thousands of images, the American Civil War has always suffered from a dearth of accurate renderings of its events, particularly in color.

Part of the reason for this lay in the lack of artists who had the skills and the interest to depict the war. The skill came from both artistic ability and actual witnessing of the events; the interest in the artist's own inclination to record what he saw. Winslow Homer, perhaps the best of the Northern wartime artists, produced only a few war-related paintings before he turned to other work, and none of them of battle. Alfred Waud, an Englishman who produced views for the illustrated newspapers, worked mostly in pencil. Conrad Wise Chapman, the Confederacy's best artist, produced only a few paintings that have survived, including his superb series of thirty-one small paintings of the siege of Charleston. Edwin Forbes, whose etchings of the Army of the Potomac won him fame in the 1880s, only rarely worked in color. Thus, from the time the war ended until perhaps the last twenty years, we have seen the Civil War primarily through a black and white lens.

Today, reconstructing the events and particularly the uniforms of the war involves piecing together every detail that can be gleaned from photographs, comments in letters or diaries, quartermaster or ordnance receipts, inspection reports, and a variety of other sources. These sources exist in many places, and often the most revealing are the financial records associated with the equipping of a unit. Revealing, but often deadly dull. Even when all of these details are painstakingly pulled together, much may remain unknown. Further, just getting the uniform itself right may be only half the battle. If one is to depict a unit at a given time, say, just before a particular engagement, it is important to know what kind of condition these men were in. Had they just marched thirty miles? Was the weather hot or cold? Had they had a chance to shave? Were they inordinately dirty, or had they just received a new issue of clothing? All of these details, added together, help to re-create the soldier of the past. Although there may still be questions, much of today's research has gone far beyond what was known in the past.

It is one thing for an artist to copy what he sees, or thinks he sees, from a photograph, or to take a modern, live human being, dress him up in a reproduction uniform, and paint the scene. The result may be artistically pleasing, but it is not likely to really show history as it was. To do that, one must know the period, the uniforms, hairstyles, body shapes and builds, the weather of the event, the terrain, and, above all, to be able to show how those elements affect the scene. It isn't enough to know that a four-button sack coat was blue and had four buttons; one must know the cloth, the texture, the actual pattern of the coat; how it hangs, how it feels in hot weather. It is not enough to merely draw a horse; it has to be the right horse, the right size, with the right gear.

Over the years, very few artists have proven capable of really understanding what it takes to depict the soldier as he was, but in the last twenty-odd years, one man, Don Troiani, has moved to change our view of the war to one that the veterans themselves might well have recognized. In so doing, he has combined a highly talented artistry with a standard for research and accuracy that ensures that his paintings have lasting value. Few others can match his uncompromising standards of excellence and authenticity. He chooses his models with the greatest care to achieve the proper look of the men in mid-Victorian America. The garb and gear of each figure are painstakingly researched. Appropriate backgrounds are found and studied, sometimes sending the artist hundreds of miles from home to examine battlefields and structures firsthand. Often, because of the amount of research involved, it may be years between a painting's conception and the actual moment the brush is put to canvas.

To support his art, for a quarter century Don Troiani has methodically built one of the great private reference collections of Civil War, War of 1812, and Revolutionary War uniforms, equipage, insignia, and weapons. An expert researcher himself with a personal Civil War library of more than 2,500 volumes, he is assisted in his quest for truth by a select network of advanced collectors, curators, and historians with whom he corresponds regularly and who open their own collections to him.

In all this, Don Troiani he has taken his cue from the great French masters of the nineteenth century, Édouard Detaille, Jean-Louis-Ernest Meissonier, and Alphonse de Neuville, who showed soldiers as believable human beings. The French artists knew their subjects intimately; they marched with them, saw them on parade, knew their hopes and fears. And, to ensure that they were painted accurately, these artists built large personal collections of original objects to use as props. Those collections later formed the basis of the great French military museum, the Musée de l'Armée in Paris.

Don Troiani has tried to do the same thing. Although he did not, in fact, know the actual veterans of the war, his interest in them, his nationally important collection of their objects, and his eye for what made them distinctive has resulted in a body of work that is, by and large, as good as any produced by the artist veterans themselves. For him, the life of the common soldier of the Civil War is as familiar and vivid as the surroundings of his Connecticut studio. No other modern artist has approached this subject with the same enthusiasm, insight, and dedication as this accomplished recorder of drama and detail.

Leslie D. Jensen

## CHAPTER 1

# *Militia and Early Volunteers*

THE CONTRIBUTIONS OF THE AMERICAN MILITIA to the Civil War are largely unrecognized. The first troops to respond to the call for war, both North and South, came from the states' organized volunteer militias. Militia-trained officers and enlisted men moved to command positions in the newly recruited volunteer regiments because of their prior military training and social position in their communities as units were raised locally. Some militia regiments even served throughout the war with the volunteer armies. It was the American militia system that in many ways set the entire tone for the raising of the volunteer armies that ultimately fought the war.

In the chaos of the early days of the war, several units claimed "firsts." Clearly it was the militia of the South that first went to war. Militiamen throughout the South began seizing Federal arsenals and forts as their states declared they were seceding from the Union. In Charleston, South Carolina, the hotbed of secession, there was a well-organized volunteer militia, completely uniformed and equipped, its weapons largely drawn from the Federal government's support of the state militias. In fact, the cadets of the Citadel, one of the most celebrated military academies of the South, may actually be entitled to the claim of opening hostilities by firing upon a Union supply ship, the *Star of the West,* on January 9, 1861. South Carolina's militia had been called into service by Gov. Francis W. Pickens on December 17, 1860, and prompted the move of the Federal garrison from Fort Moultrie to the unfinished Fort Sumter. By January 1861, the South Carolina militia had been recruited to full strength and had effectively besieged the small garrison of Federal troops at Fort Sumter. The die was now cast, and the hand that cast it was that of a state militia force.

The American militia system originated in the "trained bands" of the colonial era. These groups had their origin in the English tradition that free men were entitled, as well as obligated, to participate in their own defense. Colonists armed and trained themselves for the common defense from Native Americans and foreign invaders. By 1860, the trained bands had become the states' volunteer militias. By law, all able-bodied white males of appropriate age had been required to be part of the enrolled or common militia. As threat of attack by Native Americans or foreign invasion faded, however, so did the impetus to actively participate in the militia system.

By the 1830s, the annual assemblage of the common militia had been reduced to the level of a holiday celebration. Lampooned in cartoons and folk art, the image of the militia muster in the early nineteenth century was that of a drunken frolic, with the militiamen armed with sticks and umbrellas. This is the image that still pervades the common conception of the American militia system. It overlooks, however, the parallel growth of the volunteer militia companies

*U.S. model 1851 cap of then-colonel George A. McCall, who later became a major general. Although superseded shortly before the war, this French-inspired cap was a major fashion influence on militia headgear of many states prior to hostilities.* WEST POINT MUSEUM.

that began in the colonial era among a citizenry that was attracted to military life. The volunteer militia company was generally chartered by the state and composed of men who had volunteered to uniform and equip themselves at their own expense and submit to military discipline and drill to become a military organization. Every good-sized urban area had such companies. They were, to a large degree, social organizations, providing a sense of community and commitment, but some grew into respectable military units.

In the eighteenth and early nineteenth centuries, these volunteer companies were usually attached to the common militia paper regiments as "flank" or elite companies. Whereas the common militia officers were usually that in name only—the origin of the fabled "Kentucky colonel"—the officers of the volunteer companies frequently took their duties and obligations seriously, devoting time and often their own money to see that these military companies were properly trained and equipped. By the 1840s, the states were giving up on the common militia. The movement now known as Jacksonian democracy had advocated the abolition of the common militia as a social inequity, and Jacksonian politicians did nothing to encourage its invigoration or reform. Militia laws were ignored, and the common militia became virtually extinct. To fill the gap, the states rewrote their militia laws, replacing the common militia with the volunteer companies as the "active militia," while retaining on paper the manpower count of their citizenry as a potential militia body.

The volunteer militias, once completely drawn under state authority, often continued to demonstrate the individuality with which they had been conceived. They continued to wear their distinctive uniforms of their own design. These often reflected the origins of the company and ranged from the national blue of the American Guard of the 71st New York State Militia to the Irish green coatees of the Montgomery Guards of Charleston, South Carolina. The traditionalists, such as the 7th Regiment of New York City, often continued to wear gray. By the 1850s, however, as New York and other states tried to impose regimentalization upon what had previously been independent companies, uniforms became more standardized. In the North, dark blue frock coats and uniform caps of the Federal 1851 pattern were common. In the South, as in Virginia, gray frock coats and coatees were common, but as company, rather than regimental, uniforms. As late as the mid-1850s, the uniform in Georgia was half seriously said to be "a Shirt-collar and a pair of Spurs."[1] Yet the reformers had their way, and before the war began, much of the militia had been revitalized.

No state better typified the results of this reorganization than the state of New York. On the eve of the Civil War, New York's military force comprised some 19,000 rank and file, with a staff of 532 officers. These men were organized into a force of 62 active regiments. These ranged in size from smaller, rural regiments of 400 men to the elite 7th Regiment of New York City, with over 1,000 soldiers. Some were still armed with inadequate or antiquated weaponry, such as altered flintlocks, but efforts had been made to acquire better weapons, such as the M1855 rifle muskets and rifles of the 7th Regiment. When war began in 1861, New York had a militia force that could immediately be placed at Federal call.[2] In December 1860, the editor of the *Military Gazette*

*Coat worn by Col. Elmer Ellsworth of the 11th New York Volunteers when killed on May 24, 1861, in Alexandria, Virginia. After receiving his uniform from the tailor, Ellsworth stated prophetically, "It is in this suit I shall die." The coat bears the damage of the shotgun blast in the chest, although the bloodstains were washed out many years ago.* COLLECTION OF NEW YORK STATE DIVISION OF MILITARY AND NAVAL AFFAIRS.

*Trousers with red-edged gold stripe worn by Col. Elmer Ellsworth at the time of his death.* COLLECTION OF NEW YORK STATE DIVISION OF MILITARY AND NAVAL AFFAIRS.

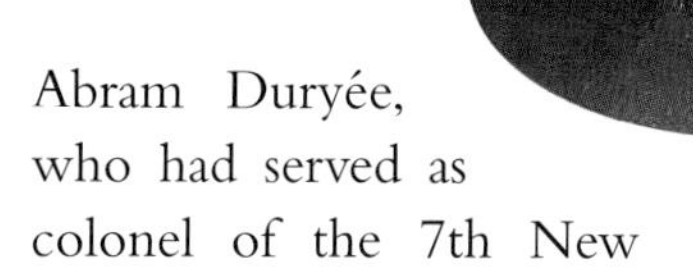

*Forage cap patterned on the U.S. model 1839 worn by Capt. H. M. Nelson of Virginia's Clark Cavalry before the war and possibly as a captain of the 1st Virginia Cavalry at Manassas in 1861. There appears to have been a six-pointed star (now missing) on the front.*
TROIANI COLLECTION.

wrote, "Every day brings news of Military preparations at the South, and we sincerely hope that it will only do for the Southern Militia what the Anti-Rent War preparations did for this State—enlist their best men, and raise a fine force, ready for use against a foreign foe, or preserve internal tranquility, but never against their brethren of other States, or against the Union!"[3]

Thus when the war began, the militias of both North and South provided the first men in service. Whether the 7th of New York, "the regiment that saved the capitol," or the Charleston Zouave Cadets at Fort Sumter, militiamen usually began the great American conflict dressed in their militia uniforms. The first Massachusetts troops to leave the state wore their individual company uniforms, with only gray overcoats procured by the state's governor John Andrews for uniformity. The men of the 7th New York went to Washington in natty gray fatigue uniforms of jackets and chasseur caps. The first Rhode Island troops wore loose blue flannel smocks with gray trousers in place of their militia uniforms. The South Carolina forces at Charleston ranged from the gray and red of the Charleston Zouave Cadets to the green smocks of riflemen. Together they presented a veritable military kaleidoscope of uniforms.

Whereas the militias could provide the first troops for what was to become a long and protracted struggle, the militia force itself was incapable of sustaining the war effort. On May 3, 1861, Pres. Abraham Lincoln called for 42,000 three-year volunteers and 22,000 more men for the Regular service. With the defeat at Bull Run, he called for an additional 500,000 volunteers. Confederate president Jefferson Davis began accepting volunteers as early as February 1861, and after a series of calls for volunteers, the South began conscription in April 1862. North and South alike, these volunteers represented a new breed of soldiers.

Because the central governments in 1861 lacked the structure and resources to form these volunteers into viable military units, that task was left to the individual states. Each state had an allotted number of regiments to provide, even though in the first days there were generally more volunteers than required. Following the militia tradition, regiments were generally recruited by a central prospective unit commander. Especially in the first days, these men were frequently from the militia system. One of the war's premier regiments, the 5th New York, Duryée's Zouaves, was the creation of Col. Abram Duryée, who had served as colonel of the 7th New York State Militia Regiment from 1849 to 1859. Robert G. Shaw, colonel of the 54th Massachusetts Volunteer Infantry, the famed African-American regiment, had first gone to war as a private in the same regiment when the 7th marched to "save" Washington in April 1861.

In a few cases, whole militia regiments volunteered for war service. The 2nd, 9th, 14th, 20th, and 79th Regiments of New York State Militia became, respectively, the 82nd, 83rd, 84th, 80th, and 79th Volunteer Regiments during the war. More frequently, a militia regiment became the recruiting core for volunteers. The 6th New York brought forth the 66th New York, which had as its lieutenant colonel Samuel Zook of the old 6th Regiment. Zook later became colonel of the 57th New York and died at Gettysburg as a brigadier general. After the 69th New York Militia Regiment served at First Bull Run, it returned to New York City, where it raised a volunteer 69th Regiment, the core of the famed Irish Brigade, and later the 182nd New York of the Corcoran Brigade. The link between the militia and volunteer regiments in the early days of the war was especially strong.

Although militia troops could go to war in their own privately purchased uniforms, providing uniforms for the influx of civilian volunteers completely strained the resources of even the prosperous and industrial North. Jackets were manufactured in stopgap fashion throughout the North. In New York, they were to have eight-button fronts and be of blue cloth, but immediately jackets of shoddy gray were accepted to meet the demands of uniforming the new recruits. In Pennsylvania, jackets with nine-button fronts made of cloth of varying shades of gray and light blue were issued to the first volunteers.[4] Jackets of blue and gray were common issue throughout Ohio, Indiana, and Illinois as well.

In the South, the first regiments of new volunteers wore locally manufactured uniforms often based upon those of the militia. The Virginia militia companies in their distinctive uniforms were joined into regiments lacking in uniformity. In Louisiana, with the urbane center of New Orleans, there were uniformed Zouaves and chasseurs in tribute to the Creole heritage of the city. The blue-coated Washington Artillery of that same city, as trim and proper as any Northern militia unit, went to war in gray jackets in the East, while its Western companies served in blue denim jackets and trousers. Southern volunteers went to war in blue as well as gray, just as in the North. Some states devised distinctive uniforms. In North Carolina, the regulation uniform for state troops was a six-button sack coat of gray with black stripes on the shoulder for infantry, red for artillery, and yellow for cavalry. In 1861, Mississippi troops were to wear shirts of distinctive colors—red for infantry, gray for artillery, and blue for cavalry. Their hats were to be black felt, looped up on three sides. With each state, and often each locality, providing its own clothing at the war's start, the diversity was unending. Only later would some uniformity be established with the issue of uniforms produced in regional clothing depots.

This mixture of blues and grays within both the Union and Confederate forces, along with the colorful Zouave and other distinctive uniforms common to both sides, inevitably led to confusion on the battlefront. At Big Bethel in June 1861, the gray uniforms of the 3rd New York caused other Union soldiers to fire upon them.

The problem had been foreseen, and attempts for easy identification were attempted without great success. As early as May 1861, several Southerners had suggested badges for identification. From New Orleans, a "C. Schumacker" offered distinctive arm badges. A lady, F. B. Johnston of Salem, Virginia, offered to make "a rosette of red and blue ribbon" for the same purpose. In August 1861, Stonewall Jackson's men adopted their own device—"a Sherr [sheer?] strip of white cotton cloth about an inch wide and six long attached to the top of the cap"—as a means of distinction.[5] In the North, the gray-clad 47th New York was ordered to wear "a broad stripe of red, white and blue" on the left sleeve to distinguish "Union troops when on the field of battle." None of these devices was ever truly successful, but in the end, the economy of mass production solved these problems as the blue and the gray sorted themselves out.

Neither professional soldiers nor citizen soldiers, the volunteers of 1861 personified the American nation. They were a cross section of a boisterous and rambunctious populace about to be forged into a new nation in the crucible of war.

*Prewar Connecticut militia shako of an unidentified unit, bearing the state seal and infantry hunting horn device. This item was made by John A. Baker of New York City, who supplied headgear to state militias across the country in the prewar years.* MIDDLESEX COUNTY HISTORICAL SOCIETY.

*Emblazoned in gold embroidery on a blue velvet band on this forage cap, the legend "Scott Life Guard" proclaimed to all the title of the 4th New York Volunteers. It was worn by Capt. William B. Parisen, who served with the unit from April 1861 until its muster out in August 1863.* TROIANI COLLECTION.

# 6TH REGIMENT, MASSACHUSETTS VOLUNTEER MILITIA, 1861

On the anniversary of the battles of Lexington and Concord, April 19, 1861, Massachusetts "minutemen" were again under fire. These militiamen had mustered on April 17, 1861, from their widely scattered homes in Middlesex and Essex Counties for the defense of the nation's capital. Their journey south had taken them through New York and New Jersey to Philadelphia. The 6th Massachusetts left that city for Washington at 1 A.M. on the nineteenth, but its route was through Baltimore, and that city was in turmoil, with secessionists vowing to stop the passage of reinforcements to the Capitol.

Col. Edward F. Jones of the 6th simply stated, "My orders are to reach Washington at the earliest possible moment, and I shall go on." Eventually six of the regiment's companies had safely traversed Baltimore, but the last four—C, I, D, and L—were trapped by a murderous mob. Brickbats and bullets flew at these unfortunate soldiers, who fought back, firing at rioters who were foolhardy enough to openly attack. Even Baltimore's mayor, marching with the column, joined in, taking an M1855 rifle musket from a fallen soldier to shoot his attacker.

When the regiment reunited, four men had been killed and thirty-six officers and men wounded. The march through Baltimore was not a battle, but the blood had been drawn. Their arrival in Washington was described by the *Washington Evening Star:* "The Massachusetts volunteers are provided with the dark-gray overcoat, water-proof knapsacks and haversacks, regulation caps and new rifle muskets. Each man is provided with two flannel shirts and two pairs of drawers and stockings. Many of them being hastily recruited, were not fully uniformed. The uniformed companies have black pants, with red and orange stripes down the sides, and dark blue infantry coats." Clad in state-purchased overcoats and militia shakos, the 6th Massachusetts had gone to war as citizen soldiers. They were true descendants of their Revolutionary ancestors.

PRIVATE COLLECTION

# PRIVATE, MARYLAND GUARD, 1861

DAVID RANKIN, JR.

The Maryland Guard was organized and raised in Baltimore in late 1859. The guard was formed as a battalion of four companies and became part of the 53rd Regiment of the Maryland Militia. Over the next months, two more companies were added. As with many of the finely dressed militia companies in the large cities of the eastern United States, the Maryland Guard was composed of young men of the best class. An advertisement that appeared in the local newspapers, such as the *Baltimore American and Commercial Advertiser,* touted the fact that the uniform each member was required to buy was "simple and cheap," costing $42.68. Recruits were given three months to fully outfit themselves. The ad described the uniform as consisting of an overcoat; full chassseur uniform, which included a light blue flannel shirt with ornamental brass buttons, jacket and pantaloons trimmed with yellow, red cummerbund, and gaiters; cap; knapsack; blanket; body belt; and undress jacket. Both the full dress and undress uniforms were predominantly blue, except for the undress pantaloons, which were black. The belts were changed from white to black for parade and fatigue.

The color of the uniform doomed it to a short history. Secessionist sentiment ran high in Baltimore, and most of the Maryland Guard immediately cast their lot with the South when war came. Although the uniform of the Maryland Guard was short-lived, its style represents well the feeling and spirit during the months leading up to the war.

Many members of the battalion made their way to Richmond. Once there, they were outfitted by the state of Virginia. The uniform they received was described by one guardsman, James McHenry Howard, as "coarse gray, but very durable." The Maryland men were not destined to serve as a unit, however. Two companies were sent from Richmond to Winchester, Virginia, to form the nucleus of the Confederate 1st Maryland Regiment. Left behind was one company under Capt. J. Lyle Clarke, which became Company B, 21st Virginia Infantry, and served as such for the duration of the war. Both regiments saw extensive action with the Army of Northern Virginia.

# 7TH REGIMENT, NEW YORK STATE MILITIA, 8TH COMPANY, 1861

Few militia units have ever gained the fame of New York's 7th Regiment. In 1861, the 7th was considered the epitome of a militia unit. Whereas most state militias consisted of underorganized companies, each with distinctive uniforms, loosely coalesced into paper regiments, the 7th numbered a full 1,000 men with a regimental staff, even a surgeon and a chaplain. Before the war, in common with other New York militias, there was a company of cavalry and a mountain howitzer battery in the regiment as well.

Although called a "silk-stocking" regiment, it drew largely from New York City's burgeoning middle class, with young clerks, salesmen, and junior professionals filling its ranks as enlisted men. Its officers were mainly successful businessmen, with a dedication to the regiment that surpassed a hobby. Thus when President Lincoln called for volunteers in 1861, he expected the nation's militias to respond, and the 7th was the first to leave New York City. Gen. Winfield Scott felt that the 7th's national reputation made it ideal for the defense of the nation's capital, and it has been called the regiment that "saved the Capitol" because of its dramatic appearance on the streets of Washington, D.C., just as Lincoln despaired of troops. It was described as it marched in Washington: "The infantry is armed with improved regulation muskets [M1855 rifle muskets] and bayonets, the troop of horse with pistols and heavy swords,

PRIVATE COLLECTION

*Worsted epaulets for dress coatee worn by Lewis C. Parmelee of the 7th New York State Militia.* TROIANI COLLECTION.

and the engineers with rifles [M1855] and sabre bayonets. Almost every man is armed with a pistol, including musicians and servants, and some have heavy dirks and knives."

Its gray fatigue uniforms were trimmed with black, a color combination chosen in the 1820s and retained by the regiment through the twentieth century. The white-buff belts supported the accoutrements of the men, which were supplemented with personal, nonissue blankets of various colors and designs. Gray knit sack coats, nicknamed "Aspinwalls" after their donor, were also worn in Washington. Their uniforms were never stained with the soil of combat, for the 7th did not go to Bull Run, returning to New York City and mustering out early in June 1861. That does not mean that these men saw no combat, however, for by war's end, 606 of these enlisted men and officers accepted commissions in various other organizations of the Regular army and volunteer forces. One of them was Pvt. Robert Gould Shaw, who later served as colonel of the 54th Massachusetts Volunteer Infantry.

*Dress shako worn by Lewis C. Parmelee as a member of the 7th New York State Militia from 1859 until 1861. As an officer in the 2nd U.S. Sharpshooters, Parmalee was killed at Antietam while capturing a Confederate flag, an act for which he was awarded the Medal of Honor.* TROIANI COLLECTION.

*A .69-caliber cartridge box made by L. S. Baker and used by Parmelee in the 7th New York State Militia before the war. The heavily varnished flap bears the gilt brass device "NG," for National Guard.* TROIANI COLLECTION.

# 1ST REGIMENT SOUTH CAROLINA RIFLES, 1861

The 1st Regiment South Carolina Rifles was raised in the extreme western part of the state and was the first South Carolina regiment mustered into Confederate service. As with many early Confederate regiments, its first uniform was dark blue trimmed in green, the traditional color for a rifle regiment, although the arms supplied it by the state were old smoothbore muskets. In June 1861, the Confederate government published regulations requiring its troops to be uniformed in gray. Following this, dress of the 1st Rifles was changed to conform. The green trim was retained, as were the hats with rifle insignia. The arms were upgraded, but only to the more modern M1842 musket. The regiment did not obtain rifled arms until well after it had joined the Army of Northern Virginia.

PRIVATE COLLECTION

The 1st Rifles was the first South Carolina regiment to change its original enlistment from one year to the open-ended "for the war" required by the Confederate government. This decision ordained that the men of the 1st Rifles would see action in all the major engagements of the famed army in which they served. By the fall of 1862, the original uniforms of many of the enlisted men had begun to wear out, and regimental records show a rapid replacement by uniforms with jackets rather than coats. At the battle of Fredericksburg, December 13, 1862, the 1st Rifles sustained heavy casualties. Among the mortally wounded was Ordnance Sgt. H. Berry Arnold, who had been first sergeant of Company L. Sergeant Arnold died at Chimborazo Hospital in Richmond, leaving behind clothing and items that most certainly reflect what he brought with him from home, including all or part of his original uniform, as recorded in the Compiled Service Records:

| | |
|---|---|
| 1 - coat | 2 - pair socks |
| 1 - vest | 1 - pair boots |
| 1 - pair pants | 1 - knapsack |
| 2 - pair drawers | 1 - pocket book |
| 3 - shirts | 1 - silver pencil and gold pen |
| 1 - hat | $102.40 |

The 1st South Carolina Rifles served the Confederacy until the end of the war, seeing action in nearly every important battle fought by the Army of Northern Virginia. At Appomattox, only a surviving 157 officers and men were present. They could return knowing that no Confederate regiment could boast a more gallant record of service.

# DRIVE THEM TO WASHINGTON

The battle of First Manassas on July 21, 1861, made it painfully evident that the war, which had initially been expected to be a short one, was likely to extend at least into the following year. Also evident was the fact that unless some effort was made to dress both armies in distinctive uniforms, there would be continued instances of soldiers from the same command firing on friendly forces. It was during this battle that Thomas J. Jackson received his famed nickname of "Stonewall," at the head of the brigade that would share that name. No clearer picture of the lack of uniformity exists than that of Jackson at the head of the 4th and 27th Virginia Regiments, but dressed in the uniform of a colonel of the Federal army. Arrayed behind him, ready to drive the Yankees from the field, his Virginians were virtually indistinguishable from many on the opposite side of the battlefield. Most had received locally made uniforms, many wearing battle shirts that were not uniform even within the same regiment. To add to the problem, inspection reports from the end of June showed that during the short time since leaving home, the soldiers' clothing had become worn, further blurring distinction between Northern and Southern troops.

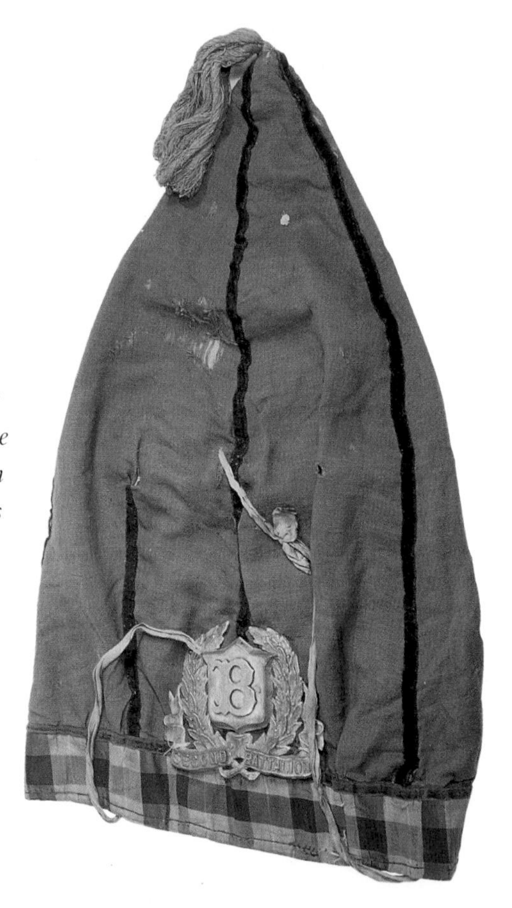

*Influenced by the dress in Garibaldi's campaigns of liberation, this distinctive Sicilian style headgear was popular in the South during the opening months of the war. It was often worn in company with a hat or kepi. This rare specimen bears a brass badge marked "8th Regt, 2nd Batt."*

COLLECTION OF NEW YORK STATE DIVISION OF MILITARY AND NAVAL AFFAIRS.

BOOTH WESTERN ART MUSEUM, CARTERSVILLE, GEORGIA

# PRIVATE, COMPANY I, 4TH VIRGINIA INFANTRY C.S.A., THE LIBERTY HALL VOLUNTEERS

Civil War regiments, and the various companies they comprised, tended to be made up of men from the same general geographic area or who shared a common heritage. Company I of the 4th Virginia Infantry was composed primarily of students from Virginia's Washington College, which from 1776 to 1798 was known as Liberty Hall Academy. With obvious pride in their school, the young men who volunteered for the great adventure did so as the Liberty Hall Volunteers. Before the end of the academic year, the company they formed had been receiving military training from cadets of neighboring Virginia Military Institute. By the time they were mustered into Confederate service on June 2, 1861, to serve for a period of one year, the men of Washington College were considered a well-drilled command, at least by 1861 standards. But the young men learned quickly that cannonballs and bullets had no respect for academic achievement. At the battle of First Manassas, the men from Liberty Hall saw six of their number killed and several wounded.

DAVID RANKIN, JR.

The Liberty Hall Volunteer shown here is dressed as men of his company appeared on the field at Manassas in July 1861. His uniform consists of a battle shirt instead of a jacket, accoutrements described in the service records as "old and indifferent," and a .69-caliber smoothbore musket altered from flintlock to percussion. When originally outfitted, the company had no bayonet scabbards and no cap boxes, both of which were privately obtained and paid for by the company commander, Capt. James J. White.

Regimental returns of the 4th Virginia for the first three months of the war show that Company I was typical. The service records list six companies of the regiment as armed with the altered muskets, one with the cadet musket, and two with Harpers Ferry rifles, better known as Mississippi rifles. In every company, the uniforms were reported as "much worn and in bad condition."

On April 14, 1862, Company I was reorganized for the duration of the war, with the addition of forty-nine men from the militia and eleven transfers from other units, and it lost much of its academic flavor. The 4th Virginia served with the Army of Northern Virginia until the end of the war. It was organized along with the 2nd, 5th, 27th, and 33rd Virginia Regiments to make up the famous Stonewall Brigade, a fact that, as veterans, the men who had left school to fight for the Confederacy as members of the Liberty Hall Volunteers most certainly boasted of in years to come.

# FLAT RIVER GUARD, COMPANY B, 6TH NORTH CAROLINA STATE TROOPS INFANTRY

With "military fever" running high in April 1861, the young men of Orange County, North Carolina, flocked to the colors in numbers sufficient to quickly raise two companies of infantry. One of these companies, the Flat River Guard, numbered fifty enlisted men under the command of Capt. Robert F. Webb. Through the efforts of the ladies of the county, the company was uniformed and prepared for war. Because North Carolina was a major textile manufacturing state, it is likely that the cloth for these uniforms was of local manufacture of what was termed "North Carolina gray cassimere," according to Frederick P. Todd in *American Military Equipage, 1851–1872.* The hat worn by the guards was likely issued by the state. It is similar to the U.S. regulation hat but bears the early-style hunting horn insignia, as well as the letters FRG.

In May, Captain Webb was ordered by the adjutant general of North Carolina to move his company to Raleigh. It was here that the guards were mustered as Company B, 6th North Carolina Infantry, commanded by Col. Charles Fisher, who, according to Richard W. Iobst in *The Bloody Sixth,* had determined to raise a regiment of "smiths, carpenters, masons, and engineers." Colonel Fisher had been a member of the North Carolina Senate and president of the North Carolina Railroad and was obviously a man of wealth. He supplied the regiment with knapsacks, bayonet scabbards, and canteens and was likely responsible for unique belt plate that was manufactured for, and proudly worn by, the men of his command.

The 6th Regiment was immediately sent to Virginia and assigned to the brigade commanded by Brig. Gen. Bernard E. Bee. It received its baptism of fire on the field of Manassas. The regiment charged Ricketts's and Griffin's Federal batteries and sustained heavy losses, not only from the batteries and their infantry support, but also from Confederate troops in their rear who fired into them. Among those killed was Colonel Fisher.

DAVID RANKIN, JR.

# CLINCH RIFLES, GEORGIA MILITIA, APRIL 1861

The Clinch Rifles were formed in Augusta, Georgia, in 1852. Named in honor of a hero of the War of 1812, Gen. Duncan Clinch, the company was typical of the numerous elite militia organizations that could be found in the large cities of the United States in the decade prior to the Civil War. These companies were often composed of the best and the brightest young men of the urban areas, most of whom had sufficient financial backing to outfit themselves in the height of military fashion.

Membership in the Clinch Rifles was both an honor and a privilege that was not granted lightly. A young man aspiring to membership would be voted on and was expected to pay dues, outfit himself in the company's uniform, and attend regular meetings. The purchase of one uniform was usually not enough, as style changes would dictate that those wishing to remain must be ready to conform to the decision of the majority. The meticulously kept minutes of the meetings of the Clinch Rifles show that on May 30, 1859, a resolution was adopted to "change the uniform by making the coat a frock coat." This was followed just over a year later in July 1860 by a decision to discuss a design for a new uniform. These uniforms would be tailor-made in Augusta. For those wishing to belong, peer pressure certainly was alive and well.

In keeping with the European tradition of green for riflemen, and adding an elegant gold braid trim, the Clinch Rifles' uniform made it a distinctive and easily recognized company. The new uniform was based in style, if not in color, on the latest issue of the Regular army. The French-style forage cap had been adopted by the Regulars in 1858 for fatigue purposes. The frock coat for full dress had replaced a similar, less practical pattern the same year. Whereas the Regulars would not wear the two items together, the decision to do so by the Clinch Rifles made for a smart and practical uniform by the standards of 1860.

DAVID RANKIN, JR.

Unlike many units raised in 1861 that bore the title of Rifles, the men of the Clinch Rifles were armed as a true rifle company, carrying the 1841 Mississippi rifle modified to use the deadly looking saber bayonet. These rifles had been issued by the state of Georgia, which had received them from the Federal government, which, under a law dating from 1808, had issued the various states arms for their militias. The belt, the U.S. rifle belt model of 1855 with an attached frog to hold the scabbard for the saber bayonet, also stood out as unique to a rifle company. The cartridge box for the Mississippi rifle had no provision for a shoulder belt and was worn on the right side of the waist belt. Although the saber bayonet had the appearance of a formidable arm, it was not well liked by the men who used it. One primary reason was the fact that it made the arm difficult to load quickly when it was in place on the rifle. Another negative factor was the weight of the weapon, which, when added to the weight of a full cartridge box, added to the soldier's already significant burden.

*Silver and star crescent badge belonging to Pvt. J. Macready of Company A, 7th Louisiana, who enlisted at New Orleans on April 22, 1861.* WILLIAM ERQUITT COLLECTION.

ANDREW B. BOOTH, *RECORDS OF LOUISIANA SOLDIERS AND COMMANDS* (SPARTANBURG, S.C.: REPRINT PUBLISHERS, 1984), 832.

*Gray cloth-covered Virginia militia shako made by Wm. B. Richards of Alexandria, Virginia, bearing a brass state seal. This pattern was used by the Old Dominion Rifles, which became Company H of the 17th Virginia Infantry. The January 31 and March 23, 1861,* Alexandria Gazette *described the manufacturer's business: "Mr. Richards enjoys peculiar facilities for getting up military apparel and has during the past winter completely uniformed several companies of our section of the state and several from a distance."* ANDREW PELLS COLLECTION.

*A prewar South Carolina die-stamped belt plate of a style in wide use before and during the early part of the war by troops of that state. The plate bears the state seal originally designed in 1776, with the device of a palmetto tree, hearkening back to the defense of Charleston Harbor in 1776 when the palmetto trees at Fort Moultrie absorbed the fire from British cannonballs.*

WEST POINT MUSEUM.

*Prewar coatee worn by Capt. Hugh Mortimer Nelson of the Clark Cavalry of Virginia. In 1861, this unit formed a company of the famed 1st Virginia Cavalry, commanded by J. E. B. Stuart.* TROIANI COLLECTION.

# THE FIRST BATTLE FLAGS

As the summer of 1861 passed, it was evident that the war that had begun in April was not going to be over in the few months many had originally believed. Also evident was the fact that Confederate regiments needed a distinctive flag to be carried into battle—a flag that would be easily recognized at a distance on a smoke-shrouded field by friend and foe alike. The confusion and tragic instances of troops killed by friendly fire in some of the first battles had resulted in part from the wide variety of uniforms being worn and in part because the flags being carried could easily be mistaken for that of the enemy. By late fall, the problem of uniforms was on its way to being rectified, as the Richmond Clothing Depot and other facilities were now beginning to produce a uniform that, if not standard in the strictest sense, was at least distinct from that worn by the Union army. At the same time, there emerged a proud new banner that would eventually become one of the most enduring symbols of the Southern Confederacy. In November 1861, near Centreville, Virginia, the first issue of the new battle flag was made.

The officers receiving the flags included men whose names were already becoming household words in the Confederacy: Joseph E. Johnston, James Longstreet, Gustavus Smith, and Earl Van Dorn. The uniforms worn by these men reflected a mixture of Federal and Confederate regulations, with a generous dose of personal taste. According to Lt. Colin Selph, an officer on General Johnston's staff who was assigned the duty of obtaining the silk for these flags, they varied in color from light pink to red due to the unavailability of scarlet silk. Because of a scarcity of silk in the South, subsequent issues of the battle flag were made of scarlet bunting, which bore the strain of use in the field much better. It was not, after all, the type of material, but the cause the flags represented that made those who followed them into battle willing to sacrifice all in their defense.

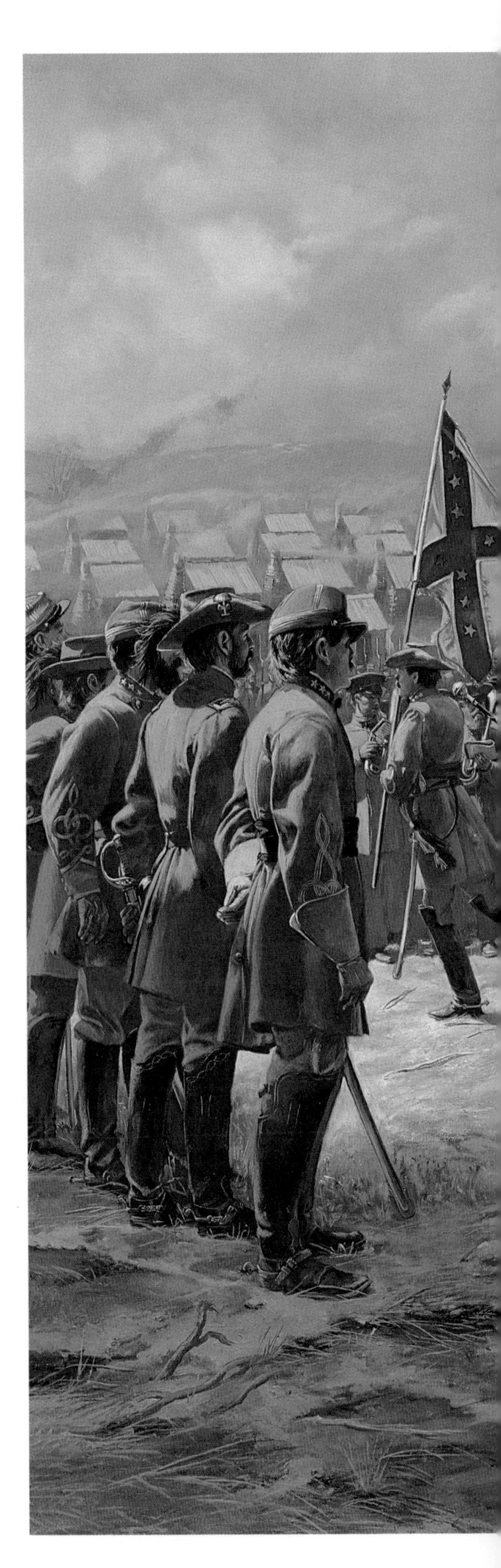

*Stiffened officer's kepi with gray satinette cloth covering and gold tape trimming. The design appears to have been based loosely on what was in fashion in Europe at the time. This cap belonged to Lt. William R. Macbeth of Company B, 16th Louisiana Battalion (Confederate Guards Response Battalion), who was killed on April 6, 1862.* CONFEDERATE MEMORIAL HALL, CLAUDE LEVET PHOTOGRAPH.

BOOTH WESTERN ART MUSEUM, CARTERSVILLE, GEORGIA

# 3RD ALABAMA INFANTRY, COMPANY A, MOBILE CADETS, 1861

DAVID RANKIN, JR.

For the young men of the Mobile Cadets, the heady excitement of the first months of 1861 must then have seemed like a dream come true. Here at last was the opportunity to make the fantasies of military glory a reality. The company had been formed in 1845, and then as now contained some of the finest youth from the wealthiest families of Mobile, Alabama. Since the early days, the cadets, while excelling at military drill and target practice, had been little more than a social club. Now, with the Federal evacuation of Fort Sumter, the possibility of war seemed very real. So real, in fact, that the captain of the cadets was waiting in the telegraph office following the news of the evacuation when the call for volunteers was received. A return message was immediately sent to the Alabama governor offering the services of the Mobile Cadets to the Confederacy. Within days, the cadets moved to Montgomery, where they were designated

*Frock coats were more prevalent in the Confederacy during the early part of the war, until economical considerations dictated a shift to jacket manufacture. This early specimen is believed to have been worn by a soldier in the 5th Louisiana Regiment.* TROIANI COLLECTION.

*Knit woolen smoking cap, or tam-o'-shanter, worn by Pvt. Edward N. Whittier of the 1st Rhode Island Detached Militia. Informal caps of all sorts were favored by troops during quiet moments in camp.* TROIANI COLLECTION.

Company A, 3rd Regiment Alabama Infantry. The 3rd was the first Alabama command to leave the state for Virginia, where on May 4, 1861, at Lynchburg, they were mustered into Confederate service.

The early uniform of the Mobile Cadets had been patterned after the undress uniform of the U. S. Military Academy at West Point. Between the time the company was mustered into actual service and its movement to the seat of war, it had received more suitable attire consisting of cadet gray jackets with matching trousers and forage caps all trimmed in black. Probably while at Lynchburg, the cadets received M1841 Mississippi rifles with saber bayonets, which were shipped to that point from Alabama's Mount Vernon Arsenal. From Lynchburg, the 3rd Alabama was ordered to Norfolk, Virginia, where it remained until the city was evacuated on May 5, 1862. The Mobile Cadets found the action they had looked for in the Seven Days' battles before Richmond. At Seven Pines and Malvern Hill, the 3rd Alabama lost a total of 367 men killed and wounded. At Malvern Hill, the dead of the 3rd Alabama included two Mobile Cadets, both killed bearing the regimental colors.

# 1st Rhode Island Detached Militia, 1861

PRIVATE COLLECTION

Of all the volunteers and militiamen who gathered in Washington, D.C., in early 1861, few were so distinctly dressed as the Rhode Island troops of Col. Ambrose Burnside. Recruited from several militia companies and battalions, the 1st Rhode Island Detached Militia wore a simple blue overshirt or smock, gray trousers, and black-brimmed hats or blue chasseur caps. Often their caps sported the white linen covers called havelocks after the English general who sported

*Wool flannel shirt blouse worn by Pvt. Edward N. Whittier of the 1st Rhode Island Detached Militia at the battle of Bull Run in 1861. Manufactured by the firm of Macullar, Williams, and Parker, they were merely shirts worn outside the trousers and adorned with small brass flower buttons. A company of carabineers armed with Burnside carbines wore rifle insignia on the sleeves.* TROIANI COLLECTION.

ALAN H. ARCHAMBAULT, "THE FIRST REGIMENT RHODE ISLAND DETACHED MILITIA, 1861," *MILITARY HISTORIAN AND COLLECTOR* 53, NO. 3 (FALL 2001): 105–6.

*Kepi worn by Pvt. Edward N. Whittier of the 1st Rhode Island Detached Militia at First Manassas. Originally dark blue, it has faded to a brownish hue because of the noncolorfast logwood dyes used by contractors. The color breakdown could occur rapidly, as attested to by one Union soldier who was quoted in the November 23, 1861,* Boston Evening Journal *shortly after leaving home as saying that "the rusty gray pants and blue caps turned to reddish brown and are not particularly becoming."* TROIANI COLLECTION.

such devices in India. It was a simple and practical uniform shared with Rhode Island's other infantry regiment, the 2nd.

These militiamen marched to First Bull Run with Burnside, who was now a brigade commander. The line companies were armed with M1855 rifle muskets, but a special carbineer company formed for skirmishing was issued breech-loading carbines of Burnside's own design. It needed these arms, as it was thrust into the fighting early on, spearheading the assault on Matthew's Hill. Despite their valiant performance, by the end of the day's battle, the stalwart Rhode Islanders joined in the general withdrawal and eventual rout of the amateur Federal army.

# 11TH VIRGINIA INFANTRY, COMPANY E, THE LYNCHBURG RIFLES, JULY 1861

The use of battle shirts in place of jackets or coats was a common practice in many Confederate regiments in the early days of the war. These shirts could be produced with comparative ease by local tailors or ladies' sewing circles and presented the proud volunteers with a distinctive garb they could wear to meet the Yankees. Had the war lasted only the few weeks or months as predicted by many, this may have been the only uniform many Southern boys would have worn. However, fate and the Federal army determined otherwise, and these distinct and often colorful garments soon disappeared. By the end of the summer of 1861, the image of the ragged Confederate was a reality. Uniforms made of cloth that would hold up well in civilian use started before long to disintegrate under the harsh reality of military service. These were soon replaced by uniforms made in Confederate government facilities from Richmond to Houston, Texas.

TIMOTHY OSTERHELD

Company E, 11th Virginia Infantry, the Lynchburg Rifles, contained many faculty members and students from Lynchburg College. The company was commanded by Capt. James E. Blankenship, who had been a professor of mathematics and a member of the school's military department. Captain Blankenship was certainly qualified by education to command, as he had graduated at the head of his class from Virginia Military Institute in 1852.

The Lynchburg Rifles was outfitted locally. The *Lynchburg Daily Virginian* reported that the company was uniformed in "gray goods trimmed with blue," and existing photographs show that the men wore battle shirts into service. They also had locally made equipment and were armed with Springfield muskets.

The 11th Virginia was quickly sent forward to join the Confederate army near Manassas, Virginia. During the battle of First Manassas, both Companies E and H were engaged with the enemy at Blackburn's Ford. It was here that Captain Blankenship showed that schooling did not necessarily make effective leadership—when things got hot during the fight, he turned and ran. Following the battle, the men of the 11th Virginia scoured the field and equipped themselves with new weapons and all other needed accoutrements. By the end of July, the company was outfitted as well as any in the Southern army.

# CHARLESTON ZOUAVE CADETS

Southern militiamen were no more immune than their Northern brethren to the Zouave craze fostered by the tour of Elmer Ellsworth's U.S. Zouave Cadets in the summer of 1860. In Charleston, South Carolina, a notice in the *Daily Courier* called for the raising of a military company to be named the Charleston Zouave Cadets. By the middle of August, the first meeting of the organization established a constitution for the company, and in October, officers were elected.

Determining a uniform was not as easy, and in the end, although the original constitution had called for a dress uniform "similar to the full uniform of the French Zouaves," when the company paraded for the first time, the men wore gray fatigue jackets and pants with red trim, accented "with white crossbelts." This was not a Zouave uniform, and even when the company adopted a full dress, or winter, uniform in November, it too was gray.

This winter uniform was worn for the first time at a drill on December 14, 1861, six days before South Carolina announced its secession from the Union. Actually a modified French chasseur uniform, it featured a tight-fitting gray short coat with slits at the sides, again trimmed with red. White gaiters and leather greaves (leggings worn between knee and ankle) helped give their straight-legged gray trousers the appearance of Zouave trousers. Officers wore dark blue uniform coats and trousers trimmed with red facings and gilt lace. All members wore exceptionally natty red and blue forage caps, the officers' trimmed with gilt lace.

The Charleston Zouave Cadets had devised an attractive and efficient uniform, but it could not be accurately described as Zouave. The Zouave Cadets' main contribution to the war was guarding Union prisoners from the battle of Bull Run who were housed in Charleston's Castle Pinckney. There they wore their short fatigue jackets and trousers without gaiters or leather greaves. By February, the Zouave Cadets had disbanded, although some of the members went on to serve in an artillery company guarding Charleston Harbor.

DICK AND M. E. CLOW

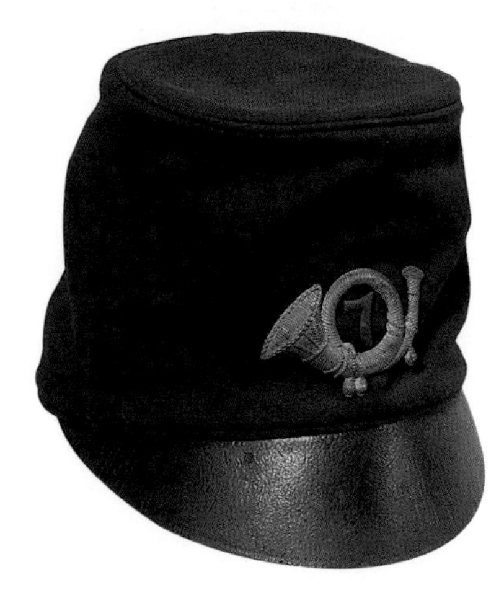

*An Austrian-style officer's forage cap* (Lager Mutze) *worn by Capt. Charles Burton of the 7th Connecticut Volunteers in the early part of the war. This style of cap, with a downward-pitched visor, was widely favored by both sides. Although christened a McDowell cap by modern collectors after the general who wore one, the evidence points to its origin in Europe as early as the 1850s or before.* TROIANI COLLECTION.

*An unusual enameled officer's belt, probably dating from before or very early in the war, with interlocking tongue-and-wreath Georgia buckle. The yellow coloring may indicate use by a cavalry officer.* WILLIAM ERQUITT COLLECTION.

*Typical of prewar firemen, this ornate belt and buckle are distinctively marked to the band of the 2nd Rhode Island Detached Militia. It was worn by musician William S. Dillway, who served about four months in late 1861.* JOHN OCKERBLOOM COLLECTION.

*White linen havelock worn by Sgt. Rollin B. Truesdell of Company F, 27th New York Volunteers. The regiment's historian commented: "On the march and in this battle [1st Bull Run] many men in the regiment wore white linen 'havelocks' with long capes over the back of the neck. These had been recommended to protect the wearers from the effect of the sun. The only good purpose they served, however was to furnish lint and bandages for the wounded, and were never worn much after this battle."* TROIANI COLLECTION.

C. B. FAIRCHILD, *HISTORY OF THE 27TH REGIMENT N.Y. VOLUNTEERS* (BINGHAMTON, N.Y.: CARL MATTHEWS PRINTERS,1888), 15.

*Early-war Federal gray felt overcoat of substandard quality. Describing similar inferior overcoats, a reporter wrote in the December 19, 1861,* Boston Evening Journal*: "Holding the cloth up to the light, you can see the cheat; using a little strength, you feel it; it is like brown paper. The wind will blow through them as if they were sieves; the least strain tears them." This coat, in unused condition, still bears the contractor's paper size label on the front.* TROIANI COLLECTION.

# 1ST MINNESOTA INFANTRY, JULY 1861

DR. J. LINDSTROM

The 1st Minnesota Infantry was raised in April 1861 from various small towns along the St. Croix and Minnesota Rivers. Most companies came together at Fort Snelling. The state made every effort to arm the proud, new regiment with the best weapons in its arsenal. Three companies received the M1855 rifle musket, while the rest were armed with a combination of M1841 rifles and smoothbore muskets altered from flint to percussion. Clothing was a more difficult problem. Only one company had uniforms, which had been made for the men by the women of their hometown. As luck would have, it the women had outfitted their soldiers in the color soon to be adopted by the enemy—gray. The remainder of the regiment received trousers and red woolen shirts purchased by the state from the stock of a St. Paul mercantile house. Several companies that had been temporarily stationed near Fort Ridgely, Minnesota, received old U.S. Army uniforms. Army forage caps were procured and issued in June, before the regiment left the state.

During May and June, the 1st Minnesota drilled and received a continual flow of visitors to their camp. On June 14, orders were received to move the regiment to Washington. As a parting gift, the men received 600 white cloth havelocks made for them by a local Ladies' Aid Society. These items, designed to fit over the army cap and extend down to cover the back of the neck, were touted as being indispensable to the soldiers' comfort. As the 1st Minnesota moved east, the Chicago press reported that the men in their red shirts were "looked upon as heroes of romance, frontiersmen and Indian fighters," according to the *St. Paul Pioneer and Democrat*.

It was expected that when the regiment arrived in the East, it would be outfitted in the regulation uniform. But when the army finally moved across the Potomac to meet the Rebels, the men still wore the same basic dress they had on when they left home, including the red shirts that marked them as frontiersmen. They lost 160 of their number, killed and wounded, on the field of Bull Run. Soon after the battle, the entire regiment finally received its first issue of regulation army uniforms. It served the rest of the war in the common garb of the Union soldier, but the record of valor it gained in the hard-fighting II Corps was anything but common. The final record showed a total loss in combat of 10 officers and 177 enlisted men killed and mortally wounded.

# 6TH TEXAS INFANTRY, PRIVATES, COMPANY G, 1861–62

Throughout the Civil War, the state of Texas made every effort to take care of her sons serving in the Confederate army. This extended to all aspects of the soldiers' lives, be it arms, uniforms, or hospital care. This was particularly evident in 1861, but to the degree possible, it continued for the entire war.

Company G, 6th Texas Infantry, is an excellent example of the early state effort. The company was raised as the Travis Rifles in Austin during the summer of 1861. With patriotic fervor high, the people of Austin procured the material for tents and uniforms, and the ladies of the city used their sewing skill to make both. The first uniform was described as "a dark pepper and salt grey" and, as appropriate to a rifle company, it was trimmed in green. Like many early units, both Union and Confederate, despite its name, the company did not carry rifles. The original arms of the Travis Rifles were flintlock muskets that were rifled and altered to percussion ignition.

Despite the patriotic intentions, the uniforms manufactured for the Travis Rifles by the industrious women of Austin seem to have lasted for only a short time. The company moved from Austin to Camp McCulloch, Texas, where it became Company G of the new 6th Texas Infantry. While here, the entire regiment was outfitted in new uniforms made of a light brown material manufactured at the Texas State Penitentiary. They also received new smoothbore M1842 Springfield muskets, which fired a formidable buck and ball load, as well as new accoutrements, including belts and cartridge boxes. The regiment finally received rifles in early 1862, when several issues were made of M1841 Mississippi rifles.

DAVID RANKIN, JR.

The 6th Texas remained west of the Mississippi until early 1863, when it moved east to the Army of Tennessee. Here it was consolidated with the 10th Texas Infantry and the 15th Texas Dismounted Cavalry and, under Col. R. Q. Mill of the 10th, was assigned to Churchill's Brigade in the division commanded by the hard-fighting Irishman Patrick Cleburne.

# 62nd Pennsylvania Infantry (33rd Independent Regiment), 1861

The 62nd Pennsylvania Infantry was recruited in the counties of Allegheny, Clarion, Jefferson, and Blair in July 1861 by Col. Samuel W. Black as the 33rd Independent Regiment. The original numerical designation lasted only a short time, however, until a controversy was settled relating to the commissioning of officers. In early correspondence, the 62nd was most often referred to simply as Colonel Black's regiment, and it was by this designation that the initial uniform was supplied by the U.S. Quartermaster's Department. In early August, Colonel Black requested and received permission from Gen. George B. McClellan for his new regiment to be uniformed in the sky blue jackets of the style worn by the U.S. Army in the Mexican War. It serves as a testimony to both the efficiency and versatility of the Quartermaster's Department that it was able to quickly respond to this request, which was only one of hundreds received from the volunteer regiments being mustered for Federal service.

Within less than a month, the army had contracted with the firm of George W. Colladay in Philadelphia, and by August 31, the regiment received the initial delivery of the requested uniforms—247 pairs of sky blue trousers and 449 sky blue jackets. By early September, the regiment was uniformed and equipped and on its way to Washington. On the eleventh, it crossed the Potomac River into Virginia.

PRIVATE COLLECTION

The sky blue uniforms of the 62nd served the regiment for less than six months. On January 22, 1862, Colonel Black's regiment, along with the 83rd Pennsylvania, was outfitted in the imported uniform of the French chasseur. It was in this dress that the regiment would see its first action—at Yorktown, Virginia, in April 1862. At Gaines' Mill on June 27, Colonel Black was killed in action.

By August 1862, the men of the 62nd no longer were distinguished by the uniform they wore. As they marched with the V Army Corps, they wore the standard uniform of the Federal soldier. But as one of the finest regiments in the Army of the Potomac, the 62nd needed only its record in battle to set it apart from the rest.

# 19TH ALABAMA INFANTRY, SPRING 1862

Early in June 1861, the Confederate secretary of war received a letter from Blount County, Alabama, offering the services of two companies that were "organized and . . . uniformed, drilled and ready to march." These companies, the Blount Continentals and the Blount Guards, were indeed ready to march, in uniforms with jackets cut much like a formal tailcoat. Although they surely felt every inch the warrior, the Continentals and Guards lacked one important ingredient: Like many of the brave young Southern men who were rallying to the colors of the new nation, the men of Blount County had no weapons.

By August, these companies had joined others from Pickens, Jefferson, and Cherokee Counties in camp near Huntsville and had been mustered as Companies B and K of the 19th Alabama Infantry. The lack of arms had required the new regiment to enlist for the period of the war, while others who came with their own weapons were allowed to enlist for twelve months' service. While at Huntsville, the new regiment was outfitted with all the necessities of a soldier's life. Camp kettles, tents, mess pans, axes, and spades were supplied, and each man received a tin cup and plate, but although these items prepared them for service, they would hardly strike fear in the heart of any Yankee.

It was not until January 1862, while in camp near Pensacola, Florida, that the 19th Alabama received the weapons they would carry into battle. Photographic evidence shows that at least some of the arms received were M1841 Mississippi rifles sporting an intimidating and unique bayonet, which could also serve effectively as a sword. Here at last were the tools that would allow the regiment to show what it could do. And it did not have long to wait. On April 6, as part of Gen. Albert Sidney Johnston's Army of the Mississippi, the 19th Alabama was part of the surprise dawn attack on the Union army camped around Shiloh Church, near Pittsburg Landing, Tennessee. During the heavy two-day fighting, the Alabamians suffered 219 killed and wounded, a casualty list that amounted to one-third of the number engaged.

DICK AND M. E. CLOW

*Saber bayonet made before the war by the Horstmann firm of Philadelphia for the U.S. 1841 rifle, which appears in period photographs of Alabama soldiers.* A. H. SIEBEL JR. COLLECTION.

# 2ND NEW HAMPSHIRE VOLUNTEERS, 1861

Although New Hampshire was asked for only one regiment of infantry with Lincoln's call for 75,000 volunteers in April 1861, so many responded that a second regiment was also formed from the eager volunteers. Four of its companies had been prewar militia companies, and the choice of gray for the regiment's initial uniform may have reflected this heritage. Wearing a "spike-tail" coatee with red trim, gray trousers striped with red, and "jaunty forage caps" of gray with red bands, the 2nd New Hampshire carried M1842 buck and ball muskets. One company carried Sharps breech-loading rifles provided by subscriptions of the citizens of Concord. Soon after Bull Run, the muskets were replaced with rifle muskets.

In fact, the regiment was fully equipped when it left the state for Washington in the spring of 1861. Each soldier was issued a "grey coat and pants, grey overcoat, grey fatigue cap, two flannel shirts, one pair of flannel drawers, one extra pair of socks, one pair of shoes, and one large camp blanket." He also received an "india rubber knapsack" with his accoutrements. By June, the *Washington, D.C., Evening Star* reported that the regiment's uniform included "grey caps and pants and blue jackets."

The 2nd fought at First Bull Run in its gray uniforms, but it wore Federal blue thereafter as it fought with the Army of the Potomac in every important battle to 1865.

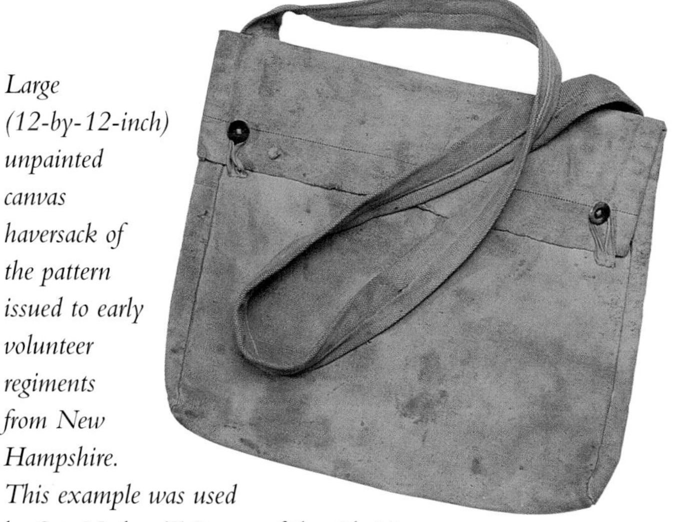

*Large (12-by-12-inch) unpainted canvas haversack of the pattern issued to early volunteer regiments from New Hampshire. This example was used by Sgt. Nathan T. Brown of the 6th New Hampshire Volunteers. Note the unusual double-button arrangement to secure the flap.* TROIANI COLLECTION.

COLLECTION OF KELLY OSMER

*Commercially manufactured forage cap provided to at least the first sixteen regiments from New Hampshire. Of a quality more often associated with officers, these caps were dressed with the silvered letters "NHV," in addition to a false embroidered hunting horn in brass or silver finish, with regimental and company designations. Some examples of this cap have horns of gilt brass despite the silver color of the other insignia.* TROIANI COLLECTION.

# SUMTER LIGHT GUARD, COMPANY K, 4TH GEORGIA INFANTRY, APRIL 1861

The Sumter Light Guard was one of numerous Georgia companies mustered into Confederate service wearing a uniform of its own design. In late April 1861, the *Augusta Chronicle and Sentinel* described the regiment: "This splendid corps arrived in town on Sunday morning. They number 83 men. They were accompanied by the American Brass Band, whose performance elicited general approval and eulogy from our citizens. They only escort the corps thus far on their journey. The Uniform of the Sumter Light Guards is a dark blue jacket, for the privates, trimmed with buff."

Within a matter of days, the Sumter Light Guard was mustered into Confederate service as Company K, 4th Georgia Infantry. The 4th Georgia was initially armed with smoothbore muskets, which were probably some of those purchased by the state in the North prior to the outbreak of the war. The regiment became part of the II Corps of the Army of Northern Virginia, and its history is interwoven with that famed army and corps.

PRIVATE COLLECTION

*A prewar stamped brass Georgia state seal hat device. Examples are known with both a gilt and silver finish and have been excavated on Civil War sites near Savannah and in South Carolina.* WILLIAM ERQUITT COLLECTION.

*Pvt. Milton J. Wolf of Company L, 28th Pennsylvania Volunteers, wore this short gray uniform jacket. Although the state of Pennsylvania contracted for a large number of cadet gray uniforms in early 1861, Col. John W. Geary chose to uniform and equip the 28th out of his own pocketbook. These garments were most likely replaced by the regulation blue before the beginning of the 1862 campaigns.* COURTESY OF PAMPLIN HISTORICAL PARK AND THE NATIONAL MUSEUM OF THE CIVIL WAR SOLDIER.

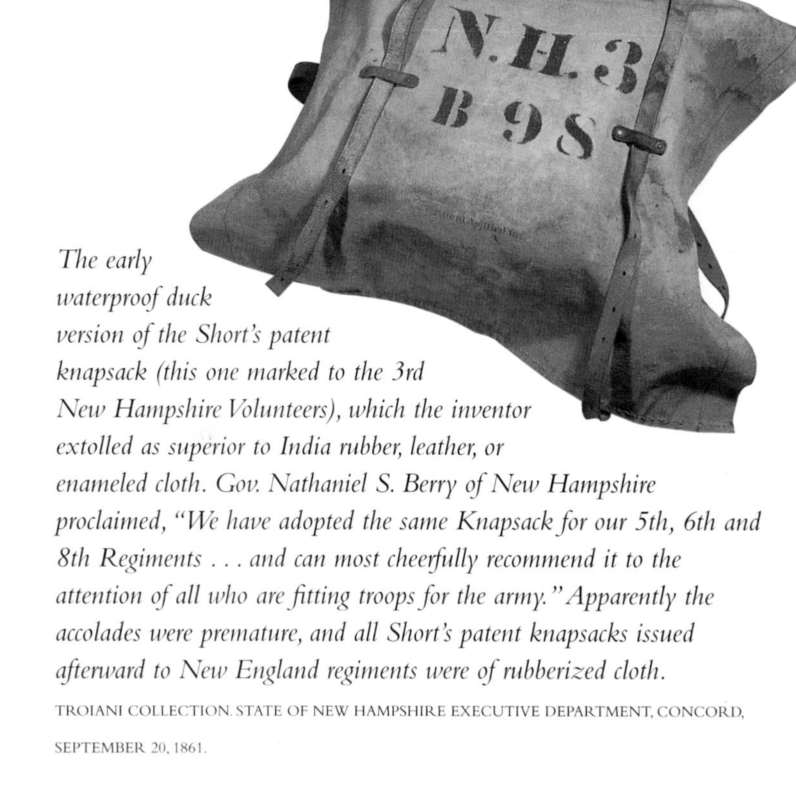


*The early waterproof duck version of the Short's patent knapsack (this one marked to the 3rd New Hampshire Volunteers), which the inventor extolled as superior to India rubber, leather, or enameled cloth. Gov. Nathaniel S. Berry of New Hampshire proclaimed, "We have adopted the same Knapsack for our 5th, 6th and 8th Regiments . . . and can most cheerfully recommend it to the attention of all who are fitting troops for the army." Apparently the accolades were premature, and all Short's patent knapsacks issued afterward to New England regiments were of rubberized cloth.*

TROIANI COLLECTION. STATE OF NEW HAMPSHIRE EXECUTIVE DEPARTMENT, CONCORD, SEPTEMBER 20, 1861.

*This whimsical camp or smoking cap was probably handmade by Pvt. Charles L. Comes of the 8th Louisiana Infantry. Such headwear was popular during idle hours in camp, which constituted much of a soldier's service. Comes was killed in action on the first day at Gettysburg.* CONFEDERATE MEMORIAL HALL, CLAUDE LEVET PHOTOGRAPH.

*Undoubtedly the most curious headgear donned in the war was the Whipple's patent cap. Patented in July 1861 by J. F. Whipple, it was produced by the Seamless Clothing Manufacturing Company and initially proved popular, especially among New England units, until the rigors of campaigning condemned it to an early extinction. There appear to have been two varieties: the solid-body felt type (shown) and a two-piece construction of a treated soft material with a center seam in the crown. The intensely bright blue cap shown here is one of the few surviving examples.*

TROIANI COLLECTION.

# 17TH MISSISSIPPI INFANTRY, COMPANY I, PETTUS RIFLES

The 17th Mississippi Infantry was mustered into Confederate service on June 1, 1861, to serve for a period of twelve months. Among those sworn to serve the new nation were the men of Company I, the Pettus Rifles, commanded by Capt. Marmaduke Bell, who had organized the company at Cockrums, De Soto County. The regiment left the state on June 13, headed for Virginia. Ahead of it lay four years of war in the ranks of the Army of Northern Virginia.

When they left Mississippi, the men of Captain Bell's company wore a uniform that, as closely as any, represented that prescribed prior to the war by the state for her troops. For reasons that may have reflected the desire for the predominance of states rights, Mississippi had decided to assign the infantry of her state army the trim color traditionally reserved for artillery—red. The company had been armed with muskets and bayonets, complete sets of accoutrements, canteens, and knapsacks. Whereas most of the uniforms were locally manufactured, the state quartermaster had supplied the buttons, described in requisitions simply as "Infantry buttons."

As with most early state-issue uniforms, that of the Pettus Rifles was replaced soon after actual campaigning had begun. By early 1862, the uniforms of the 17th were replaced by more standard Confederate issue, which the regiment wore for the remainder of the war. The original knapsacks continued in service at least until the end of 1861. The file of a private of Company C who was killed in action at the battle of Leesburg on October 21, 1861, states that because his knapsack was "thrown away on entering the fight and not found," he had no private effects to send home. It took over a year of campaigning before the soldiers of both armies learned that discarding or stacking of knapsacks before a battle usually resulted in their loss.

DICK AND M. E. CLOW

*Confederate copy of a U.S. model 1845 percussion cap pouch made in Columbus, Mississippi, during the early days of the war. The finial was often made of lead instead of brass.* NELSONIAN INSTITUTE.

# THE STANLY MARKSMEN, COMPANY H, 14TH NORTH CAROLINA INFANTRY

PRIVATE COLLECTION

The Civil War had begun. Confederate forces, in Charleston Harbor, fired upon Fort Sumter and Pres. Abraham Lincoln issued a call for 75,000 men to put down the Rebellion. In an article in the *Stanly (North Carolina) News and Press* Dr. Richard Anderson of Abemarle, Stanly County, asked of his fellow townspeople, "What was Stanly County to do?" Their own governor, John W. Ellis, wanted to recruit 10,000 volunteers to help defend Virginia. The majority of the populace of Stanly County were farmers; few owned slaves. Caring little for politics, they wanted to live and work their farms in peace. Dr. Anderson's question received no response. The crowd that had gathered in the second-story courtroom at the Abemarle Courthouse remained passively quiet. Anderson slowly rose from his chair and said, "I'm asking for volunteers to make up a company for Stanly County." The crowd now grew restless. Anderson's call for volunteers was passed from person to person, down the stairs to the first floor and out to those who gathered on the courthouse steps. One young man, Robert Carter, was told of the request for volunteers to support the secessionists. "Well, I'll go! I'll GO!" he shouted. Young Carter began pushing his way up to the second floor. All turned to look, then another young voice called out, "I'll go too! I'll volunteer!" Stanly County thus raised a company of 104 men to fight for the new Confederacy.

In the days that followed, the city of Abemarle dedicated itself to the care of the Stanly Marksmen. Young ladies tied ribbons around the arms of each new volunteer. A Committee was formed of concerned citizens to help clothe and equip the men for active service. The minute book of the committee states that gray cloth was procured for uniforms—darker gray for the coats, lighter gray for the trousers. A red grosgrain ribbon was used for the facings. The county's first sewing machine was pressed into service, as two local tailors, John Williams and Tommy Haskell, worked night and day sewing the garments. The ladies, supervised by "Aunt Tempe" Russell, cut up the cloth to pattern for the tailors.

The uniform dress of the Stanly County Marksmen was a frock coat with a high collar, "a chest full of red braid," and light gray trousers. The committee also supplied the company with twelve water buckets, seven club axes, seven hatchets, fourteen tents, thirty frying pans, ninety tin plates, and hats and shoes for all.

On May 5, 1861, they were sworn into state service as Company H, 4th North Carolina Volunteers. They later became Company H, 14th North Carolina Infantry, fighting in all the major battles of the Army of Northern Virginia. Four long years later, only 9 of the original 104 men surrendered at Appomattox Courthouse.

The history of how the Stanly County Marksmen procured their first uniforms is atypical of most early Confederate companies. Theirs were donated uniforms, made locally. Most other Confederate companies received uniforms from their home state, purchased them from private contractors, or marched to their assembly camps in their civilian clothes, hoping to buy or receive new clothing there. The new Confederate government allotted $21 to each new volunteer to spend on military clothing. But by the late summer of 1861, all the martial finery was gone. Warm winter clothing, wool socks, blankets, flannel shirts, wool overcoats, jackets, shoes, and boots were sent out to the armies. Now parades and fancy uniforms were just a fond memory for the Stanly County Marksmen.

*Dark blue satinette frock coat worn by John Crozier of Company E, 1st Delaware Volunteers, during his three months of service in early 1861. The coat is of simple construction, the only ornamentation being a light blue tape edging around the collar. There is a gap in the spacing of the buttons where the waist belt plate would have rested. The uniforms of Company D of this regiment (and possibly others) were made by the patriotic ladies of St. Paul's M.E. Church.* (DELAWARE GAZETTE, MAY 14, 1861.) TROIANI COLLECTION.

Right: *The state of New Hampshire furnished austere frock coats of its own pattern to the first eight regiments from that state. Fully lined, they were made of a shoddy material, without ornamentation of any sort except a light blue cord edging to the shoulder straps that lay under the brass shoulder scales. This example was worn in 1862 by John Currier, a forty-eight-year-old musician of the 6th New Hampshire Volunteers.* TROIANI COLLECTION.

# CHAPTER 1: MILITIA AND EARLY VOLUNTEERS


### INTRODUCTION

1. Robert Weir, *Regulations for the Uniforms and Dress of the Army of the United States* (Boston: Robert Weir Publishers, 1857), 83.
2. Frederick P. Todd, *American Military Equipage*, 1851–1872, vols. 1 and 2 (n.p.: Chatham Square, 1983).
3. *Military Gazette,* December 1860, p. 353.
4. Michael J. Winey, "Pennsylvanians in Gray," *Military Images* (July–August 1982), 92.
5. National Archives, Record Group 109, M-437, Letters Received by the Confederate Secretary of War.

### 6TH REGIMENT, MASSACHUSETTS VOLUNTEER MILITIA, 1861

Charles W. Hall, *Regiments and Armories of Massachusetts* (Boston: W. W. Potter, 1899).

*The Massachusetts Register,* (Boston: Adams, Sampson, 1862).

*Washington, D.C., Evening Star,* April 20, 1861, 3.

### PRIVATE, MARYLAND GUARD, 1861

*Baltimore American and Commercial Advertiser,* January 16, 1860.

*Reflections and Opinions of James McHenry Howard* (Baltimore: Wm. Wilkins, 1903), 27.

### 7TH REGIMENT, NEW YORK STATE MILITIA, 8TH COMPANY, 1861

Emmons Clark, *History of the Seventh Regiment of New York,* (New York: The Seventh Regiment, 1890).

*Washington, D.C., Evening Star,* April 25, 1861, 2.

### 1ST REGIMENT SOUTH CAROLINA RIFLES, 1861

National Archives, M-267, Compiled Service Records of Confederate Soldiers, South Carolina, December 17, 1862.

### DRIVE THEM TO WASHINGTON

National Archives, Record Group 109, M-468, Compiled Service Records of Soldiers Who Served in Organizations from the State of Virginia, 4th Virginia Infantry.

### PRIVATE, COMPANY I, 4TH VIRGINIA INFANTRY C.S.A., THE LIBERTY HALL VOLUNTEERS

National Archives, Record Group 109, M-324, Compiled Service Records of Confederate Soldiers Who Served from Virginia, 4th Virginia Infantry.

### FLAT RIVER GUARD, COMPANY B, 6TH NORTH CAROLINA STATE TROOPS INFANTRY

Frederick P. Todd, *American Military Equipage, 1851–1872,* vol. 2 (n.p.: Chatham Square, 1983).

Richard W. Iobst, *The Bloody Sixth* (Raleigh: North Carolina Centennial Commission, 1965), 5.

### CLINCH RIFLES, GEORGIA MILITIA, APRIL 1861

*Augusta Daily Constitution,* October 14, 1860.

*Original Orderly Book,* Clinch Rifles, July 18, 1860.

*Augusta Chronicle and Sentinel,* May 7, 1861.

**THE FIRST BATTLE FLAGS**

Letter written by Lt. Colin McRae Selph, July 25, 1905, Louisiana Historical Association Papers, Tulane University Library.

**3RD ALABAMA INFANTRY, COMPANY A, MOBILE CADETS, 1861**

William. S. Coker, ed., *The Mobile Cadets, 1845–1945: A Century of Honor and Fidelity* (Bagdad, Fla.: Patagonia Press, 1993), 19, 29.

Frederick P. Todd, *American Military Equipage,* 1851–1872, vol. 2 (n.p.: Chatham Square, 1983).

National Archives, Record Group 109, M-331, Compiled Service Records of Confederate General and Staff Officers and Nonregimental Enlisted Men, roll 265, Lt. Col. James L. White.

*www.rootsweb.com,* 3rd Alabama History.

**1ST RHODE ISLAND DETACHED MILITIA, 1861**

Augustus Woodbury, *A Narrative of the Campaign* (Providence: Sidney S. Rider, 1862).

Original Uniform of Edward N. Whittier, 1st Rhode Island Detached Militia, Don Troiani Collection.

**11TH VIRGINIA INFANTRY, COMPANY E, THE LYNCHBURG RIFLES, JULY 1861**

National Archives, Record Group 109, M-324, Compiled Service Records of Confederate Soldiers Who Served in Organizations from Virginia, 11th Virginia Infantry.

*Lynchburg Daily Virginian,* May 1, 1861.

Rusty Hicks and Adam Scher, "Piedmont Battle Shirts," *Military Images* (November–December 1995): 9–14.

Robert T. Bell, *11th Virginia Infantry* (Lynchburg, Va.: H. E. Howard, 1985), 11.

**CHARLESTON ZOUAVE CADETS**

*Charleston Daily Courier,* July 30, 1860.

Frederick P. Todd, "Notes on the Organization and Uniforms of South Carolina Military Forces," *Military Collector and Historian* 3, no. 3 (September 1951): 53–62.

Ron Field, "Charleston Tigers," *Military Illustrated* no. 103 (December 1996).

**1ST MINNESOTA INFANTRY, JULY 1861**

Annual Report of the Adjutant General of Minnesota, St. Paul, 1861.

Quote from a Chicago paper of June 28, 1861, found in the June 29 *St. Paul Pioneer and Democrat.*

Todd H. Fredericks and Stephen E. Osman, "Minnesota 1st Volunteer Infantry, 1861–1864," *Military Collector and Historian* 47, no. 2 (summer 1995): 83–89.

Frederick H. Dyer, *A Compendium of the War of the Rebellion* (New York: Thomas Yoseloff, 1959).

**6TH TEXAS INFANTRY, PRIVATES, COMPANY G, 1861–62**

Jim Turner, "Co. G, 6th Texas Infantry, C.S.A., from 1861 to 1865," *Texana* 12, no. 2 (spring 1974): 149–78.

Richard A. Baumgartner and Larry M. Strayer, *Echoes of Battle* (Huntington, W.V.: Blue Acorn Press, 1996).

National Archives, Record Group 109, Personnel Files of the 6th Texas Infantry.

**62ND PENNSYLVANIA INFANTRY (33RD INDEPENDENT REGIMENT), 1861**

National Archives, Record Group 92, entry 2194, book 3; and Record Group 94, Regimental Books, 62nd Pennsylvania Infantry.

**19TH ALABAMA INFANTRY, SPRING 1862**

National Archives, Record Group 109, M-437, Letters Received by the Confederate Secretary of War; and M-374, Compiled Service Records of Confederate Soldiers Who Served from Alabama, 19th Infantry.

John M. Murphy and Howard Michael Madaus, *Confederate Rifles and Muskets* (Newport Beach, Calif.: Graphic Publishers, 1996), 503.

*War of the Rebellion: A Compilation of the Official Records of the Union and Confederate Armies,* vol. 20 (Washington, D.C.: Government Printing Office, 1901).

**2ND NEW HAMPSHIRE VOLUNTEERS, 1861**

Martin A. Haynes, *A History of the Second New Hampshire Volunteer Infantry* (Lakeport, N.H., 1896).

*Washington, D.C., Evening Star,* June 24, 1861, 3.

**SUMTER LIGHT GUARD, COMPANY K, 4TH GEORGIA INFANTRY, APRIL 1861**

*Augusta Chronicle and Sentinel,* April 30, 1861.

National Archives, Record Group 109, M-266, Compiled Service Records of Confederate Soldiers Who Served in Organizations from the State of Georgia.

Frederick P. Todd, *American Military Equipage,* 1851–1872, vol. 2 (n.p.: Chatham Square, 1983).

**17TH MISSISSIPPI INFANTRY, COMPANY I, PETTUS RIFLES**

National Archives Record Group 109, M-269, Compiled Service Records of Confederate Soldiers Who Served in Organizations from the State of Mississippi, Records of the 17th Mississippi.

**THE STANLY MARKSMEN, COMPANY H, 14TH NORTH CAROLINA INFANTRY**

"First Stanly Civil War Unit Was Heroic, Colorful Group," *Stanly (North Carolina) News and Press,* October 10, 1962.

# CHAPTER 2

# *Volunteers of Many Nations*

THE AMERICAN NATION IN 1861 WAS BEGINNING to reflect the diversity of population that would characterize our national experience into the twentieth century. During the seventeenth and eighteenth centuries, the colonies that became the United States were composed mainly of people of English descent. A few Dutch, French Huguenot, German, and Scots-Irish immigrants were interspersed in this relatively homogeneous population and added to the vitality of the new nation. In the years before the Civil War began, however, a major wave of immigration hit the American shores, changing forever the national character and contributing to the diversity of the military uniforms worn by the Civil War soldiers.

From the 1820s through the 1850s, the numbers of these new immigrants reached levels never before seen. In the 1820s, immigration numbered around 10,000 persons a year. In 1854 alone, over 420,000 new immigrants arrived in the United States. Although these numbers would be dwarfed by the millions of immigrants who arrived in the twentieth century, they were sufficient to cause a backlash against immigration from the native-born and descendants of earlier immigrants. The Know-Nothing movement of the 1850s was a hypocritical attempt to ensure that these new Americans would not "corrupt" the values of a political system already terminally divided over the issue of slavery. It was reflected even in the militia system. New Irish immigrants formed a regiment, the 69th New York State Militia, whose ultimate purpose was the liberation of Ireland. German immigrants gathered in units such as the 5th New York State Militia to practice target shooting and celebrate the liberties found in their new home, while some native-born reacted by forming strictly "American" organizations such as the 71st New York State Militia, known as the American Guard. Each was in its own way a reflection of the national origin of its members, but the regiments also reflected the nation itself as they came together in 1861 for the war.

Since the waves of nineteenth-century immigrants tended to settle in the Northeast and Western states, most of the foreign-born volunteers served in the Northern armies. Only the more cosmopolitan cities of the South, such as Charleston, South Carolina, and New Orleans, had sufficient numbers of foreign-born to form distinctive units. In Charleston, before the war, among the militia companies at the start of the war were the German Artillery, complete with spiked helmets known as *Pickelhaubes;* the Union Light Infantry, in Scottish trews; the Lafayette Artillery, in French frock coats and red trousers; and the Montgomery Guard, in traditional Irish green coatees. In New Orleans, in 1860, the Creole Zouaves were described as wearing chasseur uniforms, including a "coat of navy blue, with gilt buttons, skirts only five or six inches deep," and "Turkish trousers of light blue, full and baggy." These national uniforms would soon disappear in the South, as the Confederate military ran into insurmountable problems of procurement and distribution. Confederate clothing manufactories were not so flexible as their Northern counterparts, and distinctive uniforms of any sort tended to disappear in the Southern forces. Irishmen, Germans, and Scots who served with the South soon lost their national flavor.[1]

In the North, the militia companies and regiments also often reflected the national origin of their members. Thus Scotsmen in kilts could be found equally in New York or Illinois, and French Zouaves and chasseurs, or at least their uniforms, ranged from Missouri to Massachusetts. Germans in spiked helmets were not found solely in Charleston, as *Pickelhaubes* appear in advertisements throughout the Northern papers. Still, despite the better resources of Northern quartermasters, there were few truly national uniforms worn by even Federal volunteers as the war progressed.

Whereas Zouave and chasseur uniforms were common throughout the war, there were few true Frenchmen wearing them. The old 55th Regiment of the New York State Militia—in existence since the 1840s as a company of French-Americans—was hard-pressed to fill its ranks with volunteers of French ancestry; nevertheless, its infantry went to war in a version of the French campaign uniform, and its Zouaves were as splendidly attired as any North African regiment. A few French veterans found their way into the 62nd New York, the Anderson Zouaves, whose flank companies also wore a full-rigged Zouave uniform, but for the most part there was more influence than service from French immigrants, whose actual numbers were few in wartime America.

The much more numerous German population often had a Teutonic flair in the manner in which it wore its uniforms, but there were relatively few volunteer regiments in German dress. When the early Ohio volunteers from Cincinnati departed for war, members of the 9th Ohio wore the white clothing of the Turner Societies—social and athletic clubs organized in a quasimilitary fashion—and some even took their target rifles with vicious-looking knife bayonets to war. The 41st New York went to war in green and red uniforms based upon the traditional garb of Prussian Rifle regiments. They did, however, somewhat spoil the effect with the addition of a French Zouave company to the regiment. The German riflemen of the 20th New York Volunteer Infantry wore Federal blue but did sport the traditional German marksman lanyard, or aiguillette, from the front of their coats. Louis Blenker's 1st German Rifles wore a simple gray and green uniform that had less German styling than practicality. Although the overall contribution of the German-American population to the war was tremendous, for the most part German volunteers blended into the mainstream.

Although often mentioned and completely romanticized, the use of Scots Highlander uniforms appears to have been limited to the original members of the 79th New York State Militia, who served with the 79th Volunteer Regiment during the war. The prewar kilts were worn by those former militiamen who had them when the regiment left New York City, but trews, trousers of tartan cloth, were worn afterward until replaced by Federal blue. The only distinctly Scots garments to see sustained service were caps of either the glengarry or tam-o'-shanter styles, worn by the 79th and other predominantly Scots units such as the 12th Illinois.

Another national uniform used during the war was the *bersaglieri,* or Italian light infantry, uniform mimicked by the 39th New York, the Garibaldi Guard. The men of the 39th New York, however, were not all of Italian descent, and even the regiment's colonel, Frederic George D'Utassy, was not Italian. In fact, D'Utassy's regiment was one of the most cosmopolitan of all the volunteer regiments. It was reported that the regiment included "three companies each of German and Hungarians and one company each of Frenchmen, Italians, Spaniards and Swiss."[2] The loose, red "Garibaldi shirt," patterned after those worn by the original Italian national patriots of Garibaldi's army, was, however, a frequently mentioned garb of early war volunteers.

Perhaps most surprising is the lack of any distinctly Irish garb among the volunteers. The Irish-American population was quite sizable during the American Civil War and was second only to the number of German-Americans in the Union armies. Irish-Americans, however, did not go to war in green uniforms like those worn earlier in the century by Irish militia companies. Instead, except for Thomas F. Meagher's green general's uniform and a reported green vest in the Irish Brigade, most Irishmen went to war in the issued uniform of a state or the Federal government. Even the Irishmen of New York's 69th State Militia Regiment had given up their green uniforms for regulation blue years before the war began.[3] Still, the Irish green battle flags of regiments from several states dotted many a Civil War battlefield.

Foreign volunteers fought and died, North and South alike. Their contributions to our history are invaluable, and even though most of the volunteers of the war—fully three-quarters of the Union army—were native born, the very real color their few distinctive uniforms added to the war only highlights their story.

# Irish Jasper Greens, Lance Corporal, Fall 1861

On August 24, 1861, with all the eloquence of nineteenth-century oratory, the Irish Jasper Greens of Savannah were presented with a new flag. The flag was a gift from several young ladies of the city and symbolized both allegiance to the state and the ethnic makeup of the organization. One side was of white silk, with the coat of arms of Georgia surmounted by eleven gold stars, and the reverse side was of green silk, upon which was embroidered the Harp of Erin along with the name of the company and the date of its organization, 1842. At the time of presentation, the Greens numbered about 100 men, commanded by Capt. John Foley. A detachment of the company had been ordered to garrison Fort Pulaski in January, and now the entire unit was preparing to move to augment the garrison of the fort.

DR. COYLE S. CONNOLLY

Militia units such as the Irish Jasper Greens were very much a part of the fabric of prewar Savannah. The rules and minutes meticulously kept by the Greens leave no doubt that these sons of Erin were among the best. In 1861, the company had both a fatigue and a dress uniform, both of dark blue trimmed in green. It was the fatigue uniform that the men wore to duty at Fort Pulaski. In the organization's rules, it is described as "a blue jacket with green collar and cuffs, 10 buttons in front, straps on the shoulders to pass the belts under." The trousers for both uniforms were the same but were dependent upon the season—for summer, white linen with no stripe, and for cooler weather, dark blue with a $1^{1}/_{2}$-inch green stripe edged with buff down the outer seam. Rank was indicated by chevrons of "green army lace on green cloth laced with buff showing green between the chevrons . . . pointing upwards." The rank of lance corporal, indicated by a single chevron, placed its wearer in a command structure between a private and a full corporal. No description of the headgear of the company is recorded, but several references are made to white plumes, which would have been used with the shako popular at the time. The meeting minutes of April 19, 1860, show that the company also purchased fatigue caps. Given the meticulous care invested in the design of the rest of the uniform, these caps most certainly were designed to complement the rest of the fatigue dress. The property returns of the Irish Jasper Greens for December 1861 indicate that while the muskets carried by the company belonged to the state of Georgia, most accoutrements worn to war were the property of the Confederate States. Of plain leather, these replaced the white buff belts worn prior to the war.

# COMPANY K, 69TH NEW YORK STATE MILITIA

Irish-Americans in New York City had formed militia companies since the eighteenth century, but the most Irish of all militia regiments, the 69th New York, was not organized until October 1851. It was formed from eight existing militia companies and confirmed by General Order No. 489 on November 1, 1851. The 69th is a part of New York's military heritage to this day, and its name became legendary during the Civil War, beginning at the battle of First Bull Run.

The colonel of the 69th, Michael Corcoran, gathered many Irish volunteers to bring the militia regiment to war strength, including a new Company K to replace the troop of cavalry in the militia organization. The new company, known as the Irish Zouaves, was recruited by Thomas Francis Meagher. Meagher, in exile from his native Ireland, was a political activist and Irish-American politician, and a major force in attracting volunteers. His men did not wear full Zouave uniforms, retaining only the short, open jacket and vest of the French originals. Meagher and the other officers of the Irish Zouaves wore similar uniforms, with gold braid on their jackets and crimson and gold stripes on their pants. Their weapons were M1816 muskets altered to the Maynard primer system and rifled, while the rest of the regiment carried M1842 muskets.

The 69th lost nearly 200 men at Bull Run as casualties and prisoners. Corcoran was captured and taken to Richmond as a prisoner. Meagher was wounded and carried from the field while unconscious. His Zouaves fought bravely, one of them saving the regimental color from capture at the end of the battle. The battered regiment returned to New York City, where a new volunteer 69th was raised. It became the core of the famed Irish Brigade, commanded by Gen. Thomas Francis Meagher.

WILLIAM RODEN

*This model 1858 U.S. canteen with blue woolen cover belonged to Pvt. Daniel O'Hare of Company B, 69th New York State Volunteers. O'Hare joined on September 21, 1861, and deserted the same day, taking his newly issued canteen with him.* TROIANI COLLECTION.

# 8TH AND 20TH NEW YORK VOLUNTEER INFANTRY, 1861

The large German-American population of the North was among the first to rally to the defense of the Union in 1861. In all, over 200,000 of these immigrant Americans would enlist in the Federal armies. Some of them were not only eager volunteers, but distinctly dressed as well. Two New York City German regiments, the 8th and 20th Volunteer Infantry, wore uniforms reflecting the Germanic tradition of marksmanship and the use of rifles.

The 8th, calling itself the 1st German Rifles and commanded by Louis (Ludwig) Blenker, was actually issued M1842 muskets rather than rifles, but still placed the distinctive green trim of a rifle unit on their gray uniforms. Uniformed in a gray sack with a strap and buckle behind, gray pantaloons with a broad green stripe down the side, and a gray cap with green cord, the 1st German Rifles was only one of several Union regiments in gray in 1861. More distinctive was the regimental engineer corps—the Pioneers, a splendid body of handicrafters, all equipped with India rubber aprons, axes, hatchets, knives, and other paraphernalia. These men led the regiment into Virginia in July 1861, where they served in the reserves at First Bull Run, though they did help turn back Confederate cavalry in the rearguard action of the Union retreat.

The 20th, called the United Turner Rifles, was issued and continued to carry throughout its service the M1841 rifle, also popularly called the jaeger or Mississippi rifle. This was truly a regiment of riflemen from its inception, having received 720 U.S. rifles with saber bayonets and 240 with socket bayonets fitted by an Albany, New York, mechanic named Frederick H. Grosz upon muster from the state of New York.

The United Turner Rifles, named after the Turnverein, German athletic societies that also fostered the use of firearms for marksmanship, also wore a distinctive uniform. Their dark blue frock coats had shoulder straps and were trimmed with a Germanic marksman lanyard, or aiguillette, worn looped from the shoulder. Their Federal-style uniform or Hardee hats were trimmed with rifle insignia, and all trim, including the hat cords, was in rifle green. At Antietam, with their Swedish colonel, Ernst von Vegasack, the 20th stormed across the open fields between the East and the West Woods to the Dunker Church, their regimental colors in the front, Vegasack crying of the colors, "Let them wave. They are our Glory!"

PRIVATE COLLECTION

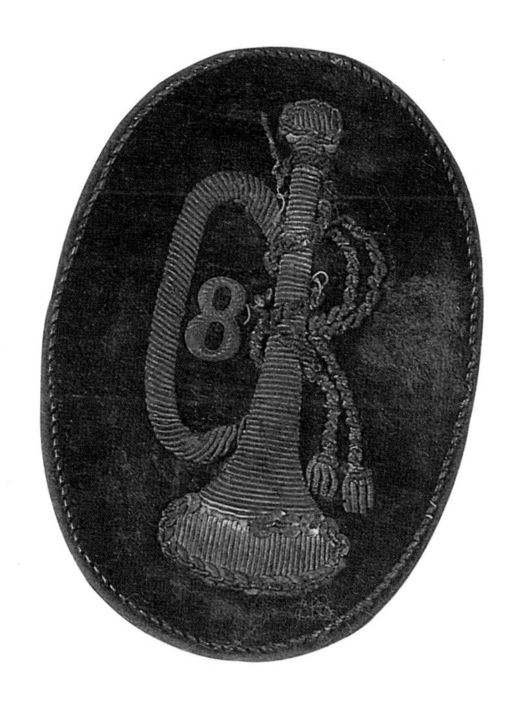

*Officer's metal-backed hat insignia of the 8th New York Volunteers, with an embroidered trumpet and silver number 8 on a dark green velvet ground.*

TROIANI COLLECTION.

# 79TH NEW YORK HIGHLANDERS, 1861

DICK AND M. E. CLOW

Most militia regiments that served in the American Civil War limited their service to thirty to ninety days, the legal limits set on required participation. Some units were so eager to go war in 1861 that they forfeited their militia status to serve longer periods. The 79th New York State Militia was such a regiment. It was added to New York's militia rosters in 1859, but only after some controversy, as state authorities were not eager to add another regiment of immigrants into a system they sought to regiment by eliminating distinctiveness. Indeed, the regiment's required bill of dress stipulated that only trousers be worn, although they could be of plaid cloth. If the state had its way, the new regiment, which was allowed to take the regimental number 79 in honor of Great Britain's regiment of Cameron Highlanders, even though it was out of sequence, would have been just another militia regiment.

The Scotsmen of the 79th, however, were not to be just another regiment. This became clear at the regiment's first parade, when the men marched in Manhattan wearing not pants, but kilts. Though these Scots wearing "short petticoats and bare knees" were described as being "in poor taste and barbarous," the 79th persisted, and the men thereafter wore their kilts in every parade until the war came in 1861. To go to war, the regiment had to nearly double its size with recruits, but it was impossible to obtain sufficient material for kilts for the new members. Another result of getting these recruits was that enough other militia units had already gone to war to fill the state's quota. If the 79th were to go to war, it would have to go as a Federal volunteer regiment, which it willingly agreed to do in order to fight.

On June 2, 1861, the 79th went to war, with the screech of bagpipes and here and there the bare knees of men in kilts. The original militia members of the 79th wore their kilts in this parade, with the officers in the colors of their clans. The new men wore plaid trousers, with the cutaway kilt jackets of the regiment, trimmed with red and white. Armed with converted flintlock muskets, it was still obviously an ethnic regiment, but more importantly, it was a regiment with pride that would carry it through three years of war. From First Bull Run, where the 79th lost its colonel, James Cameron, the brother of Lincoln's secretary of war Simon Cameron, to such far-flung actions as Secessionville in South Carolina, Antietam, Vicksburg, Knoxville, the Wilderness, and Spotsylvania, the Scotsmen of the 79th were true to their regiment.

# 12TH ILLINOIS INFANTRY, 1ST SCOTTISH REGIMENT

Like many of the early Union volunteers, the 12th Illinois Infantry, originally known as the 1st Scottish Regiment, left for war dressed in gray. This regiment was raised in different parts of the state, and for the first months of service, its men wore a variety of dress that reflected the tastes of the individual counties and towns, as well as their ability to clothe their sons for battle. By August 1861, the need to enlist soldiers for more than a few months' service prompted the state of Illinois to offer a fine, new gray uniform for the first six regiments, now designated as the 7th through 12th Illinois Volunteers. The coat was to have a short skirt extending midway to the knee and be trimmed in light blue. In addition, the men would receive a fatigue uniform consisting of a shirt and pantaloons of fine hickory cloth and a Zouave cap. A hat of gray felt was also included with the dress uniform, but contemporary photographs of men of the 12th show them in Scottish tams, which were worn to honor their first colonel, John McArthur of Chicago. Although the uniform itself was consistent within the various regiments, Regimental Special Order No. 21 was issued at Paducah, Kentucky, on October 9, 1861, to address the fact that sergeants and corporals of the 12th were wearing chevrons of differing colors. The order specified that all chevrons and trouser stripes would in the future be of light blue worsted wool or cloth. It also established chevrons of three stripes and a single tie for company quartermaster and commissary sergeants.

PRIVATE COLLECTION

On September 23, 1861, a War Department order mandated that all regiments in U.S. service discontinue wearing gray, the color adopted by the enemy. It was not until March of the following year, however, that the regiment received blue replacement uniforms.

The early muster rolls of the various companies refer to the arms of the regiment simply as "old Muskets," which is consistent with those issued to nearly all of the early Illinois regiments. By the fall of 1862, the Federal government had gotten the arms situation in hand with a combination of imported and domestic firearms. The 12th would be rearmed with both Enfield and Springfield rifle muskets.

The battle history of the 12th Illinois was second to none. Beginning at Fort Donelson and continuing through the campaign under General Sherman in Georgia and the Carolinas, it fought with valor and distinction.

# SONS OF ERIN

It was midmorning on September 17, 1862, near the town of Sharpsburg, Maryland. The battle of Antietam had been raging for several hours as a brigade of the Army of the Potomac's II Corps moved forward toward the position held by Confederate troops of Gen. D. H. Hill's Division. This brigade, composed of three ethnic Irish regiments—the 63rd, 69th, and 88th New York—along with the 29th Massachusetts, was destined to gain everlasting fame as the Irish Brigade. When the day was done, the Confederate position would also have a name; it would be known forever as the "Bloody Lane."

Leading the brigade was a true son of Erin, Gen. Thomas Francis Meagher, known for his elegant uniforms. At the battle of Savage Station in June, he had worn a suit of dark green velvet, trimmed with gold lace. Today, mounted on a magnificent bay horse with the flags of the 69th New York behind him, he was the picture of glory. The regiment, and indeed the brigade, was uniformed in the eight-button jacket issued by the state of New York. This jacket had been adopted pursuant to the recommendations of a military board appointed by the state in 1861. The men of the color guard were identified by their nonregulation chevrons surmounted by embroidered crossed U.S. flags. The brigade's knapsacks had been stacked in the rear prior to the assault, and a few young soldiers had chosen to remove their shoes and move forward barefoot. Within a short time, the Confederates were driven from their post, but the cost to the Irish Brigade was high: 113 killed and 422 wounded.

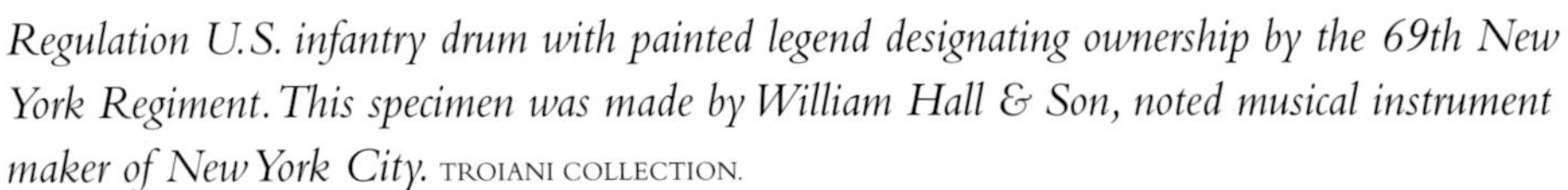

*Regulation U.S. infantry drum with painted legend designating ownership by the 69th New York Regiment. This specimen was made by William Hall & Son, noted musical instrument maker of New York City.* TROIANI COLLECTION.

MARYANNE TRUMP BARRY

# 41ST NEW YORK VOLUNTEER INFANTRY, DE KALB REGIMENT, 2ND YAEGER REGIMENT

Besides the well-known French Zouave uniform and Highlander's kilt, another distinctive foreign uniform was worn during the Civil War by an American volunteer regiment—the green and red of the German jaeger, or rifleman. German riflemen had traditionally worn green since the eighteenth century. During the American Revolution, German mercenaries had included a Rifle Corps, equipped with short and stubby, but efficient, rifles and uniformed in green coats faced with red.

The 41st was raised mainly from the German-born immigrants of New York State. As one of four regiments that the Union Defense Committee was authorized to recruit and equip, the 41st was exempt from any state regulations as to its uniforms and equipment. The regiment originally was known as the De Kalb Regiment, after German general Johann de Kalb, who was killed in the Patriot cause during the American Revolution. It was also known as the 2nd Yaeger Regiment, as there was already a 1st German Rifles in service under Col. Louis Blenker.

The 41st chose the distinctive green and red of German riflemen for its uniform, which was described in detail by the New York City newspapers:

> The dress consists of a dark green frock coat, trimmed with red on the collars and cuffs, gray pantaloons, trimmed with a red cord, and cloth caps of the same color as the coats faced with red. The troops are also provided with an overcoat of gray pilot cloth, made after the Prussian Army regulation; in fact, the complete outfit of the regiment is on the plan of the Prussian Army. The knapsacks are to be of the most approved style, being sloped, so as to fit in the hollow of the back, and of a size and weight to contain a good store of outfit—the officers' uniforms are precisely the same as that of the men, with the only distinction of their shoulder straps and the lace on their caps.

DICK AND M. E. CLOW

Armed with M1842 muskets, the regiment was ready for war by June 1861, when it was presented with an American standard of silk with gold fringe. On the blue field was a shield surrounded by thirty-four stars and with the inscription "De Kalb Regiment, N.Y.V." By July, the regiment was paraded with "neat havelocks," which "were found of unusual benefit in keeping the sun off."

The 41st served in the XI Corps of the Army of the Potomac until after Gettysburg, when it was transferred to South Carolina. Reenlisting in 1864, the 41st continued as a veteran regiment, fighting in the Shenandoah Valley at Cedar Creek and mustering out at City Point after serving in the siege of Petersburg.

# DE KALB ZOUAVES, 41ST NEW YORK VOLUNTEER INFANTRY, 1861

The 41st New York was raised mainly among the German-American immigrants of New York. Recruited and equipped by the Union Defense Committee of New York City, it was free to design its own uniforms. Most of the regiment, known as the De Kalb Regiment after Revolutionary War hero Johann de Kalb, a Prussian general who gave his life in the winning of U.S. independence, chose green rifle coats trimmed with red like those of Prussian jaegers, or riflemen. The regiment was also known as the 2nd Yaeger Regiment, because Blenker's 8th New York was already called the 1st German Rifles, but like the 8th, it had to content itself with M1842 muskets rather than rifles. It was not until 1863 that these riflemen received M1861 rifle muskets.

Even with its Germanic heritage, the 41st could not resist the influence of that French craze—the Zouave uniform. The regiment's Company A was known as the De Kalb Zouaves or Duysing's Zouaves, after its captain, and wore "a dark blue jacket (braided with red) and pantaloons with the yellow and black leggings of the Turcos, the blue sash and the red fez and blue tassel" like the French Zouaves. The elaborate yellow trim on the sleeve was not, however, a part of the French uniform, and is found on an original jacket in the collection of the Smithsonian Institution.

By 1862, when the regiment served as part of Blenker's division at Cross Keys, Groveton, and Second Bull Run, it was garbed in the blue jackets of New York Volunteers. The regiment participated in the XI Corps' disasters at Chancellorsville and Gettysburg and was in Hilton Head, South Carolina, when its service expired. It mustered out on June 9, 1864. A reorganized veteran 41st went on to the end of the war, seeing action at Cedar Creek and Petersburg, Virginia.

TIM OSTERHELD

# BROTHERS OF IRELAND

As Gen. George B. McClellan's Penninsula campaign ground to a halt outside Richmond, the forces of Robert E. Lee were on the offensive. After failing to destroy Union forces at Mechanicsville late in June 1862, Lee pressed the Federal defensive lines near Gaines' Mill. He threw his best at the beleaguered Federals, including Stonewall Jackson's seemingly invincible brigade. Among the first hit were the Irish volunteers of Col. Thomas Cass's 9th Massachusetts Volunteer Infantry.

Seeing the green flag of the 9th, Jackson growled that his men should sweep away "that damned brigade" and threw them at Cass's regiment. The gallant little regiment refused to be swept away and, though it lost men, stubbornly held its ground. Then, just as it seemed about to be overrun, the green flags of the real Irish Brigade came up in relief, as the Irishmen of the 63rd New York joined the Irishmen of the 9th Massachusetts in combat. Together they thwarted Jackson.

Irish green had saved that part of the field. It was seen in the battle flags of both regiments and in the unique green velvet uniform worn by that most Irish of all Irishmen, Gen. Thomas Francis Meagher. Meagher's gaudy outfit was topped off with a green-plumed straw hat. The men of the 9th wore no green, only the standard blue of the Federal soldier. The men of the 63rd New York also wore Federal blue, but they stripped to their multihued shirts in the June heat of Virginia's Peninsula. On that day, all their clothing was begrimed by black powder, smoke, and blood, as these brothers of Ireland held the field.

JOHN KERR

# 55TH NEW YORK, LAFAYETTE GUARD, 1861

On April 17, 1861, the French-American 55th New York State Militia voted unanimously to offer its services to the national government. It was accepted about the first of May and set up camp on Staten Island to organize for war. But the militia's colonel became hopelessly ensnared in military red tape, and as delays mounted, the regiment began to disintegrate, as whole companies deserted to other volunteer regiments that were leaving for the war. To get the regiment to the front, its officers appealed to Baron Philippe Régis de Trobriand to take the colonelcy and lead the regiment to war.

De Trobriand's regiment, now called the 55th New York Volunteer Infantry, or Lafayette Guard, retained the uniforms of its French heritage: "Regiment will assemble on Wednesday, 31st inst. In fatigue dress (overcoats with epaulettes, red pants, small caps, shoes and gaiters). Armed and equipped with knapsacks containing the necessary underclothing." The New York City firm of Brooks Brothers contracted for uniforms for the regiment, including "60 French Imported Scarlet Fez Caps at $1.25 ea." As there was not sufficient red cloth for the regiment's trousers, Brooks Brothers manufactured "Brown Drilling Pants" as substitutes. At the end of August, the 55th finally went to war, trained and equipped, and drilled by an amateur colonel soon became professional. "They went away in heavy duck pantaloons and blue overcoats, except one company wearing French Zouave uniforms."

De Trobriand's already undersize regiment suffered severely in the Peninsula, and in September 1862, its survivors were consolidated into a four-company battalion. De Trobriand lamented: "Where were the red pantaloons? Where were the Zouave jackets? And above all those who had worn them, and whom we looked in vain among the ranks to find." Within months, the 55th disappeared, consolidated into the 38th New York, with de Trobriand becoming a brigadier general after commanding a brigade in the III Corps.

COLE UNSON

*These simple brigadier general's shoulder straps belonged to Philippe Régis Denis de Keredern de Trobriand, an immigrant from France. The embroidered hat insignia dates from his colonelcy with the 55th New York Volunteer Infantry, Lafayette Guard.* COLLECTION OF NEW YORK STATE DIVISION OF MILITARY AND NAVAL AFFAIRS.

*Cartridge box plate of the 55th New York Volunteers recovered from a camp site in Virginia. Another variation of this type has also been excavated, but with the numbers in script.* WEST POINT MUSEUM.

# 39TH NEW YORK, GARIBALDI GUARD

JOHN H. KURTZ

Almost certainly the most cosmopolitan of all volunteer regiments, the 39th New York Volunteer Infantry was also plagued with the most notorious of colonels. Col. Frederic George D'Utassy gathered a polyglot regiment of Hungarians, Spanish, Italians, French, Swiss, and Germans to form the Garibaldi Guard, or perhaps more appropriately, the 1st Foreign Rifles. D'Utassy's personal history is clouded, but his conduct with his regiment is well documented. Almost immediately his regiment staged a minor mutiny over being issued M1842 muskets rather than the rifles they expected. There was friction between the diverse elements of the regiment, and the inept officers D'Utassy gathered were incapable of instilling discipline. D'Utassy himself was almost immediately under suspicion of having bilked the government by charging for 900 rations when only 700 men were in the regiment. Eventually D'Utassy was court-martialed, found guilty, and sent to New York's Sing Sing Prison for multiple frauds committed against his own regiment and the government.

In the beginning, though, the regiment was cloaked in the romance of its name, uniforms, and multiple national flags. Before they received their full uniforms, the men of the regiment paraded in red Garibaldi shirts, of which it was said that "the warm scarlet color . . . , reflected upon the men's faces as they stood in line, made a picture which never failed to impress the reviewing officer." The regiment's full uniform eventually consisted of "blue frock coats, blue pants trimmed with red cord, red undershirts, and felt hat ornamented with feathers and green leaves. Their knapsacks contained blankets and comfortable under clothing, while the haversacks were crammed with bread, cheese, bologna sausages, etc." Ultimately the 39th shed itself of both its bad officers and distinctive uniforms, becoming one of the Army of the Potomac's steady regiments.

# GARIBALDI LEGION, 1861

With thousands of immigrants only years, or even months, away from their native land, ethnic pride was very evident in nineteenth-century America. Substantial communities of these new Americans existed, particularly near the various ports of entry from Boston to New Orleans. Many who had come to this country seeking a new life were veterans of European armies. These men, and those who would find a common bond with them, flocked to the colors of their adopted land. Even before war became a reality, companies of militia were being formed that had a distinctive European flavor both in appearance and name. In 1861, the major influx of immigrants of Italian and southern European heritage was still several decades away. By this time, however, both New York and New Orleans could boast substantial numbers of arrivals from Italy. Many of these were followers or admirers of the Italian revolutionary Giuseppe Garibaldi.

When the shooting finally started, both the Union and Confederate armies had within their ranks units of Italian-born volunteers. The Garibaldi Guard, later to become the 39th New York Infantry, served in the Union Army of the Potomac's famed II Corps. In the South, the *New Orleans Bee* reported that a battalion "composed exclusively of Italians," which would be known as the Garibaldi Legion, would be raised in that city and went on to describe in detail the uniform it would wear.

> Hat: high peaked black felt, moderate sized brim turned up on left side with a small bunch of green, black and white feathers . . . around the crown a green silk cord terminating behind in a tassel and fixed in front with a gilt button
> Jacket: a round jacket of red woolen cloth
> Trousers: bottle green pantaloons cut wide and reaching below the knee, there held by gaiters or leggings of the same material buttoned on the outer side
> Accouterments: a black belt and cartridge box

WILLIAM RODEN

The *New Orleans Daily Picayune* reported on the "dashing red uniforms and plumed hats" of that city's Garibaldi Legion. Although the future of the Southern Garibaldis would be quite different from that of their Northern brothers, the short history of the New Orleans legion would do credit to the ethnic population of that city.

By October 1861, it was reported by another New Orleans newspaper, the *Daily True Delta,* that 30,000 Louisiana troops had been sent out of the state in service of the Confederacy. With New Orleans and the state itself vulnerable to attack, the troops left behind—the volunteer militia, including the flamboyant Garibaldis—would be responsible for their defense. These soldiers likely would have given a good account of themselves if a fight for the city had become a reality. As it was, the city administration elected to surrender on April 29, 1862, rather than face destruction at the hands of Union naval gunboats on the Mississippi. Following the surrender, the Garibaldi Legion ceased to exist as a military organization. Some of the members likely found their way into other Confederate regiments, but their flamboyant uniforms were left behind, along with the short history of the Southern Garibaldis.

## New York Independent Battalion, *Les Enfants Perdus*

This unusual unit was organized in New York City during August and September 1861 from various immigrant groups by Lt. Col. Felix Confort, a former French Army captain. The term *Les Enfants Perdus* seems to have been derived from the Crimean War, when *enfants perdus* referred to groups of soldiers engaged in what might be called a "forlorn hope" task, such as an assault upon an impregnable position or other post of extreme danger. Confort's men were supposedly "intended for special service as tirailleurs and scouts." Instead, they were first engaged in McClellan's bungled Peninsula campaign, where they were described as "foreigners, the rough-scuff of New York City," and it was noted that "some twenty tried to desert to the enemy after the first pay day." Assigned later to the XVIII Corps, *Les Enfants'* most active service came in the siege of Battery Wagner, South Carolina, and Morris Island.

DR. DAVID YANKE

The first uniform was a triple-breasted chasseur-style coat with yellow trim and a detachable yellow plastron. It was described in 1861 as "an improvement on the well known Zouave costume. The trousers are not so baggy, the jacket has short tunic lapels and the cap is of the kepi instead of the fez pattern. In color the uniform is throughout, dark blue, trimmed with yellow; is made of serviceable cloth, and will wear well, at the same time it looks so handsome." According to a later description, it was a "smart blue tirailleur uniform with yellow breast pieces, shoulder knots and facings, and the rakish 'plume de coq' which garnished their hats, gave them a decidedly foreign appearance." A later uniform was made "without plastroon [*sic*] (or yellow front piece) and substituting in lieu of the three rows of round buttons, one row of 9 New York State buttons—Trimmings of Infantry Blue instead of Yellow as present." Fancy dress, however, does not make a soldier, and *Les Enfants* never matched the brilliance of their uniforms.

# CLEAR THE WAY

All regiments of the Irish Brigade suffered severely on the bloody day at Antietam, their ranks thinned and their flags shredded. In November 1862, the 28th Massachusetts, an Irish-American regiment in the IX Corps, exchanged places with the Yankee 29th Massachusetts of the Irish Brigade. Thus, on the coming bloody day in December, the Irish Brigade would be composed fully of Irish-American regiments.

At Fredericksburg, Virginia, on the cold morning of December 13, 1862, cloaked in sky blue great coats, their dark blue forage caps pulled tightly down on their heads, the men of the Irish Brigade were deployed in a sunken road bordered by a thick stone wall. They were about to make a desperate assault, and their precious green battle flags were gone, sent home for replacement. Only the new 28th had unscathed colors to take onto the field of battle. As Gen. Thomas F. Meagher gave a fiery oration, his staff officers handed out sprigs of green boxwood for the men's caps. The Irish Brigade would go into battle under green colors, even if most of its regiments lacked their flags.

In the noise of battle, the Irish cheer "Faugh-a-Ballagh!" was heard from the 28th: "Clear the Way!" It was the regimental motto. Yet despite all their courage, the wearing of the green, and the regimental motto, the Irish Brigade could not overcome the sheets of flaming lead that tore through their ranks. Their gallant assault upon the Confederates at Fredericksburg failed. No dead were closer to the Confederate lines than those of the 28th and the other regiments of the Irish Brigade.

*Forage cap of the 63rd New York Volunteers, which formed part of the Army of the Potomac's famed Irish Brigade. The cap bears the red trefoil badge of the 1st Division, II Army Corps, with the regimental number and company letter.* COLLECTION OF NEW YORK STATE DIVISION OF MILITARY AND NAVAL AFFAIRS.

PRIVATE COLLECTION

ISH BRIGADE

# IRISH BRIGADE BAND

By August 1862, the famed Irish Brigade had not been at war for a year, but its commander, Gen. Thomas F. Meagher, was in New York City to recruit new men for his brigade. His task had been made easier by the members of the Produce Exchange, who appropriated money for a bounty of $10 each to the first 300 recruits for the brigade. Along with the state and Federal bounties, this meant that a recruit would receive about $140 on joining his regiment. The recruits took a new brigade band along with them to the war. A reporter for the *Irish-American* described the scene as Meagher left for Harrison's Landing with recruits and the new band: "The new band for the Brigade went out with Gen. Meagher in the *Key West*. They are under the leadership of Edward Manahan. The members wear a tasteful gray uniform faced with green, and make a handsome appearance. They will be a great addition to the Brigade, and will cheer the tedium of camp life with some of the fine old music of Fatherland, to which every true Celt is so passionately attached."

With less than a year's service, the Irish Brigade had already fought at Fair Oaks, Gaines' Mill, Savage Station, White Oak Swamp, and Malvern Hill. Still ahead were Antietam, Fredericksburg, Chancellorsville, and Gettysburg. The Celts of the Irish Brigade would have reason to seek comfort in music in the long, sad months ahead.

DR. COYLE S. CONNOLLY

# PRIVATE, 45TH NEW YORK INFANTRY, JULY 1863

PRIVATE COLLECTION

The 45th New York Infantry can be considered one of the very best of the ethnic German regiments to serve in the Union army. Recruited in New York City as the 5th German Rifles, and mustered in September 9, 1861, the regiment was made up entirely of immigrant Germans. Orders were given in the native tongue, and until forbidden by the army, the regimental books were written in German. The early regimental assignments were varied and included time in the Union Army of Virginia under Maj. Gen. John Pope. By September, the 45th was part of the 1st Division of the Army of the Potomac's XI Corps.

The arms and uniform of the 45th New York were, as befitted their German ancestry, carefully documented in the meticulously kept regimental books. In January 1862, the following accounting was made of the regimental ordnance:

737 - Remington rifles, Cal. 54
88 - Enfield rifles, Cal. 577
733 - Sword bayonets for Remington rifles
735 - Sword bayonet scabbards, Remington rifles
88 - Sword bayonets, Enfield rifle
48 - Swords, N.C.O.
133 - Belts & Plates, N.C.O.
622 - Belts & Plates, privates, N.Y.
95 - Belts & Plates, U.S.
832 - Cartridge boxes
832 - Cap pouches
832 - Frogs

The men of the 45th New York wore the state-issued jacket into the Gettysburg campaign. By direction of the commander of the XI Corps, each soldier was ordered to carry two pairs of shoes. The men were also directed "to take on the march, overcoats, India Rubber Blanket, and Shelter tent." It was left to the discretion of the regimental commander whether the men would also carry woolen blankets.

The 45th New York was thrown into the fighting north of Gettysburg on July 1 and made a heroic stand in the streets of the town during the retreat of the XI Corps. The regiment would continue to serve in the XI and later the XX Corps until July 1864, when it was ordered to the defense of Nashville and consolidated with the 58th New York.

*One of a pair of the first national Confederate guide flags of the 5th Louisiana Battalion (later Kennedy's 21st Louisiana Volunteers). These small silk banners, measuring 31 1/2 by 18 1/2 inches, were stationed on the flanks of the regimental line to aid the men in keeping proper alignment. The 5th Battalion served at Island Number 10, the battle of Belmont, and in operations around Corinth. This small unit was composed almost exclusively of German immigrants, with a sprinkling of French, Belgians, and Scandinavians.* TROIANI COLLECTION.

# CHAPTER 2: VOLUNTEERS OF MANY NATIONS


### INTRODUCTION

1. Frederick P. Todd, *American Military Equipage, 1851–1872,* vol. 2 (n.p.: Chatham Square, 1983).
2. *Washington, D.C., Evening Star,* May 30, 1861.
3. Maj. Robert Taylor, Inspector 4th Brigade, October 25, 1859 report, in *Annual Report* (Albany, 1860).

### IRISH JASPER GREENS, LANCE CORPORAL, FALL 1861

*Savannah Morning News,* November 30, 1927.

Georgia Historical Society, Savannah, Irish Jasper Greens Papers, vol. 2, Rules and Minutes, January 31, 1856–January 30, 1862; and box 3, folder 8, Property Returns, 1861.

### COMPANY K, 69TH NEW YORK STATE MILITIA

*Washington, D.C., Evening Star,* Thursday, May 23, 1861.

*Irish American,* August 17, 1861.

New York State Archives, *Commissary General of Ordnance for 1861,* Reports, 91.

Michael Cavanaugh, *Memoirs of General Thomas Francis Meagher,* Worcester, Mass.: Messenger Press, 1892.

### 8TH AND 20TH NEW YORK VOLUNTEER INFANTRY, 1861

C. Eugene Miller, *Der Turner Soldat: A Turner Soldier in the Civil War, Germany to Antietam* (Louisville, Ky: Calmar Publications, 1988).

### 79TH NEW YORK HIGHLANDERS, 1861

*Military Gazette,* September 15, 1860, 277.

William Todd, *The 79th Highlanders, New York Volunteers in the War of the Rebellion, 1861–1865* (Albany, N.Y.: Branlow, Burton, and Co.), 1886.

### 12TH ILLINOIS INFANTRY, 1ST SCOTTISH REGIMENT

National Archives, Record Group 94, Order Book, 12th Illinois Infantry.

### SONS OF ERIN

Frederick P. Todd, *American Military Equipage,* (Providence, R.I.: Company of Military Historians, 1977), 2:358.

### 41ST NEW YORK VOLUNTEER INFANTRY, DE KALB REGIMENT, 2ND YAEGER REGIMENT

Ron Field and Roger Sturcke, "41st New York Volunteer Infantry Regiment, (De Kalb Regiment or 2nd Yaeger Regiment) 1861–1865," *Military Collector and Historian* 39, no. 2 (summer 1987): 76, 77.

*New York Herald,* June 9, 1861, 5.

*New York Daily News,* June 20, 1861, 8.

*New York Herald,* July 4, 1861, 8.

### DE KALB ZOUAVES, 41ST NEW YORK VOLUNTEER INFANTRY, 1861

*New York Tribune,* June 8, 1861, 8.

National Archives, Record Group 156, Ordnance Returns, U.S. Regiments, 41st New York Volunteer Infantry.

Frederick Phisterer, *New York in the War of the Rebellion, 1861–1865,* vol. 3 (Albany, N.Y.: J. B. Lyon, 1912), 2237–38.

### BROTHERS OF IRELAND

Alonzo Foster, *Reminiscences and Record of the 6th New York V.V. Cavalry* (privately printed, 1892), 35.

### 55TH NEW YORK, LAFAYETTE GUARD, 1861

Régis de Trobriand, Four Years in the Army of the Potomac (Boston: Ticknor, 1889).

*New York Evening Express,* July 29, 1861, 3.

*New York Tribune,* September 1, 1861, 5.

Brooks Brothers contract, August 3, 1861.

### 39TH NEW YORK, GARIBALDI GUARD

Ella Lonn, *Foreigners in the Union Army* (Baton Rouge: Louisiana State University Press, 1951).

William L. Burton, *Melting Pot Soldiers* (Ames, New York: Fordham University Press, 1988).

*New York Herald,* May 29, 1861, 8.

### GARIBALDI LEGION, 1861

*New Orleans Bee,* January 28, 1861.

*New Orleans Daily Picayune,* June 11, 1861.

*New Orleans Daily True Delta,* October 20, 1861.

**NEW YORK INDEPENDENT BATTALION, *LES ENFANTS PERDUS***

*New York Herald,* December 7, 1861.
*Irish-American,* March 22, 1862.
Francis Balace and John R. Elting, "Les Enfants Perdus, 1861–1864," *Military Collector and Historian.* 22, no. 1 (spring 1970): 26–27.
National Archives, Record Group 92, entry 999, vol. 20, 423.

**CLEAR THE WAY**

Capt. O. P. Conyngham, *The Irish Brigade and Its Campaigns* (1867; reprint, Baltimore: Butternut and Blue, n.d.), 341.

**IRISH BRIGADE BAND**

*Irish-American,* August 16, 1862.
Joseph G. Bilby, *Remember Fontenoy: The 66th New York and the Irish Brigade in the Civil War* (Hightstown, N.J.: Longstreet House, 1995).
William F. Fox, *Regimental Losses in the American Civil War* (Albany, N.Y.: Albany Publishing Co., 1889).

**PRIVATE 45TH NEW YORK INFANTRY, JULY 1863**

National Archives, Record Group 393, entry 5323, Special Orders XI Corps, Order's No. 68, April 14, 1863.
New York Monument Commission, *New York at Gettysburg,* vol. 1 (Albany, N.Y.: J. B. Lyon, 1900), 375–81.
Frederick H. Dyer, *A Compendium of the War of the Rebellion,* vol. 3 (New York: Thomas Yoseloff, 1959).

# CHAPTER 3

# *Zouaves and Chasseurs*

THE MOST EXOTIC AND COLORFUL OF ALL THE uniforms worn during the American Civil War were those derived from the French Zouave regiments. Uniforms of chasseurs, cousins to the Zouaves, were not as elaborate but just as distinctive. Together they were an expression of the Gallic influence of Napoleon III's ill-fated second empire. France's military machine appeared to be a formidable force in the 1850s, as it came out of successful campaigns in the Crimean War and the war with Austria in 1859. American officers, including George B. McClellan, who served as military observers with the French armies became proponents of the French systems. The influences of their observations were manifested in many forms. Just prior to the war's start, the U.S. Army replaced Winfield Scott's venerable drill manual with Hardee's *Tactics*, a revised French manual for light infantry drill and formations. During the war, Federal quartermasters issued leggings and shelter tents modeled after the French originals. And soldiers of both the North and the South wore homegrown versions of the French Zouave and chasseur uniforms.

In 1861, there were three regiments of Zouaves in the French Army. Their origins went back to 1830, when many of the French expeditionary troops were withdrawn from North Africa, and General Clausel recruited native North African troops as replacements. Among them were the *Zoudaouas,* the former ruling dey's militia, who offered their services to the French general. He accepted, and thus were born the legendary Zouaves. In 1831, King Louis-Philippe officially sanctioned the Zouave Corps as part of the French colonial forces. By 1835, there were two battalions of six companies in the corps. Two companies of each battalion were composed of French citizens at this time, but by 1841, only one company of nine was of native North African soldiers. By 1852, the three battalions were all European (the native troops were now in sharpshooter battalions known as the *Tirailleurs Algériens*), and the original battalions became the three regiments of Frenchmen now known as Zouaves.

Despite the Europeanization of the Zouaves, their uniforms remained that of the native North African. By the time of the American Civil War, they were well established, if not indeed traditional. The Zouave was distinguished by his

*These once luxurious and expensive red velvet shoulder straps are of the type labeled "extra rich" in a Schuyler, Hartley & Graham military goods catalog. No artillery colonel wore these straps, however, for they belonged to Gouverneur Kemble Warren and were worn by him while commanding the famous Duryée Zouaves, the 5th New York Volunteer Infantry.* WEST POINT MUSEUM.

short, dark blue jacket, worn open and without buttons on the front. Under this was a closed, dark blue vest, fastened at the side rather than the front. The Zouave's trousers were of madder red wool, made without individual legs and ending just below the knees. A blue sash was wrapped about the waist, covering the top of the trousers, and a pair of gaiters secured the bottom of the trousers. The gaiters were covered at the top with leather greaves, or *jambières* (leather leggings worn over garters). For headgear, the Zouave wore a fez, wrapped originally in a green turban. Later the turban was made of white cloth. Ornamentation on these uniforms was limited to red tape edging on the jackets at the edges and cuffs, and on the body in the form of a false pocket known as a *tombeau*, shaped like a circle culminating in a stem topped with a trefoil. The *Tirailleurs Algériens* wore the same uniform, but in light blue with yellow trim.

In Crimea in 1854 and Italy in 1859, Zouave and Turco (the popular name for the native *Tirailleurs*) figured prominently in the campaigns. At the opening Crimean battle of the Alma, Zouaves bravely scaled the heights under Russian fire, and at the climactic battle of Sebastapol, it was again Zouaves who launched foolhardy assaults upon the Russian fortifications. In Italy, Zouaves and Turcos fought in the bloody battles of Magenta and Solferino, and they appeared in press releases, lithographs, and heroic oil renditions of the battles. Their bravery and exotic dress, along with stories of their notorious foraging and petty thievery, made them gallant rascals who captured the imagination of the European, and soon the American, public. Zouave soldiers figured prominently in the illustrated American weeklies of the 1850s, which included sidebars and short features on Zouave antics and foibles. Perhaps the color and caprice of these soldiers were a seductive distraction in the normally staid life of the Victorian age. For whatever reason, the allure of the Zouave uniform reached the United States in the 1850s and took solid root.

It was not until 1860, however, that the Zouave movement reached its true zenith. That year, a highly trained Zouave drill team from Chicago, led by E. Elmer Ellsworth, undertook a national excursion, challenging local militia units to drill competitions, and appearing on the front pages of newspapers throughout the nation. Ellsworth's U.S. Zouave Cadets wore a uniform based upon, but not copied from, the French uniform: "A bright red chasseur cap with gold braid; light blue shirt with moire antique facings; dark blue jacket with orange and red trimmings; brass bell buttons, placed as close together as possible; a red sash and loose red trousers; russet leather leggings, buttoned over the trousers, reaching from ankle halfway to knee; and a white waistbelt."[1]

This flamboyant uniform actually had more circus than military in its ancestory, but Ellsworth's design influenced numerous imitators within the year, from the Albany Zouave Cadets to Baxter's and Gosline's Pennsylvania Zouaves, with their button-trimmed jackets. Elmer Ellsworth became a national hero. His Zouave Cadets disbanded after the tour, but many later became officers of volunteer Zouave regiments. In 1861, Ellsworth raised a regiment of Zouaves from New York City firemen and became the first national martyr,

*Zouave uniform of Sgt. William D. Porter, Company K, 155th Pennsylvania Volunteers. This regiment was transformed into Zouaves in early 1864 by the acquiescence of the army Quartermaster Department, which economized by cannibalizing the remaining stock of imported French chasseur clothing. The trousers and leggings were enlarged, and jackets were cut from the hooded talmas. This uniform is a slate blue-gray in color, referred to in official documents as "French dark sky-blue kersey." Sergeant Porter wore this uniform when with the color guard at the battle of Five Forks, Virginia, in 1865.* TROIANI COLLECTION.

killed by a prosecessionist after seizing a Confederate flag. His Zouave tour had sown the seeds that grew into dozens, if not hundreds, of militia and quasimilitary Zouave companies throughout the nation. Their uniforms were often poor imitations of the French originals or reflected an originality of design that probably would have embarrassed a French Zouave, but they became an integral part of the history of the uniforms of the war.

The first regiments of volunteer Civil War Zouaves wore a vast variety of uniforms. Hawkins' Zouaves of New York wore proper Zouave jackets and vests, but with dark blue trousers that, while baggy, were not of true Zouave proportions. Duryée's Zouaves, a highly professional set of volunteers, wore close copies of the true blue and red French uniform. Wallace's Zouaves of Indiana came to war in gray uniforms and kepis rather than "heathen" blue and red Zouave garb. Even Ellsworth's Fire Zouaves were originally uniformed in gray uniforms with red fire shirts. Wheat's Tiger Rifles of New Orleans had blue jackets and fezlike caps, but wore red shirts and white-and-blue-striped trousers. Baxter's Philadelphia Fire Zouaves came to war in short blue jackets ornamented on the edges with brass buttons, light blue trousers, and dark blue chasseur-style kepis. Coppen's Louisiana Zouaves, with many French-American volunteers, came close to the French, even to the use of *vivandières* (women licensed to act as sutlers in a regiment) to assist the soldiers.

The uniforms of these volunteers reflected the individuality of the regiments as much as they did the Zouave originals. They were procured in the initial rush to arms with public and private funding. In the North, the Federal government assumed the task of clothing the volunteers and attempted to standardize, but never eliminated, the Zouave uniform. In the South, the Zouave uniform disappeared in the scramble among state and central governments to procure and distribute clothing to the Confederate soldiers. In 1863, a second wave of Northern Zouaves was created in the Army of the Potomac, and new Zouave uniforms were fashioned for them. When the war ended in 1865, and the triumphant Armies of the Republic paraded in Washington, D.C., there were more regiments in Zouave uniform than there had been in the army of 1861. Zouaves fought in their distinctive uniforms in every major battle of the war. Their contributions are measured in the valiant dead they left upon those many fields.

In Europe, the chasseur could be a light infantryman or a light cavalryman. In the United States during the Civil War, only the light infantry chasseur's uniform was mimicked. The use of light infantry was indeed largely due to the colonial experience in North America. Irregular warfare in the vast forests of the New World reshaped the European style of warfare, as well as the uniforms worn by the Regulars of

*A dark blue jacket with yellow-orange cording and small brass ball buttons worn by a member of the Boston Light Infantry, a well-known independent company in the Massachusetts Volunteer Militia. Written in the sleeve is the inscription "Worn at Fort Warren 1861."* WEST POINT MUSEUM.

Europe. In Napoléon III's second empire, all infantry became light infantry, with quicker tactical movements, more open formations, and uniforms meant to reflect that style of warfare. In the 1850s, the *Chasseurs à Pied de la Garde Impériale,* or Foot Chasseurs of the Imperial Guard, wore a distinctive uniform that consisted of a short frock coat *(habit-tunique)* extending a few inches below the waist, vented at the bottom edge with a slit; "voluminous breeches" tucked into *jambières* and gaiters; and a low, plumed shako for headgear. For fatigue purposes, the chasseurs wore the distinctive kepi that had originated in the desert warfare of North Africa, known in the United States as the chasseur kepi.[2]

In 1860, as a part of the movement toward greater battlefield mobility, all French infantry were ordered into uniforms like those of the Imperial Guard Chasseurs. The short-skirted *habit-tunique* and baggy trousers were adopted, along with a new short leather shako. The *habit* was of dark blue with chasseur yellow facings, and the trousers were of light blue-gray. The gaiter-*jambière* combination was also adopted for all, and a fatigue jacket of plain dark blue was also provided. It was a highly attractive and stylish uniform, which would influence many American volunteers during the Civil War, although not to the extent of that of the Zouaves.

The uniform of 1860 was selected as an experimental purchase and issue by the Quartermaster General, Montgomery Meigs, in 1861 and 1862. Meigs ordered 10,000 complete uniforms of this pattern from the firm of Alexis Godillot in July 1861. They were received in New York in late December and were issued to a number of regiments of the Army of the Potomac in 1862. The experiment was largely a failure because the uniforms were made in sizes too small for the average American soldier.

Still, the chasseur-style uniform of 1860 nearly became the uniform of the U.S. Army. In 1862, at the height of the war, a uniform board was convened to consider the adoption of a new uniform. Its recommended uniform was based upon the French chasseur garb of 1860. Interestingly, prominent on this board was Gen. Daniel Butterfield, whose 12th New York State Militia Regiment had adopted the French chasseur uniform in 1861 while on duty in Washington, D.C. The board's recommendation, however, was shelved and never adopted.

The only chasseur uniforms worn in the war were those purchased by volunteer regiments, such as the 65th New York and several regiments of New York's Excelsior Brigade, or provided some Pennsylvania regiments by the Federal government. At war's end, only the distinctive Zouave uniform remained in the armies of the Republic. The chasseur uniform had been infrequently worn, except by the militia, where it remained popular, especially in New York, New Jersey, Pennsylvania, Massachusetts, and California. Clearly, though, of all the uniforms based upon those of a foreign nation, those of France were the most widely used. It would take the humiliating defeat of the soldiers of Napoléon III in the Franco-Prussian War of 1870 to dim the luster of the French soldiers.[3]

RICHARD CONTE

# 6TH NEW YORK VOLUNTEERS, WILSON'S ZOUAVES

What is a Zouave? Is it simply a soldier in a fancy uniform, or is it a soldier with an attitude? In the case of Billy Wilson's Zouaves—the 6th New York Volunteer Infantry—there were no fancy uniforms, but plenty of attitude. Organized by William Wilson, a New York City politician, from the "roughs and b'hoys" of the city, the 6th styled itself the Union Zouaves but was unable to provide Zouave uniforms for itself. Instead, upon signing the enlistment roll, each man was given "a new thick grey shirt, and a tricolor cockade for his breast." Wilson, a showman as well as politician, swore in his new regiment with a ceremony as rowdy as a political rally. Waving the American flag, Wilson called on his men to swear to support the flag and never flinch through blood or death. Waving their brown felt-brimmed hats or brandishing their seven-inch Bowie knives, Wilson's men responded with shouts of "Blood! Blood!" They had attitude.

What they did not have, in the beginning, though, was good leadership. Shipped to Florida in June 1861, the 6th New York did little except help man the guns of Fort Pickens. On October 9, 1861, a surprise Confederate attack upon the regiment's island camp caused a rout and the burning of their tents. It took Regular infantry to drive off the Rebel troops. Wilson's Zouaves needed a dose of discipline. After a purge of "its bad officers and soldiers," the regiment proved worthy of its initial attitude and served with credit in the XIX Corps against Port Hudson, Louisiana. Billy Wilson took his "b'hoys" home in June 1863.

TIMOTHY OSTERHELD

*This kepi belonged to Pvt. Sullivan Wiley, Company I, 8th Massachusetts (Salem Zouaves–Salem Light Infantry). Wiley served with this unit from April 30 to August 1, 1861, when he joined the 12th Maine Volunteers.* JOHN OCKERBLOOM COLLECTION.

## SALEM ZOUAVES, 8TH MASSACHUSETTS VOLUNTEER MILITIA, 1861

TIMOTHY OSTERHELD

By 1860, many of the old independent militia companies were feeling their age in that they suffered declining numbers and were losing popularity to more modern militia organizations. Among these well-established units was the venerable Salem Light Infantry, chartered by the state of Massachusetts in 1805. The Salem Light Infantry held a banquet for Comdr. William Bainbridge of the U.S. frigate *Constitution* in 1813 in celebration of that ship's victories in the War of 1812. In the ensuing years, the company was prominent in all of the celebrations and parades, both in Salem and throughout the state. In 1859, as it tried to keep up with the fashions of the time, the company adopted the French

Zouave drill under the tutelage of its captain, Arthur F. Devereux. The next year, 1860, it hosted the U.S. Zouave Cadets of Elmer Ellsworth during their East Coast tour.

The initial uniform of the Salem Zouaves, as the company came to be known, was not a Zouave uniform. Instead, the men of the Salem Zouaves wore a closed shell jacket of medium blue, trimmed with imitation frogging in red on the breast, medium blue pants, and red fatigue caps. With the outbreak of the war, the company was placed in the 8th Regiment, Massachusetts Volunteer Militia, for three months' service as Company I (alternately recorded as Company J). The regiment left for Washington on April 18, 1861, and the Salem Zouaves under Captain Devereux found themselves providing part of the ship's crew sailing the USS *Constitution* from Annapolis to the Brooklyn Navy Yard to save it from secessionists. The historic militia company had again done honor to a ship that has become a national treasure.

Returning south, the Salem Zouaves were stationed in Baltimore when they received their first true Zouave-style uniform, delivered on June 26, 1861. The jacket, vest, and pants were made of a navy blue woolen twill fabric with crimson trim. The cap had a red crown with dark blue band and was quartered with gold braid. An original uniform is in the collection of Salem's Essex Institute, and several photographs clearly preserve the unusual features of this Americanized Zouave garb. Armed with M1855 rifle muskets, the Salem Zouaves were examples of militia service in war, answering the first call for defense.

*Officer's jacket and vest of the Salem Zouaves. The officers' clothing was trimmed with gold, in contrast to the red trim of the enlisted men.* JOHN OCKERBLOOM COLLECTION.

# 11TH INDIANA ZOUAVES

Col. Lew Wallace, acting adjutant general of the state of Indiana, appointed himself the colonel of one of the six new three-month regiments assembling in Indianapolis in April 1861. Numbered the 6th through the 11th in memory of the five regiments raised for the war with Mexico, Wallace chose the final, the 11th, as his regiment. The men of this regiment wanted to be Zouaves from the start, and they were known as the 11th Regiment—Indiana Zouaves.

Wallace, a devout Christian who later wrote the novel *Ben Hur,* wanted "nothing of the flashy, Algerian colors" in his regiment. Instead, the 11th wore a conservative gray modified Zouave garb:

> Our outfit was of the tamest twilled goods, not unlike home made jeans—a visor cap, French pattern, its top of red cloth . . . ; a blue flannel shirt with open neck; a jacket Greekish in form, edged with narrow binding, the red scarcely noticeable; breeches baggy, but not petticoated; button gaiters connecting below the knees with the breeches, and strapped over the shoes. The effect was to magnify the men, though in line two thousand yards off they looked like a smoky ribbon long-drawn out.

Later the regiment received blue replacement Zouave uniforms of an entirely different style, which were worn through much of the war.

Wallace's Indiana Zouaves reorganized for three years' service in August 1861. They went on to serve in the Western Theater at such places as Shiloh and Vicksburg, and after transfer to the East, at Opequon and Cedar Creek. Wallace was promoted to major general, serving on the courts-martial of both the Lincoln conspirators and Andersonville commandant Henry Wirz.

PRIVATE COLLECTION

*This flamboyant cap was worn by Gouverneur Kemble Warren as colonel of the 5th New York Volunteer Infantry, the famed Duryée Zouaves, between August 1861 and September 1862. In the painting* A Picnic on the Hudson, *by Thomas Prichard Rossiter, he is seen lounging in a conspicuous pair of scarlet trousers and a cap such as this one.*

WEST POINT MUSEUM.

# 5TH NEW YORK VOLUNTEERS, DURYÉE ZOUAVES

PRIVATE COLLECTION

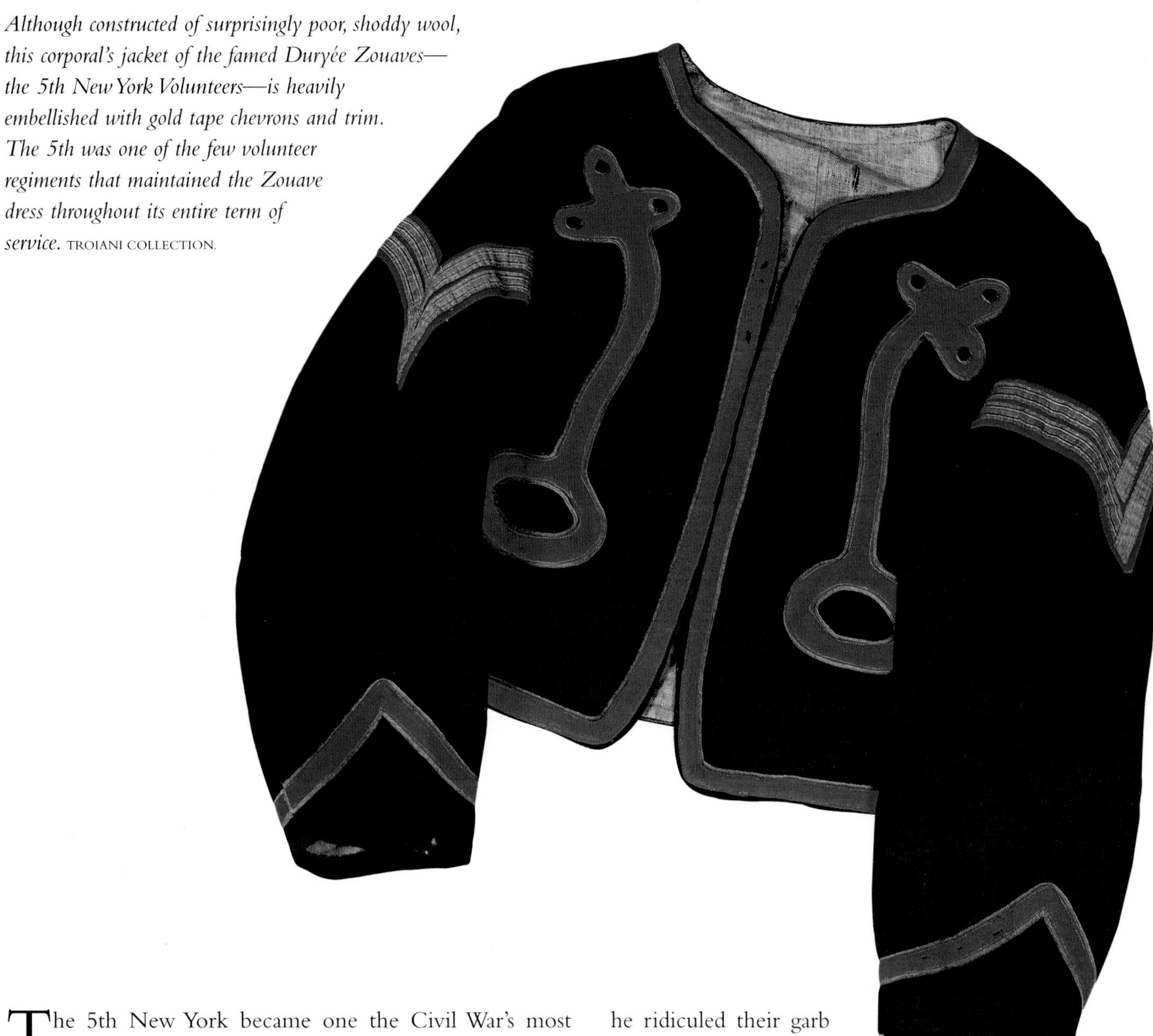

*Although constructed of surprisingly poor, shoddy wool, this corporal's jacket of the famed Duryée Zouaves—the 5th New York Volunteers—is heavily embellished with gold tape chevrons and trim. The 5th was one of the few volunteer regiments that maintained the Zouave dress throughout its entire term of service.* TROIANI COLLECTION.

The 5th New York became one the Civil War's most famous regiments for many reasons, not the least of which was its prowess on the battlefield. Part of its success, however, came from the pride the men of the 5th felt over their distinctive dress. From the beginning, the regiment's officers concerned themselves with details of its uniforms as well as its training. At Fort Schuyler in New York, they voted upon the infantry manual for the regiment as well as making decisions about their uniform. The pants would be "red and large, no stripe, the Full Dress cap, the Col. Made a motion that it should be Scarlett & Blue trimmed with Gold according to Rank, of the Zouave style."

The enlisted Zouave uniform was first made by Devlin, Hudson & Co. of New York City, evidently in haste, for there was much dissatisfaction with its appearance and fit. The manufacturer blamed part of the problem on the fact that the Zouaves persisted in wearing regular trousers under the Zouave pants, destroying the fit. When William Howard "Bull Run" Russell, the English journalist, saw them in July, he ridiculed their garb as "ill-made jackets" and "loose bags of red calico hanging from their loins." It was hardly a uniform to inspire great deeds, but Col. Abram Duryée pushed for better uniforms. By late summer, he had replaced the original uniforms with better-fitting and better-made close copies of the true French Zouave dress. He even succeeded in obtaining proper leather greaves, or *jambières,* to wear at the top of the white leggings over the bottom of the trousers. When the 5th New York was reviewed by Spanish general Juan Prim in June 1862, the Spaniard at first believed he had found a transplanted regiment of Frenchmen.

It was in these uniforms that the 5th New York made its gallant stands at Gaines' Mill and Second Bull Run, placing it forever in the "Fighting 500" regiments of the war. Uniforms may not make the soldier, but a regiment's *esprit de corps* can be inspired by many things, including its distinctive dress.

# 10TH NEW YORK VOLUNTEER INFANTRY, NATIONAL ZOUAVES

Providing uniforms for the Civil War soldier was always a demanding process for the quartermaster. Procuring and issuing sufficient clothing for the ever-increasing number of troops recruited for the war was taxing to a system based upon a peacetime establishment of a mere 16,000 men, but when the Federal volunteers demanded special regimental uniforms, quartermasters faced a procurement nightmare. The uniforms required for the 10th New York were a perfect example.

The 10th was recruited around a prewar organization known as the National Zouaves, which wore a "neat and attractive" Zouave uniform "affording perfect action of the limbs," and was expanded into a regiment under Col. Waters W. McChesney. The 10th's first wartime uniform was a hastily improvised "dark blue flannel costume, of the Zouave pattern, with grey fatigue caps." This uniform rapidly fell apart in active use, and sometime in June 1861, a new Zouave uniform of "the same pattern as the old, but of heavier cloth, the color being dark brown with red trimmings," was paid for by the state. In September, another new Zouave uniform was given to the regiment, this one beginning the practice of wearing light blue trousers with the Zouave jackets. These uniforms were evidently lost during the Peninsula campaign of spring 1862, when the regiment's baggage was burned during the evacuation of the army's base camp at White House Landing.

On September 5, 1862, an order was issued for the procurement of new Zouave uniforms manufactured by "Messer Wm. Seligman & Co. who made the old uniform," and once again the 10th was in a distinctive regimental uniform. With dark blue jackets, red vests, light blue trousers tucked into white leggings, and knapsacks painted with "10–NZ," the National Zouaves went back to war. From the bloody fields of Fredericksburg to the end of the war, there were veteran soldiers of the 10th New York in Zouave uniform. It would have been simpler to replace the 10th's uniforms with simple sack coats and forage caps, but the quartermasters of the Civil War understood the value of *esprit de corps* and of regiments such as the National Zouaves who possessed it.

WILLIAM RODEN

# LOUISIANA ZOUAVE BATTALION, COPPEN'S ZOUAVES, 1861

The mystique of the French Zouaves had taken a strong hold on the imagination of the young men who came forward to fight for the Union or the Confederacy in 1861. Given the long-standing French heritage of New Orleans, it was only natural that this city was the only one to send several companies of men dressed in true copies of Zouave attire to serve in the Confederate army. Whereas other localities in all corners of the South had Zouave companies among their troops, all the other uniforms only approximated that of the French Zouaves, and some companies boasted nothing but the title. Of the New Orleans companies, those of the 1st Louisiana Zouave Battalion, raised by Georges Augustus Gaston De Coppens, most closely resembled the true Zouave. The resemblance was more than simple appearance; the men of the battalion quickly gained a reputation as tough fighters.

As reported in the *New Orleans Commercial Bulletin:*

> The Richmond correspondent of the *Savannah Republican* thus speaks of our Zouaves: The roughest men I have seen on our side are the Louisiana Zouaves, about 600 strong, who have been at Pensacola. They are a tough, dare-devil, hardy looking set of fellows—excellent prototypes of the original French Zouaves. They have the regular Zouave uniform and that dashing rakish air supposed to belong to the originals. I don't wish "Old Abe" any worse fate than a consignment to their tender mercies. They are unquestionably the very spawn of war—that reckless breed that time of turmoil engender in malignant profusion. We have very few such soldiers in our army, however—less I presume than ever tainted any army the world has known. But it is one of the horrors of war to breed such characters.

DAVID RANKIN, JR.

The battalion served the Confederacy until the very last days of the war, seeing action from the Peninsula campaign of 1862 to the trenches of Petersburg in 1864–65. It is likely, however, that little of the color and distinction of the Zouave uniform was ever worn into battle. By November 4, 1861, the rigors of military life in the field had taken their toll. A requisition stating that "the Battalion is greatly in need of clothing not having received any since the 27th of March 1861, and is consequently entirely destitute" resulted in the battalion receiving a complete refitting, consisting of the following:

| | | |
|---|---|---|
| 449 caps | 898 flannel shirts | 449 Jackets |
| 449 overcoats | 898 drawers | 49 blankets |
| 449 trousers | 480 pr. Shoes | 449 pants |

Subsequent issues show no sign of the return to the grand uniforms in which they left for war. Within the battalion, however, the spirit of the Zouaves never died.

# 34TH OHIO VOLUNTEER INFANTRY, PIATT'S ZOUAVES

The Zouave volunteers raised in the West—Ohio, Indiana, Illinois, and Missouri—were not so gaudily dressed as their Eastern brethren. Wallace's Indiana Zouaves wore somber gray uniforms with scant red trim. Ohio's initial regiment of Zouaves was raised by Abram Sanders Piatt, a farmer and editor of the *Macacheek Press.* Piatt originally recruited the 13th Ohio Infantry, a ninety-day regiment that did not leave Ohio before its enlistment expired. The 34th Ohio, which later bore his name, never wore the baggy trousers or open oriental-style jacket of the true Zouave.

Called the 1st Ohio Zouaves, its sister regiment, the 54th, being the 2nd Zouaves, the 34th was organized at Camp Lucas, Ohio, but moved to Camp Dennison on September 1, 1861. Piatt was appointed its colonel on September 2. At Dennison, the regiment was hastily prepared for field service, there adopting its distinctive uniform and its nickname of Piatt's Zouaves. The 34th and 54th wore the same uniform, a short, dark blue jacket trimmed on the edges with red tape. Their sky blue trousers were trimmed with double stripes of red trim and tucked into russet leather leggings. The 34th wore its fezzes uncrushed, standing erect as in the Ottoman armies, the blue tassels dangling against their sides. Both regiments also wore a "three cornered hat with red tassel," similar to those worn by early Massachusetts troops.

The 34th spent its first winter in service on guard and scout duties against guerrillas in the Kanawha River Valley in what would soon become the state of West Virginia and remained there for much of the war. Originally armed with M1842 muskets, the regiment was armed with Enfield rifle muskets in 1863 and 1864. In 1864, it was moved to the Shenandoah Valley, fighting at Winchester, Opequon, and Fisher's Hill. The regiment's original colonel, Abram Piatt, was promoted to brigadier general of volunteers in April 1862. He fought in Virginia at Second Bull Run and later at Fredericksburg, where he was injured in a fall from horseback. Piatt then resigned his commission and returned to Ohio, where he resumed farming. Although never a fully rigged Zouave regiment, the 34th did serve as mounted infantry during its campaigns in the mountains of West Virginia, adding to the regiment's unusual history as Zouaves.

WILLIAM RODEN

# 9TH NEW YORK VOLUNTEER INFANTRY, HAWKINS' ZOUAVES

Rush Hawkins was a meticulous man. It showed in the way he dressed and in the efforts he lavished later in life on his collection of rare books. It was only natural that when he created a regiment of volunteer Zouaves, he would be as attentive to the details of its organization.

This highly ordered regiment, the 9th New York Volunteers, originated from the New York Zouaves, a private military club formed in New York City on July 23, 1860. The New York Zouaves' by-laws, written by Hawkins, stated that "[t]here must, of necessity, be many absolute and positive rules, which must be carried out to the letter." Rush Hawkins was a man to enforce rules. When war broke out, Hawkins rushed to Albany to offer a regiment, which was sworn into state service on April 23 and mustered into Federal service as the 9th New York on May 4, 1861.

On his own initiative, Hawkins contracted for all the regimental equipment except the blankets, overcoats, and weapons. "When I commenced the formation of my Corps I had but one idea, and that was to make it a light Rifle regiment. Thus far the idea has been strictly addressed to in every minute particular. The accouterments are made after a pattern which I sent to France after, and are those which are now used by the three regiments of zouaves in the French Army. The material is a most excellent quality of flexible bridle leather." Hawkins paid attention to the details; as a result his regiment and its uniforms left an indelible mark upon the Federal armies.

MRS. DONALD BLYN

After distinctive service with Burnside's expedition to South Carolina, the 9th joined the Army of the Potomac for the Maryland campaign. At the battle of Antietam, the 9th lost 240 of its 373 men in a charge that nearly broke the Confederate lines and reached Sharpsburg, giving the regiment's name a place in history. After Hawkins' Zouaves were mustered out of service on May 20, 1863, their uniform was chosen by the Federal quartermasters as a standard pattern for other Zouave regiments, such as the 17th and 164th New York. As Hawkins would say, "[A] uniform of glaring colors neither makes a man or a soldier." He should have known, for he created a regiment of soldiers.

# 18TH MASSACHUSETTS VOLUNTEER INFANTRY, 1861–62

Gen. Montgomery C. Meigs's Quartermaster Department was fully taxed trying to meet the demands of the growing Federal armies in the summer of 1861 and was eager to find a way to quickly supply the much-needed uniforms and equipment of these new troops. As an experiment, Meigs ordered 10,000 complete uniforms of the French chasseur, or light infantry, pattern from the firm of Alexis Godillot, the manufacturer for the French Army. It was hoped that these uniforms would solve some of the American supply problems and perhaps even set the patterns for redesigned Federal uniforms.

In what would today be considered a contracting miracle, the order was placed, and the uniforms and equipment were manufactured and actually shipped by late November 1861. These uniforms were remarkably complete and included every item a soldier needed, from "uniform coat with epaulets" to "blue cotton cravat" to "2 handkerchiefs." Moreover, the shipment included "hair tanned knapsacks" and a "*sac le petite,* containing five brushes for various purposes, needle case, with combs, thread, spool, cloak pin, and various other conveniences." It had to have been the most complete set of uniforms and equipment ever issued soldiers of the American army to that time.

The question of which regiments would receive them was settled with a drill competition, with three regiments of Gen. Fitz-John Porter's division of the Army of the Potomac winning the uniforms as prizes for the best performance. Among the winning regiments was the 18th Massachusetts. Unfortunately, the uniforms had been made in European sizes, too small to fit the American soldiers. Although larger sizes were evidently drawn from the remaining surplus, these elaborate uniforms were not at all popular with the soldiers, and as their novelty wore off, they were packed up and left in storage in Washington. Later in the war, bits and pieces of the uniforms were used for other purposes, but the 18th Massachusetts did not wear it to any of its battles with the Army of the Potomac.

PRIVATE COLLECTION

*Chasseur dress jacket* (tunique, modèle *1860) worn by Jacob Martin of Company J, 62nd Pennsylvania Volunteer Infantry. With the exception of the cuff details and pewter eagle buttons, these extremely well-made garments were nearly identical to those produced for the French Army.* JOHN HENRY KURTZ COLLECTION.

*Snugly tailored fatigue jacket* (habit-veste) *of the imported French chasseur uniforms issued to the 18th Massachusetts and the 62nd and 83rd Pennsylvania Regiments. At least one regiment of New York's famed Excelsior Brigade received these uniforms in late 1862.* TROIANI COLLECTION.

*French Army pattern of 1858 cloth-covered tin canteen* (bidon petit de 1 litre) *imported with the 10,000 chasseur uniforms and equipment. The user was provided with two spouts, one for drinking and a narrow one for taking small sips on the march.* TROIANI COLLECTION.

*The French infantry leather shakos of 1860 were the very latest pattern when purchased by the U.S. government. They were issued to the troops with full dress dark green-black feathers, while the field service green pom-poms remained in quartermaster stores. The 18th Massachusetts and 62nd and 83rd Pennsylvania do not seem to have been issued the brass eagle plates, but evidence shows at least one regiment of New York's famed Excelsior Brigade were.* TROIANI COLLECTION.

# 65TH NEW YORK VOLUNTEER INFANTRY, 1861, 1ST U.S. CHASSEURS

Although not so exotic in appearance as the Zouaves of the French Army, chasseurs had their own distinctive garb, which also influenced the dress of American Civil War soldiers. Chasseur soldiers were light troops, originally tasked with the role of scouting and skirmishing against Regular troops, who moved and fought in solid formations. By the 1850s, the French Chasseurs of the Imperial Guard wore a new style uniform coat known as a *habit-veste*, which was simply a short frock coat, slit at the bottom edge on the side as vents. It provided more freedom of movement than the long-skirted frock coats worn by French infantry since the 1840s. For trousers, the Imperial Chasseurs wore baggy trousers tucked into *jambières* and leggings like those of the Zouaves.

Also like the Zouaves, chasseurs got considerable newspaper coverage. Woodcut illustrations of the *Chasseurs de Vincennes* drill were nearly as common as charging Zouaves. It was understandable that these French uniforms were copied along with the Zouave dress. The 65th New York adopted a uniform based upon the French style: "Their uniform is neat, military and allowing free motion to the soldiers. It is army blue, chasseur jacket, trimmed with light blue braid, cadet gray pantaloons and gray caps." The light blue braid ran along the edges of the coat, with trefoil knots on each cuff and sprouting from the corners of the vents created by slitting the sides of the coat skirts. Along with the gray kepis issued in New York, the regiment received M1858 uniform hats, more popularly called Hardee hats, trimmed with bugle horn insignia with the numeral 1 in the loop, and sky blue hat cords to match the coat trim.

PRIVATE COLLECTION

The 65th New York went to war in September 1861, spending most of its term in the VI Corps of the Army of the Potomac. Present at all major battles from the Peninsula through the Appomattox campaign, it lost a total of 146 men in combat or captivity. One of its colonels, Alexander Shaler, received the Medal of Honor for bravery at Marye's Heights. At war's end, all four of the men who had led the 65th as colonel had been promoted to general.

# 76TH PENNSYLVANIA VOLUNTEER INFANTRY, KEYSTONE ZOUAVES

RICK AND JOAN DAVIES

The Zouaves of the 76th Pennsylvania, formed as the Keystone Zouaves, wore a unique variation of traditional dress. The 76th's original Zouave dress, which was not well documented, was replaced with regulation Federal clothing. It was not until November 1862 that its colonel, DeWitt C. Strawbridge, requested a new set of Zouave uniforms. These were supplied by Philadelphia's Schuylkill Arsenal and included light blue trousers, dark blue fezzes, and gray false vest fronts sewn to the jacket fronts. The regiment seems to have retained this uniform for dress throughout most of its remaining service, with photographs showing the use of veterans' stripes late in the war.

The 76th was on the Carolina coast for much of its military service, first garrisoning Hilton Head, South Carolina. Its first major combat came on July 11, 1863, in the form of assaults on Fort Wagner, where it fought its way to the parapets. The regiment lost 180 men, but made a second assault a week later. In that attack, Brig. Gen. George C. Strong was fatally wounded alongside the flag of the 76th. The regiment went on to Virginia, where it fought through Grant's Virginia campaign of 1864 at Cold Harbor, the Crater, and Petersburg. Transferred to the South again, the 76th was in the operations against Fort Fisher in 1865. By war's end, the regiment had lost 9 officers and 161 men killed or mortally wounded.

# 53RD NEW YORK VOLUNTEERS, D'EPINEUIL ZOUAVES

The 53rd New York Infantry was organized in New York City in the fall of 1861 by Col. Lionel J. D'Epineuil, a former officer in the French Army. The recruiting went forward at a slow pace, despite the fact that the colonel had received permission to outfit his men in the uniform of the French Zouaves of the Imperial Guard. The regiment eventually attracted men from other parts of the state, mostly of French descent, but also included one company of American Indians from the Tuscarora Reservation.

The New York City newspapers seemed to take particular interest in the uniform of the 53rd. "The uniform is that of the Blue Zouaves of France, which consists of dark blue jacket, trimmed with yellow braid, vest of the same, and full pants of light blue, red fez, with blue tassel and duck leggings. The cloth will be of the best quality, as good, in fact, as is used in the French army, and not the cheap flannel that was hitherto given some of our Zouaves."

"The uniform of the men is an exact copy of the 6th Regiment Imperial Zouaves of France, and is to be completed by Messers Brooks Bros., by special contract with the War Department. It consists of red fez cap with long yellow tassel, dark blue jacket trimmed with bright yellow braid, blue sash, and yellow and black leggings and duck gaiters." All of this amounted to a regiment that closely resembled the original French.

The regiment left New York on November 18, 1861. The men had been armed with the Enfield rifle musket and standard accoutrements. From all appearances, the 53rd New York would make a good account of itself once it reached the seat of war. But problems appeared almost from the start. It was apparent that the officers of the regiment had been in the habit of ignoring the condition of the men under their command. Desertions became a continual problem.

RONALD AND JULIE MARRA

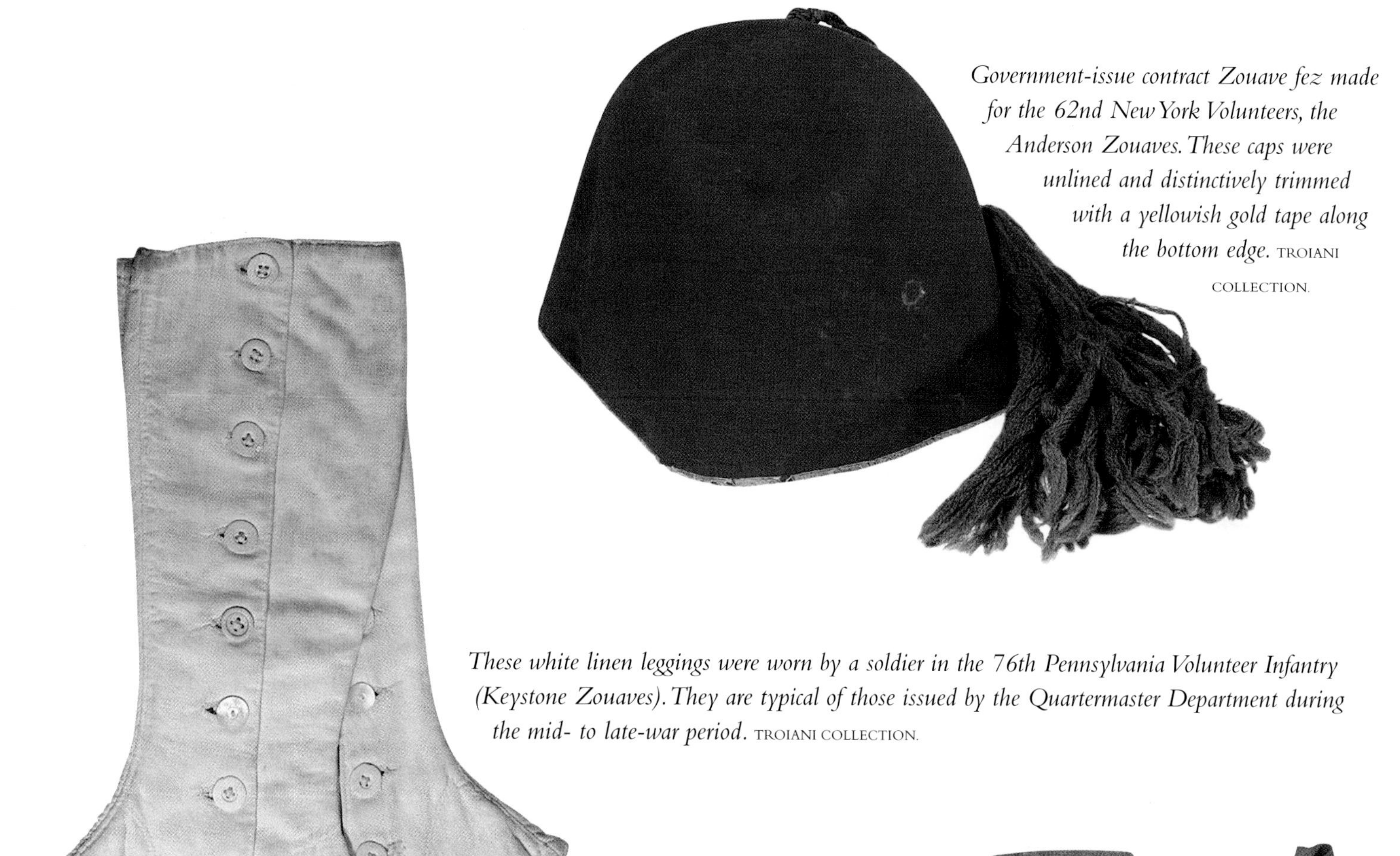

*Government-issue contract Zouave fez made for the 62nd New York Volunteers, the Anderson Zouaves. These caps were unlined and distinctively trimmed with a yellowish gold tape along the bottom edge.* TROIANI COLLECTION.

*These white linen leggings were worn by a soldier in the 76th Pennsylvania Volunteer Infantry (Keystone Zouaves). They are typical of those issued by the Quartermaster Department during the mid- to late-war period.* TROIANI COLLECTION.

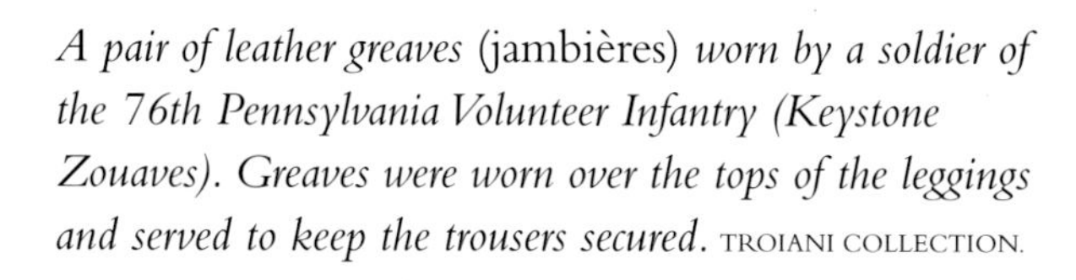

*A pair of leather greaves* (jambières) *worn by a soldier of the 76th Pennsylvania Volunteer Infantry (Keystone Zouaves). Greaves were worn over the tops of the leggings and served to keep the trousers secured.* TROIANI COLLECTION.

After being placed on board a ship for what was to be trip of several days to Hatteras, the men finally disembarked thirty-four days later at Annapolis after a series of botched attempts at landing. After this length of time, the condition of the entire command had deteriorated to a point that was beyond repair. Within a few days, nearly 400 men were no longer present for duty. An inspection of the regiment found "rifle muskets in bad order . . . uniforms very dirty, and in many cases, filthy." The fine uniforms were found to be so infested with lice that many had to be burned.

It may be that competent leadership could have salvaged the situation, but the 53rd New York was disbanded on March 21, 1862. Some of the men enlisted in the Regular army, while others were transferred to volunteer regiments from their home state.

# 74TH NEW YORK VOLUNTEER INFANTRY, 1861

The 74th Regiment, New York Volunteer Infantry, was organized in New York City as the 5th Regiment of the Excelsior Brigade. This brigade of New York Volunteer Infantry Regiments (the 70th through 74th) would suffer the greatest number of killed and mortally wounded during the war, but in the summer of 1861, when the brigade was encamped on Staten Island its future was unknown. Raised by Daniel Edgar Sickles, a volatile New York lawyer and legislator, the Excelsior Brigade was, as its name implied, meant to represent New York's best in the Army of the Potomac.

At least two of its regiments were attired in a distinctive chasseur-style uniform, but Company A of the 74th received one of the most complete French Zouave uniforms of the war:

> Attached to the regiment is a company of French Zouaves. They are dressed in the exact costume of the Imperial Zouaves of the French Army. . . . Their uniform is of the most brilliant hues of red, blue and yellow, slashed, braided and trimmed in most tasteful, dashing and expensive style.

PRIVATE COLLECTION

With the other companies of the regiment in chasseur blue, the bright uniforms of Company A stood out in striking contrast. These Zouave uniforms were careful reproductions of the French originals, from the baggy fez with yellow tassel through the richly braided jacket and vest to the ocher-colored leather *jambières*. The uniform of the Imperial Guard Zouaves, with its yellow rather than red trim, was indeed one of the most impressive of all the magnificent uniforms of Napoléon the III's armies.

The men of the 74th were equal to their uniforms and on all the bloody fields of combat from Williamsburg in 1862, through Chancellorsville and Gettysburg in 1863, to the bloodiest of fields at Spotsylvania in 1864, the regiment proved its worth. Excelsior! Ever Upward!

# 62ND NEW YORK VOLUNTEER INFANTRY, ANDERSON ZOUAVES

Named in honor of Robert Anderson, the defender of Fort Sumter, the Anderson Zouaves were recruited in and around New York City in the early summer of 1861. One company of the regiment was composed of "French adopted citizens" and constituted the Advance Guard, which wore a full French Zouave uniform, while the remainder of the regiment was in an Americanized version of Zouave garb.

The Advance Guard uniform was described as "the genuine unmistakable Zou-Zou uniform, the red fez . . . with long blue silk tassel, the immensely loose, red baggy breeches, the leggins, gaiters, long blue scarf round the middle, the queer, tight cloth waistcoat with only one arm-hole—the left—in it, fastening on the right, and the short jacket." Many of the men who wore this uniform were French Army veterans who "wore the Crimea medals . . . mounted with the names of 'Alma,' 'Inkerman,' and 'Sebastopol.'"

JO-VAL AND ELDRED CODLING

An existing uniform in the Smithsonian collection has orange inserts in the loops of the *tombeaux,* or false pockets, with embroidered letters A on the right and Z on the left for "Advance Zouaves." The deep red trousers of this uniform have dark green cord trim. It was an exceptional Zouave uniform, even by Civil War standards. Interestingly, the Seamless Clothing Manufacturing Company, which made the regiment's bright crimson fezzes, was also contracted to make "1100 felt seamless overcoats," probably of the same type made for the Berdan Sharpshooters, a garment quite unlike the Zouave cloak worn in Europe.

The 62nd New York suffered from an early reputation of poor discipline, but it ultimately served with praise in the VI Corps of the Army of the Potomac, eventually reenlisting as a veteran regiment in 1864. It mustered out at Fort Schuyler in New York Harbor on August 30, 1865. During its service, it lost ninety-seven officers and men dead or mortally wounded in combat, compiling honors as noteworthy as its original uniforms.

# RED DEVILS

Months of campaigning had taken the shine off the bright uniforms of the 5th New York Volunteer Infantry. It had not dulled the fighting edge of the men wearing them, however, as the gallant stand of the Duryée Zouaves at Gaines' Mill on June 27, 1862, proved. With Color Sgt. Francis Spelman felled with heat stroke, Sgt. John H. Berrian planted the regimental flag and dared the Confederates to take it. The Zouaves kept their flags but were so decimated by intense fire that they were pulled out of the line. Before they left the field, however, their colonel ordered them to count off and realign ranks to fill in for 162 fallen comrades.

The brilliant red of their trousers was offset by the dark blue of their Zouave jackets and vests. In many ways, the 5th's uniform was one of the closest American copies of the French original. An American touch, however, was found in the gilt lace chevrons and gold-edged trim of the regiment's noncommissioned officers. Red sashes edged with light blue, white leggings topped with yellow leather *jambières,* and red fezzes wrapped with white turbans—all the exotic trappings of the true Zouave soldier—marked the 5th New York as a distinctive regiment, but their performance at Gaines' Mill marked them as soldiers.

PRIVATE COLLECTION

# 114TH PENNSYLVANIA VOLUNTEER INFANTRY, COLLIS ZOUAVES

PRIVATE COLLECTION

On July 3, 1863, as he rode across the battlefield of the previous day at Gettysburg, an English officer "present with the Confederate Army" noted among the dead "a number of Yankees dressed in bad imitations of the Zouave costume." The dead this disdainful Englishman was referring to were from the 114th Pennsylvania, the Collis Zouaves.

The 114th was originally raised as the *Zouaves d'Afrique* by Charles H. T. Collis, a Philadelphia lawyer, to serve as a bodyguard to Maj. Gen. N. P. Banks. This company was mustered in and sent to Fort Delaware in August 1861, where it was thoroughly drilled in Zouave tactics. The *Zouaves d'Afrique* fought in several battles and skirmishes as an independent company with such success that in the summer of 1862, Collis began to recruit additional companies for an entire regiment of Zouaves.

At the end of August 1862, Collis's new regiment was in Washington, and the 114th Pennsylvania began its life as a regiment in the Army of the Potomac. It was a fully rigged

*From the start, Collis's Zouaves wore a well-designed uniform patterned after that of French Zouaves. The original company was joined by nine new companies and expanded into the 114th Pennsylvania Volunteer Infantry. Although officers wore standard frock coats, they did have the red trousers and caps of Zouaves.* WEST POINT MUSEUM.

*Uniform of the 114th Pennsylvania Volunteers worn by Thadeus Paxton of Company F. This famed regiment, also known as the Collis Zouaves, wore a jacket with light blue cuffs and chasseur trousers made of brick red imported French Army cloth. Paxton died of disease in January 1863.* TROIANI COLLECTION.

Zouave regiment, with uniforms made of cloth imported from France, but with an American twist. Its trousers, of proper madder red cloth, were not the full French Zouave style, but made less baggy and as actual trousers so they could be worn without leggings if needed. The short, open blue jacket was trimmed in red like the French originals but had light blue cuffs as well. Fezzes and turbans, for full dress, completed the Collis Zouaves' unique uniform.

The regiment participated in every major battle of the Army of the Potomac, and at Fredericksburg in December 1862, Collis himself received the Medal of Honor for his actions in leading his Zouaves in deadly battle. It was Gettysburg, however, that decimated the regiment. Although only thirteen were dead or mortally wounded there, eighty-six were wounded and sixty captured or missing. Much reduced by their casualties, the 114th was made provost guard of the Army of the Potomac Headquarters, serving with distinction through the remainder of the war.

# 95TH PENNSYLVANIA VOLUNTEERS, GOSLINE ZOUAVES

The 95th Pennsylvania Infantry, the Gosline Zouaves, was one of several regiments raised in and around Philadelphia in the fall of 1861 to receive what the U.S. Army termed a special uniform. The 95th was able to retain much of this distinctive dress for its entire term of service, being resupplied as necessary by the Quartermaster Department. In addition, in the final months of the war, this regiment was one of the very few selected to receive and try the new style accoutrements designed and patented by Col. William D. Mann, formerly of the 7th Michigan Cavalry. These accoutrements were designed to ease the burden on the individual soldier by redistributing the weight of the cartridge box. The concept had some merit and was an improvement over conventional equipment. The ending of the war, however, with the resulting vast surplus of old-style equipment, ended any chance that Colonel Mann's idea would be adopted by the army.

The uniform of the 95th remained largely unchanged from that received in 1861. The initial outfit had been contracted for by the Quartermaster Department from the Philadelphia clothing house of Rockhill and Wilson. The original uniform was described by a member of Company A as follows:

> The regimental uniform was of the zouave pattern, and differed but little from other zouave organizations—Birney's and Baxter's—then forming in the city. . . . [It] consisted of the best material, heavy marine cloth. The jacket . . . was rounded at the waist, and trimmed with broad and narrow scarlet braid. Down each side was a row of brass buttons, adding greatly to its beauty and finish. The pants were of full length, not so wide as the regular Zouave Petticoat but just wide enough to harmonize with the pleated waist, in broad folds. The over shirt was of Navy flannel, with silver plated buttons corresponding with those on the jacket, but several sizes smaller. The cap was the McClellan style, braided with narrow scarlet braid. A pair of leather leggings nearly reaching the knees finished the uniform.

PRIVATE COLLECTION

Photographs show that by late 1864, the pleated trousers and the cap were replaced by standard-issue uniform items, but the jacket and the vest remained. The 95th Pennsylvania served its entire term of service with the Army of the Potomac. From September 1862 until muster out, they were part of the famous VI Corps.

As an interesting side note, a paper from after the war gives a glimpse of how contract operations worked prior to worries about conflict of interest. On August 21, 1861, Company A's recruiting station was opened over the clothing establishment of Rockhill and Wilson.

# 72ND PENNSYLVANIA VOLUNTEER INFANTRY, BAXTER'S FIRE ZOUAVES

PRIVATE COLLECTION

Nearly every fire company in Philadelphia provided recruits for Col. DeWitt Clinton Baxter's new regiment raised in the summer of 1861. As a result, the regiment became known as Baxter's Fire Zouaves.

Their uniform was a modified and slightly less ornate version of that worn by Ellsworth's militia Zouaves, with sixteen ball buttons along each edge of the jacket, and light blue trousers that were not the full trousers of a true Zouave. Still, it was part of their identity as a regiment, and in June 1863, a month before finding themselves in the center of the fight to repulse Pickett's Charge at Gettysburg, they received new Zouave uniforms.

The 72nd had been seriously bloodied first at Antietam, where they had suffered 58 deaths in the fight for the West Woods. At Gettysburg, with only 473 men in the line, the regiment lost 64 dead or mortally wounded and an additional 125 wounded. The remnants of the gallant charge retreated to Seminary Ridge that day, leaving the exhausted survivors of Baxter's Fire Zouaves to help hold the Union line in what has been called the turning point of the Civil War. They fought on through the Wilderness and the siege of Petersburg before mustering out in 1864. After the war, many of these veteran soldier-firemen revived Baxter's Fire Zouaves as a militia unit, continuing the Fire Zouave tradition in peace as well as war.

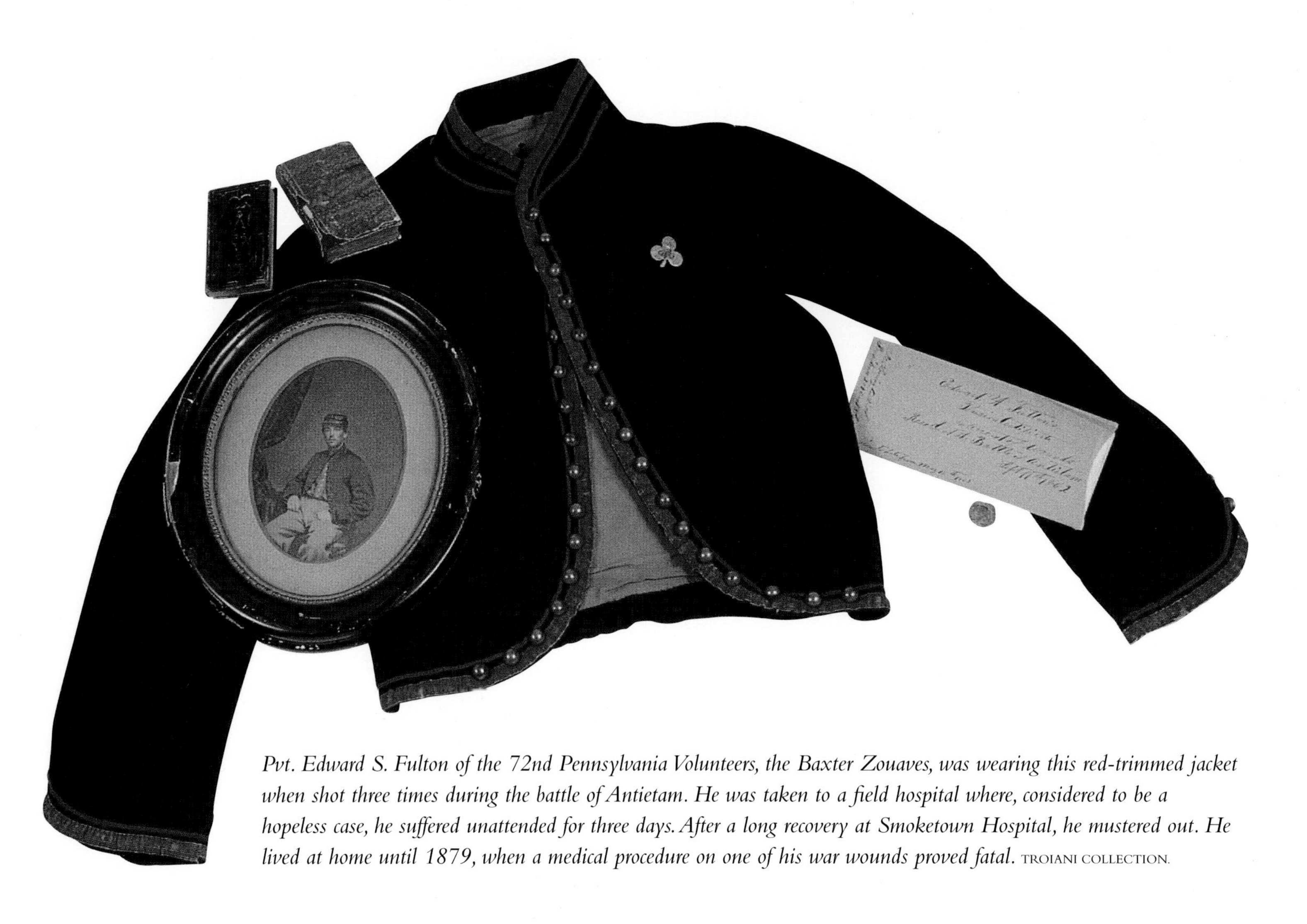

*Pvt. Edward S. Fulton of the 72nd Pennsylvania Volunteers, the Baxter Zouaves, was wearing this red-trimmed jacket when shot three times during the battle of Antietam. He was taken to a field hospital where, considered to be a hopeless case, he suffered unattended for three days. After a long recovery at Smoketown Hospital, he mustered out. He lived at home until 1879, when a medical procedure on one of his war wounds proved fatal.* TROIANI COLLECTION.

*Government-issue Zouave fez worn by Sgt. James D. Pitcher of the 146th New York Volunteers. Pitcher wore it with the brim turned up for a snugger fit, a common practice.* TROIANI COLLECTION.

*Bright red chasseur trousers worn by Sgt. Alexander Barnie, Jr., of the famed Brooklyn 14th. Well known for their picturesque garb, soldiers of the regiment searching for bodies of their friends killed at First Manassas nine months earlier wrote, "Yet here we find, unburied, the bodies of our comrades, clearly distinguishable by the peculiar uniform of the regiment. The unmistakable red pants and loose blue jacket are easily recognized."* (*BROOKLYN DAILY EAGLE*, MARCH 21, 1862.) COLLECTION OF NEW YORK STATE DIVISION OF MILITARY AND NAVAL AFFAIRS.

## 146TH NEW YORK VOLUNTEER INFANTRY

After the fierce fighting of July 2, 1863, one officer remarked that the rocky slopes of Little Round Top "seemed to be covered with corpses in light blue Zouave uniforms." These were the dead of Garrard's Tigers, the 146th New York, raised in Oneida County, New York, in 1862. Col. Kenner Garrard's regiment was placed in the V Corps; and when it was determined to honor the memory of the departed 5th New York, Duryée's Zouaves, by creating new regiments of Zouaves from line infantry, the 146th became the first to receive new uniforms in June 1863—just in time for the battle of Gettysburg.

Technically, the 146th did not get Zouave uniforms, but the yellow-trimmed light blue uniforms of the *Tirailleurs Algériens,* or Turcos, of the French Colonial Army. Made exactly like the uniforms of the European Zouaves except for color, the new uniforms of the 146th were indeed unique in all the Federal armies. Attractive and serviceable, the uniforms were not without problems. Soon it was noticed that the yellow lace trim faded quickly, and the Zouave leggings were made improperly so that they lapped to the front and snagged easily when passing through brush. Still, it was a distinctive uniform, marking an exceptional regiment.

After their successful defense of Little Round Top in July 1863, the 146th and the other regiments of the Zouave Brigade of the V Corps found themselves embroiled in the Virginia Wilderness in May 1864. There the Tigers lost 312 men, 65 of whom, including the regiment's colonel and lieutenant colonel, were killed or mortally wounded.

JOHN H. KURTZ COLLECTION

# 165TH NEW YORK VOLUNTEER INFANTRY, 1863

The severe losses within the 5th New York in its battles in 1862 made it necessary to recruit new members, and the 5th's reputation made that recruiting easy. So easy, in fact, that more recruits were signed up than were needed, and a second battalion was formed, becoming the 165th New York. The 2nd Battalion Duryée Zouaves were shipped to the West, serving with the XIX Army Corps in the Department of the Gulf from January 1863 to July 1864. At the siege of Port Hudson on the Mississippi, the 165th joined in a doomed assault that resulted in the loss of a third of the battalion, including two color-bearers, and the mortal wounding of its commander, Lt. Col. Abel Smith, Jr. In July 1864, the battalion was transferred to Washington to serve in the Shenandoah Valley and later Georgia and the Carolinas. Never as famous as the 5th, the 2nd Battalion still had an impressive record in its nearly three years of service.

The Zouaves of the 2nd Battalion wore basically the same uniform as the original Duryée Zouaves. The distinctive blue and red uniforms of the two regiments of Duryée Zouaves differed only in that the 2nd Battalion wore blue-tasseled fezzes rather than the yellow of the 5th, and the 165th often wore plain sashes rather than the blue-bound red sashes of the original regiment. It was a uniform that spanned four years and all major theaters of the war.

PRIVATE COLLECTION

# PRIVATE, COMPANY G, 109TH PENNSYLVANIA INFANTRY, APRIL 1863

The 109th Pennsylvania, originally known as the Curtin Light Guard, was one of two regiments raised in Philadelphia that received a special uniform with a coat similar to that of the French chasseur. The other regiment, the 90th Pennsylvania, also had the distinction of being the only regiment that received uniforms supplied by the United States with a button design unique to that regiment. Other than the buttons, those of the 109th being standard army issue, the uniforms of the two regiments differed only in the trim. Whereas the 90th received coats and trousers with a cord or welt of regulation infantry blue, those of the 109th were trimmed with a cord made of individual strands of red, white, and blue yarn twisted together in a candy stripe pattern. Like the buttons of the 90th, this trim was worn only by this one regiment.

PRIVATE COLLECTION

The 109th began recruiting in December 1861, two months after the 90th, and remained in the city drilling and filling its ranks until leaving for Washington in May 1862. It is interesting to note that of the regiments Pennsylvania sent to the field, the vast majority of those dressed in what the army termed "special uniforms" came from Philadelphia or its immediate area. The location in that politically important city of the U.S. Army's main clothing facility, Schuylkill Arsenal, as well as several of the country's major ready-to-wear clothing manufacturers, certainly had something to do with this. In most cases, these uniforms were supplied to those regiments throughout their term of service. The 109th was no exception. Initially many of the nonregulation uniforms were contracted from and supplied by one of several Philadelphia clothing houses. Those of the 90th and the 109th were, however, manufactured by the government, with the exception of an initial issue of "Zouave caps," which photographic evidence indicates were not resupplied. From the beginning, the 109th was armed with the M1861 rifle musket. The close proximity of the Alfred Jenks & Son factory, which by November 1861 was manufacturing the Bridesburg contract model '61, makes it likely that the regiment was armed with these.

An interesting sidelight to the history of the 109th Pennsylvania appears in an order written to the headquarters of Franz Sigel's division in June 1862, detailing items to be carried in the field. It reads in part, "The knapsack is necessary . . . but this could be dispensed with in favor of the 'shelter tent' now in use in the 109th Pa. Vols. 1st Brigade, which with the Talma [cape] and proper straps could answer the purpose of a knapsack."

# 155TH PENNSYLVANIA VOLUNTEER INFANTRY

The 155th Pennsylvania Infantry did not begin its military life as a Zouave regiment. Recruited in western Pennsylvania and organized at Camp Howe near Pittsburgh during September 1862, the 155th was trained and equipped as a standard infantry regiment. First armed with Belgian rifles and later with M1842 muskets, at Gettysburg the men of the regiment scoured the battlefield to supply themselves with M1861 rifle muskets.

In the late summer and fall of 1863, as part of Kenner Garrard's 3rd Brigade, 2nd Division of the V Corps, the 155th was presented with Zouave uniforms as a tribute to the regiment's excellence in drill. The new uniform was evidently a source of pride: "The exchange to the zouave uniform from the plain infantry uniform was enjoyed immensely by the men . . . not only on account of their having earned the recognition, but also because of the great beauty of the uniform and the greater comfort and other advantages it possessed." This new uniform had an interesting history, for it was not a standard French style. The parsimonious Quartermaster Department had decided to use up the surplus French chasseur uniforms purchased earlier in the war by giving the 155th the blue-gray chasseur trousers from those sets and fabricating jackets from the same-color talmas, or capes, from the same lot. With bright yellow *tombeaux,* or false pockets, and trim and false vest fronts sewn to the jackets, the 155th had a unique Zouave uniform fabricated with an American twist.

NATIONAL CIVIL WAR MUSEUM, HARRISBURG, PENNSYLVANIA

The 155th served with the 140th and 146th New York, which also had unique uniforms, as part of Gen. Romeyn B. Ayres's Zouave Brigade in 1864. All three regiments suffered heavy casualties in the battle of the Wilderness, but the 155th suffered greater losses in the assault on Petersburg in June. For the remainder of the war, the men of the 155th fought proudly in their Zouave uniforms, and the last Federal soldier killed before Lee's surrender at Appomattox was a Zouave of the 155th Pennsylvania.

*The 90th Pennsylvania Volunteers (National Guards) was the only regiment in the Union army to have its own distinctive button, and the Quartermaster Department in Philadelphia contracted with the firm of William G. Mintzler to supply them throughout the war.*

(NATIONAL ARCHIVES, RECORD GROUP 92, ENTRY 2195, BOOK 3.) EARL J. COATES COLLECTION.

# 33RD NEW JERSEY VOLUNTEER INFANTRY, 2ND ZOUAVES

PRIVATE COLLECTION

Not all Zouave regiments were raised in the first year of the war. Several were created later, such as the 33rd and 35th New Jersey Regiments—both recruited in the late summer of 1863—which were uniformed as Zouaves. Their uniforms were a recruiting ploy, and although the U.S. Quartermaster Department did not favor nonstandard uniforms, they relented when fancy uniforms could help induce recruits to the colors. The Zouave uniform of the 33rd was based on that of the old Hawkins' Zouaves of New York, featuring the dark blue, short open jacket, Zouave vest, and narrow dark blue trousers gathered into black leather leggings. The deep red trim adorning these garments could not be called flashy, and the uniform was indeed distinctive without being outlandish. A dark blue chasseur cap like that of the 95th Pennsylvania, a Zouave regiment raised in 1861, replaced the Hawkins' Zouaves' red fez, again making for a less exotic uniform.

The 33rd was shipped to the Western Army of the Cumberland in the fall of 1863 to serve with the XX Corps under Gen. William Tecumseh Sherman. Garbed as Zouaves, its officers in frock coats with red silk braid worked into trefoils on the cuffs and its men in their subdued uniforms, the 33rd spent its first months in service guarding bridges and doing fatigue duties, which took a toll on their uniforms. Replacements were requested by the regiment's colonel, George W. Mindil, in January 1864, before the spring campaign. Because they were distinctive, the replacement uniforms could not be readily supplied, and the regiment was "compelled to take the field in mixed dress, and as the campaign progressed the wants of the men were supplied from time to time with the regulation uniform." By late summer, the 33rd no longer wore its Zouave uniform, and Mindil informed the Quartermaster Department that any surplus Zouave clothing in store could be "passed over to some other regiment wearing this especial dress, say the 35th New Jersey or 17th New York . . . of this Army."

The quartermaster general was delighted, and Montgomery Meigs replied that if "all troops would adopt the regular uniforms no such delay [in supply] would ensue, and, it is believed that they would be as comfortably clothed." No longer Zouaves, but now battle-hardened veterans, the 33rd marched with Sherman's armies from Georgia to the Grand Review in Washington, mustering out on July 17, 1865.

*Zouave sash belonging to Cpl. James Young of the 44th New York Volunteers, People's Ellsworth Regiment. Young was killed in action on May 27, 1862, at Hanover Courthouse, Virginia.* COLLECTION OF NEW YORK STATE DIVISION OF MILITARY AND NAVAL AFFAIRS.

# 5TH NEW YORK VETERAN INFANTRY, 1864

PAUL J. SCHEIRL

In May 1863, the original 5th New York Regiment of Infantry, Duryée's Zouaves, was mustered out upon the expiration of its term of service. The regiment had fought with the Army of the Potomac for two years and gained such stature that a brigade of Zouaves was added to the V Corps in honor of its service. It was natural, then, that there was an attempt to revive Duryée's Zouaves as a veteran regiment. Enough veterans of the original regiment were reenlisted for four companies, and additional recruits were found from other regiments. Still, it was not until May 1864 that the regiment, later brought to full strength through the addition of a battalion of men from the 12th and 84th New York, joined the Army of the Potomac in its Virginia campaigns.

Like the original 5th New York, the veteran 5th was fully uniformed as Zouaves. Their initial dress consisted of a medium rather than dark blue Zouave jacket, gray shirt, leather leggings, and red fez with white turban. Its red trousers, cut more in the chasseur style than the Zouave, were trimmed with yellow cord around the pockets in imitation of the French. In typical Zouave fashion, the cartridge box was worn on the waist belt rather than from a shoulder belt. Their second uniform featured a dark blue Zouave jacket of the Hawkins' Zouave pattern, with a dark blue vest, baggier trousers, and white leggings with leather *jambières*. One soldier, who had originally called the Zouave uniform a "horror of horrors," so changed his tune that in May 1865 he wrote, "The Fifth drew a new uniform to-day,—Zouave, of course,—and they look very fine; it will be the crack regiment in the Review to-morrow."

For its whole period of service, the 5th New York Veterans fought in the V Corps of the Army of the Potomac. The regiment fought at Bethesda Church (Cold Harbor), the siege of Petersburg, Five Forks, and Appomattox. In all, it suffered 405 battle casualties. Its career was by no means so glorious as that of the original Duryée Zouaves, but it saw the war to its conclusion.

# 17TH NEW YORK VETERAN VOLUNTEERS

The image of a Union soldier wearing a Zouave uniform and mounted for battle on a mule could well be imagined as a subject for a cartoon in one of the period tabloids. The image would, however, take on anything but a comic air to many Southern civilians and soldiers in Georgia and the Carolinas in the months following the fall of Atlanta. During this time, men of the 17th New York Veteran Volunteer Infantry, uniformed as Zouaves and some mounted on mules, presented just such a picture. Two years' service in the Army of the Potomac had shown these veteran soldiers the true face of war. Now, as part of Gen. William Tecumseh Sherman's Western army, they knew they were on a campaign to punish the South and end the Rebellion. As they moved with that army toward the city of Savannah and then north through North and South Carolina, they were a force to be reckoned with.

RONALD AND JULIE MARRA

The 17th New York Veteran Volunteer Infantry was raised in and around New York City in the fall of 1863. The core of the regiment was made up of men who had served in the original 17th New York. When recruiting slowed, the ranks were filled with veteran recruits that were being enlisted for the reorganized 9th, 11th, and 38th New York Regiments, along with men who had joined a new regiment that was to be known as the Union Sharpshooters. Quartermaster records show that the Union Sharpshooters were to have received Zouave uniforms as issued to the Duryée Zouaves. As the new 17th was formed, two of the largest companies were made up of men from the original 9th New York, Hawkins' Zouaves, and it was determined that theirs would now be the uniform of the 17th Veterans. The regiment left New York on October 18, 1863, and headed West. They would serve in the XVI Corps in Mississippi and Alabama until August 1864, when they were transferred to the Army of the Cumberland and the XIV Corps, then laying siege to Atlanta. These men fit well with this army. As the regiment left Atlanta and headed east to the sea, the Zouaves were mounted on mules. They would live off the land, and as William B. Westervelt, who had served in the 27th New York and reenlisted in the 17th Veterans, remembered, "Worn out mules we left and took good ones in their place, while our cavalry were never so well mounted. All this was our gain and at the same time impoverished the South, as it left them no animals to work their land."

The 17th retained its Zouave dress until the very end. Such items as shirts, underwear, socks, and shoes were picked up along the route of march, discarded by other regiments that were oversupplied. When the regiment finally reached Washington to take part in the Grand Review in May 1865, they presented a picture that was unmistakably that of hardened veterans.

# CHAPTER 3: ZOUAVES AND CHASSEURS


### INTRODUCTION

1. Michael J. McAfee, *Zouaves: The First and the Bravest* (Gettysburg, Pa.: Thomas Publications, 1991).
2. W. A. Thorburn, *French Army Regiments and Uniforms: From the Revolution to 1870* (London: Arms and Armour Press, 1976).
3. Édouard Detaille, *L'Armée Française: An Illustrated History of the French Army, 1790–1885* (New York: Waxtel and Hasenhauer, 1992).

### TIGER RIFLES, WHEAT'S 1ST SPECIAL BATTALION, 1861

Charles L. Dufor, *Gentle Tiger: The Gallant Life of Roberdeau Wheat* (Baton Rouge: Louisiana State University Press, 1957).

Ross Brooks, "Part Irish and the Rest the Flower," *Military Collector and Historian* 51, no. 3 (fall 1999): 98–115.

### 6TH NEW YORK VOLUNTEERS, WILSON'S ZOUAVES

*Harper's Weekly,* May 18, 1861, 311.

*New York Evening Express,* April 23, 1861, 4.

Gouverneur Morris, *The History of a Volunteer Regiment* (New York: Veteran Volunteer Publishing Co., 1891).

### SALEM ZOUAVES, 8TH MASSACHUSETTS VOLUNTEER MILITIA, 1861

George W. Nason, *Minute Men of '61* (Boston: Smith and MacCance, 1910).

George M. Whipple, *History of the Salem Light Infantry* (Salem, Mass.: Essex Institute, 1890).

Collections of the Essex Institute.

### 11TH INDIANA ZOUAVES

Lew Wallace, *An Autobiography* (New York: Harper, 1906).

Harry T. Grube, "Forming and Equipping the First Six Regiments of Indiana in 1861," *Military Collector and Historian* 5, no. 1 (March 1953): 1–7.

### 5TH NEW YORK VOLUNTEERS, DURYÉE ZOUAVES

Minutes of a Board of Officers, Fort Schuyler, New York, 1861.

National Archives, Quartermaster General, Clothing Series, Letter Book 18.

William Howard Russell, *My Diary North and South* (New York: Harper and Row, 1954).

### 10TH NEW YORK VOLUNTEER INFANTRY, NATIONAL ZOUAVES

Charles W. Cowtan, *Services of the 10th New York* (New York: Charles W. Ludwig, 1882).

National Archives, Record Group 92/99, Book 20, 173.

### LOUISIANA ZOUAVE BATTALION, COPPEN'S ZOUAVES, 1861

*New Orleans Commercial Bulletin,* June 22, 1861.

National Archives, M-320, Compiled Service Records of Confederate Soldiers from Louisiana, Records of Maj. Waldemar Hyllested.

### 34TH OHIO VOLUNTEER INFANTRY, PIATT'S ZOUAVES

Ezra J. Warner, *Generals in Blue* (Baton Rouge: Louisiana State University Press, 1984).

*Cleveland Leader,* January 11, 1862.

Photographs, Michael J. McAfee and Dan J. Miller.

### 9TH NEW YORK VOLUNTEER INFANTRY, HAWKINS' ZOUAVES

Ruth Hawkins, *By-Laws of the "New-York Zouaves"* (New York: L. H. Frank, 1860).

National Archives, Record Group 156.

Don Troiani and Brian Pohanka, *Don Troiani's Civil War* (Mechanicsburg, Pa.: Stackpole Books, 1995).

### 18TH MASSACHUSETTS VOLUNTEER INFANTRY, 1861-62

Don Troiani, Earl J. Coates, and James L. Kochan, *Don Troiani's Soldiers in America, 1754–1865* (Mechanicsburg, Pa.: Stackpole Books, 1998), 150–53.

A. M. Judson, *History of the Eighty-third Regiment* (Erie, Pa.: B. F. H. Lynn, 1865).

Michael J. McAfee, "18th Massachusetts," *Military Images* 20, no. 3 (November–December 1998): 40–41.

### 65TH NEW YORK VOLUNTEER INFANTRY, 1861, 1ST U.S. CHASSEURS

*New York Herald,* July 31, 1861, 8.

*New York Quartermaster General Report* (Albany: Comstock and Cassidy, 1862).

Photographs, Michael J. McAfee.

### 76TH PENNSYLVANIA VOLUNTEER INFANTRY, KEYSTONE ZOUAVES

National Archives, Record Group 92.

William Fox, *Regimental Losses in the Civil War* (Albany, N.Y.: Albany Publishing Co., 1889).

Original uniform of William Mallory, 76th Pennsylvania, Don Troiani Collection.

### 53RD NEW YORK VOLUNTEERS, D'EPINEUIL ZOUAVES

*New York Times,* August 10, 1861.

*New York Tribune,* September 12, 1861.

National Archives, Record Group 94, Regiment Papers, 53rd New York Infantry.

**74TH NEW YORK VOLUNTEER INFANTRY, 1861**

*New York Tribune*, August 13, 1861, 8.

Frederick P. Todd, *American Military Equipage, 1851–1872*, vol. 2 (n.p.: Chatham Square, 1983).

William F. Fox, *Regimental Losses in the American Civil War, 1861–1865* (Albany, N.Y.: Albany Publishing Co., 1889).

Mark Mayo Boatner III, *The Civil War Dictionary* (New York: David McKay, 1959).

**62ND NEW YORK VOLUNTEER INFANTRY, ANDERSON ZOUAVES**

Bureau of Military Statistics, *Fifth Annual Report* (New York: Weed, Parsons, 1868), 115–16.

Frederick Phisterer, *New York in the War of the Rebellion 1861 to 1865* (Albany, N.Y.: J. B. Lyon, 1912).

Roger Sturcke, "62nd Regiment, New York Volunteer Infantry (Anderson's Zouaves), 1861–1865," *Military Collector and Historian* 35, no. 1 (spring 1983): 32–33.

Collections of the Smithsonian Institution.

**114TH PENNSYLVANIA VOLUNTEER INFANTRY, COLLIS ZOUAVES**

Frank H. Taylor, *Philadelphia in the Civil War* (Philadelphia, 1913).

*Philadelphia Evening Bulletin,* November 3, 1864.

Frank Rauscher, *Music on the March* (Philadelphia: Wm. F. Fell, 1892).

Michael J. McAfee, "114th Pennsylvania: The Collis Zouaves," *Military Images* 13, no. 1 (July–August 1991): 29.

**95TH PENNSYLVANIA VOLUNTEERS, GOSLINE ZOUAVES**

National Archives, Record Group 94, Regimental Papers, 95th Pennsylvania Infantry.

G. Norton Galloway, *The Ninety-fifth Pennsylvania Volunteers ("Gosline's Pennsylvania Zouaves") in the Sixth Corps* (Philadelphia, 1884).

U.S. Army, Military History Institute, Carlisle, Pa., Photographic Collection of Soldiers of the 95th Pennsylvania Volunteers.

**72ND PENNSYLVANIA VOLUNTEER INFANTRY, BAXTER'S FIRE ZOUAVES**

Charles H. Banes, *A History of the Philadelphia Brigade* (Philadelphia: J. B. Lippincott, 1876).

Michael J. McAfee, "72nd Regiment, Pennsylvania Volunteer Infantry (Baxter's Fire Zouaves)," *Military Images* 11, no. 6 (May–June 1990): 27.

**146TH NEW YORK VOLUNTEER INFANTRY**

Thomas W. Hyde, *Following the Greek Cross* (Boston: Houghton Mifflin, 1894), 149.

Mary Genevie Brainard, *Campaigns of the 146th Regiment* (New York: G. P. Putnam's Sons, 1915).

Michael J. McAfee, "The 146th New York Volunteer Infantry," *Military Images* 18, no. 1 (July–August 1996): 35

**165TH NEW YORK VOLUNTEER INFANTRY, 1863**

John A. Vanderbilt, John A. Murray, and Peter Biegel, *History of the Second Battalion Duryée Zouaves, One-Hundred Sixty-Fifth Regiment, New York Volunteer Infantry* (New York, 1905).

Thomas S. Townsend, *Honors of the Empire State in the War of the Rebellion* (New York: A. Lovell, 1889).

**PRIVATE, COMPANY G, 109TH PENNSYLVANIA INFANTRY, APRIL 1863**

National Archives, Record Group 92, Quartermaster Consolidated Correspondence File, Pennsylvania.

Ibid., entry 2182, Miscellaneous Records Schuylkill Arsenal, Letter Sent by Military Store Keeper, July 10, 1862.

Ibid., Record Group 156, M-12281, Quarterly Returns of Ordnance and Ordnance Stores on Hand in Regular and Volunteer Organizations.

Ibid., Record Group 94, Regimental Order and Letter Book, 109th Pennsylvania Infantry, June 8, 1862.

**155TH PENNSYLVANIA VOLUNTEER INFANTRY**

155th Regimental Association, *Under the Maltese Cross* (Pittsburgh, 1910).

Don Troiani and Brian Pohanka, *Don Troiani's Civil War* (Mechanicsburg, Pa.: Stackpole Books, 1995).

William F. Fox, *Regimental Losses in the American Civil War, 1861–1865.* (Albany, N.Y.: Albany Publishing Co., 1889).

**33RD NEW JERSEY VOLUNTEER INFANTRY, 2ND ZOUAVES**

National Archives, Record Group 94, Regimental Letter Book, 33rd New Jersey Volunteers.

Ibid., Record Group 92, Quartermaster Records, vol. 23.

Frederic Ray, Jr., Roger G. Sturcke, and Michael J. McAfee, "33rd Regiment, New Jersey Volunteer Infantry, '2nd Zouaves,' 1863–1865," *Military Collector and Historian* 31, no. 3 (fall 1979): 128–29.

**5TH NEW YORK VETERAN INFANTRY, 1864**

Robert Tilney, *My Life in the Army* (Philadelphia: Ferris and Leach, 1912).

Don Troiani et al., *Don Troiani's Soldiers in America, 1754–1865* (Mechanicsburg, Pa.: Stackpole Books, 1998).

**17TH NEW YORK VETERAN VOLUNTEERS**

National Archives, Record Group 92, entry 320, vol. 22, Quartermaster Records.

William B. Westervelt, *Lights and Shadows of Army Life* (Marlboro, N.Y.: C. H. Cochrane, 1886).

# CHAPTER 4

# *The Infantry*

WITH ONLY A FEW EXCEPTIONS, THE OUTCOME of every major battle in the American Civil War was decided by the soldiers who fought on foot with handheld weapons—the infantry. Their skill and determination, combined with the leadership ability of those commanding them, made the difference on such fields as Manassas, Shiloh, Antietam, and Gettysburg. But skill, determination, and even devotion to a cause are not always enough to assure final victory. A nation must be able to equip, feed, clothe, and maintain the means of supplying her armies for the duration of the conflict. Upon this rests the chance for ultimate victory. History has shown that when a country loses this capability—by enemy intervention, a lack of resources, or a combination of the two—little, short of a major military blunder by her enemy, will prevent disaster.

When war began in April 1861, the two contending factions were ill equipped to cope with the demands of a struggle that was destined to last more than the few months envisioned at the time. Sending soldiers to fight one or two major, decisive battles was one thing; sustaining them in the field for a prolonged period was another. To do so required factories and facilities capable of turning out arms, munitions, equipment, and clothing. Raw materials were also necessary to supply these factories, and food was needed to feed the men, who made up the fighting force, and their animals. Although arms and most leather accoutrements would last for extended periods if cared for, the average uniform of a Civil War soldier in the field lasted only a few months. On a long campaign, such as Gettysburg, the infantry soldier often wore out one or two pairs of shoes from lengthy marches on rough roads. Marching also wore out trousers, the continual friction wearing holes in the legs as well as on the hips, where equipment, particularly the cartridge box, rubbed. In 1861, the professional soldiers who made up the high command of both the Union and Confederate armies, unlike many of the state and national politicians, knew well the needs they would face.

Whereas many of the best combat officers of the prewar U.S. Army resigned their commissions to serve the Confederacy, it is an often overlooked fact that, with only few exceptions, those responsible for supplying that army stayed with the Union. Prior to the outbreak of the war, the uniforms of the U.S. Army had been manufactured and supplied by a single facility, Schuylkill Arsenal, in Philadelphia. This facility was staffed and maintained by the army's Quartermaster Department, which was also responsible for getting the uniforms and other supplies to an army that, though small in numbers, was spread across the entire country. In addition, the cloth that went to make the uniforms for the army came from a single factory—the Utica Steam Woolen Company in Utica, New York.

The uniform style worn by the Federal army in 1861 had been adopted in 1858 and was to a large extent patterned after that worn by the French. By army regulation, the infantry soldier was issued a total of eight coats, seven caps, thirteen pairs of trousers, fifteen shirts, eleven pairs of drawers, twenty pairs of stockings, and twenty pairs of shoes over a five-year enlistment. Based on this regulation and years of experience, the quartermasters were able to accurately estimate the annual needs of the army, even to how many of each size garment were likely to be called for. Large numbers of uniforms were not made in advance and stockpiled, so the Schuylkill Arsenal facility could and did respond quickly to special requests. In the late 1850s, a winter expedition against the Indians in the Northwest prompted a call for overcoats with hoods instead of the regulation cape, as well as cavalry

*Detail of coat sleeve of Col. John B. G. Kennedy of the 5th Louisiana Battalion (later Kennedy's 21st Louisiana Regiment). The Austrian-inspired gold tape sleeve knots denote the rank of colonel, and the dark blue velvet cuff trim indicates the branch of service, in this case infantry. Kennedy, a veteran of the Mexican War, commanded the unit until the summer of 1863, when most of the men were transferred into the 1st Louisiana and he was assigned to the C.S.A. Quartermaster Department.* TROIANI COLLECTION.

boots with lower heels for infantry wear. These were readily supplied with no questions asked.

With the coming of war, tens of thousands of volunteers took the field in uniforms supplied by their native states. These quickly wore out, and the majority of those who had been mustered into the service of the Federal government now looked to that authority to supply their needs. Drawing on the years of experience of its senior officers, the U.S. Army Quartermaster Department moved quickly to meet the challenge. Meeting the demand necessitated contracting with existing clothing houses. The ready-to-wear clothing industry was in its infancy, but the westward expansion of the country had created a demand for clothing that was mass-produced and not made by local tailors or at home. New York, Cincinnati, and St. Louis had commercial clothing manufacturing facilities, as did Philadelphia. It was in these areas that the army first established branch clothing depots. Of these, both Cincinnati and St. Louis began actual manufacturing operations, while New York was run as a contracting depot drawing on the existing local industry, which actually extended north to Boston. As the war progressed, other, smaller branch depots were opened, most notably in Steubenville, Ohio, and Quincy, Illinois.

The situation was far more desperate in the Confederacy. Having fewer textile mills and no facility such as Schuylkill Arsenal to use as a base, the South was forced to start from scratch. Initially the Confederate government elected to begin a commutation system that called for the volunteers to supply their own uniforms to be paid for by the government. The small Confederate Regular army alone was uniformed by the government. The system resulted in uniforms of widely varying quality and styles, although by the end of 1861, the color gray was generally accepted as standard.

It did not take long, however, before reality set in. The uniforms received by many Southern soldiers did not hold up under conditions in the field. It is likely that here the enduring myth of the ragged Confederate soldier was born. It was evident that some government control was essential. If the initial determination of the Confederacy to exist as a separate nation can be seen anywhere, it is in the rapid expansion of its economy to a wartime footing. The establishment of an arms-making industry is well documented, but the equally impressive development of a system of depots to manufacture uniforms and accoutrements is often overlooked. An initial depot in Richmond, which was opened in September 1861, was eventually expanded to include depots in Nashville and Memphis, Tennessee; Athens, Atlanta, and Columbus, Georgia; Charleston, South Carolina; Marion, Montgomery, and Tuscaloosa, Alabama; Enterprise, Mississippi; Shreveport, Louisiana; Little Rock, Arkansas; and San Antonio and Houston, Texas. Not all of these operated for the entire war; some, in fact, did so only for a few months. Nevertheless, the list represents a monumental effort to ensure that the Confederate soldier was well clothed and well equipped.

Once the supply of uniforms and clothing was stabilized in both the Union and the Confederacy, the problem for soldiers in the field in general switched from one of standardiza-

*Although trousers were issued by the government, suspenders were not. Therefore, it was up to the individual soldier to find a means of keeping up his pants. The solution was civilian suspenders of every conceivable color combination and ornamentation available. This striped pair was used by a Connecticut soldier during 1862–63.*

TROIANI COLLECTION.

tion and quality to one of supply. Without careful planning, rapidly moving armies can easily outdistance their supply lines. Between early 1862 and early 1865, there were times when the soldiers of both armies were in uniforms that were well worn. Often uniform supply was dependent on the efficiency and knowledge of regimental or brigade quartermasters, many of whom brought little or no experience to the job. Because of this, ample evidence brings into question the stereotypes of the always ragged Rebel and the ever well-clothed and well-equipped Yankee. Photographs of well-uniformed Confederate dead or captured of the Army of Northern Virginia taken in 1863 and early 1865 clearly open to question the idea of undersupplied soldiers. And an inspection report of New York's famed Excelsior Brigade, dated July 27, 1863, states that "the men are sadly in need of clothing which should be supplied prior to a march, both as a sanitary measure and economy of strength."[1]

Clothing depots in both the North and South supplied uniforms to all branches, but sheer volume dictated that the vast majority of the items made or contracted for went to the infantry. Geographic location of the depots dictated to a great extent which of the field commands would draw on which depot.

From late 1862 until the collapse of the Confederate supply system in the final months of the war, there were numerous similarities in the manufacture and supply of uniforms and equipment to the Union and the Confederate infantry. Both were at times troubled with substandard material, both suffered at times from inefficient supply officers, but conversely, during this period, both generally provided clothes and adequate equipment to their soldiers. Though there were some similarities in uniform style, there were also differences that made the infantrymen of the North and the South as distinct and dissimilar as the causes for which they were fighting.

It is difficult to describe a "typical" infantry soldier of either the Union or Confederate army. Except for a small number of Regulars in the Federal army, both forces were composed of volunteers, men who valued independence and individuality. They at times either ignored or found creative ways to circumvent standardization orders that seemed to them superficial. The appearance and equipment of the men in both armies evolved during the war to the point that the typical soldier of 1861 would have been an oddity to the veterans who marched and fought on the fields of Virginia or Georgia in 1864.

## HEADGEAR

### *Union*

The Federal army issued two types of headgear to its infantry enlisted men: the pattern 1858 army hat and the pattern 1858 forage, or fatigue, cap. During peacetime, all soldiers received both—the hat for dress occasions and the cap for general use. But in wartime, economy and practical necessity made the continued issue of both a rare occurrence. In general, the Federal soldier received only the cap, though the hat was favored by some, most notably the Iron Brigade. In some commands, soldiers were allowed to purchase and wear hats similar to the army hat; these were shaped to suit the individual. By the latter part of the war, this practice was far more prevalent in the Western armies than in the East. In both Eastern and Western armies, however, many commanders preferred the fatigue cap. In the Army of the Potomac, numerous orders issued in 1864 called for all nonissue headgear to be confiscated and in some cases burned. An order issued to the 53rd Pennsylvania Infantry, near Petersburg, Virginia, September 4, 1864, for example, said, "Every enlisted man in the Regiment must be provided with a cap. . . . In the future any man appearing on duty with hats on will be sent to their companies and others detailed instead and both the officers in command of the Companies and the men themselves held accountable. The officers placed in arrest and the men punished accordingly."[2]

### *Confederate*

For Confederate regiments in both theaters of the war, there was a much greater variety and acceptance of various patterns of headgear than in the Union armies. Although in some regiments hats seem dominate, the issuance of caps was widespread. For example, requisitions for the 19th Alabama Infantry throughout 1863 and early 1864 show a decided preference for hats, whereas those for the 17th Mississippi Infantry for the same period record only caps being received.[3] One Confederate clothing facility in Charleston, South Carolina, was devoted entirely to the manufacture of caps. These were cut out by government employees at the depot and sent to 1,000 to 1,500 local "persons of a needy class" for assembly.[4]

*This Federal forage cap bears the blue cloth crescent badge of the 3rd Division, XI Army Corps. Adopted March 21, 1863, the badge was used until the XI Corps was consolidated with the XII to form the XX Army Corps in April 1864.* JOHN OCKERBLOOM COLLECTION.

*Late-war Richmond Depot–produced jacket worn by Pvt. John K. Coleman of the 6th South Carolina Infantry in 1865. Earlier patterns produced by this depot were ornamented with tape trim or featured belt and shoulder straps.* GARY HENDERSHOTT.

*Confederate "forked-tongue" brass waist belt buckle found near Sequatchie Valley, Tennessee. One of the most widely used buckles in all theaters of the war, this specimen exhibits an interesting field-made replacement tongue.* CHARLES HARRIS COLLECTION.

## COATS, BLOUSES, AND JACKETS

### *Union*

In the Regular army, enlisted infantrymen received both a frock coat for dress purposes and a fatigue blouse to be worn on other occasions. As large numbers of volunteers filled the ranks, supplying both to each man sometimes stretched the capability of the quartermasters. As production problems stabilized, however, many volunteers did in fact receive both. In the early part of the war during the summer campaign, overburdened infantrymen often threw away extra clothing to lighten their loads, so as spring approached in 1863, 1864, and 1865, the soldiers emerging from winter quarters were ordered to put excess clothing in storage. If both the frock coat and fatigue blouse had been issued, which would be worn was usually decided within the regiment, and at times within the company. Although the majority wore the much lighter and more comfortable blouse, many chose to march and go into battle in the frock coat. In addition, many New York units were issued and wore waist-length jackets from the state for a good part of the war. In some cases, troops brigaded with New York units appear to have received such jackets. The 5th Michigan Infantry, which was in the same brigade of the III Corps with the 40th New York, received a small number of these jackets in early 1863.[5]

### *Confederate*

The Confederate army began the war with uniform coats that were anything but uniform. Differences in style and color often existed within the same regiment. By mid-1863, despite some continued acquisition of frock coats, expediency had forced the Confederate army to settle on a nearly universal issue of a gray waist-length jacket for the infantry. It was here, however, that the uniformity ended. There was little overall coordination among the various depots in either cut or trim of the jacket, and the type of material varied greatly in quality and composition. All wool was desired for durability, but it was common practice for Confederate uniforms to be made of a material referred to as jean, which was woven with a wool weft and a cotton warp. Dye lots varied greatly with availability, and some uniforms that started as gray quickly faded to tan or brown. As a result, the actual color of Confederate uniforms ranged from shades of brown to dark gray.

To supplement depot manufacture, the Confederate government was able to import both manufactured garments and cloth from abroad, but this material also varied in quality. In December 1863, Capt. James L. Tait of the British Army visited the South and offered to see to it that the Confederate army was supplied with uniforms of the very best quality. His offer was to supply, among other uniform items, 50,000 suits consisting of jacket and trousers "to be ready for shipment in 3 months from 1st January 1864."[6] The jackets and other items received were manufactured by the firm of Peter Tait of Limerick, Ireland, and were, as Captain Tait promised, of the very best quality cadet gray cloth. Few, if any, of these fine jackets reached the troops in areas other than Virginia and North Carolina.

## TROUSERS

### *Union*

In the period prior to the Civil War, the army-issue trouser was dark blue, the same color as the coat. On January 2, 1862, the commander of the Schuylkill Arsenal depot received word from the office of the quartermaster general that the color of trousers for regimental officers and enlisted men would be sky blue, and that the trouser stripe for noncommissioned infantry officers would now be dark blue.[7] The trousers for all branches were to be made of a durable, heavy woolen material known as kersey. Despite their durability, the trousers of the infantrymen required replacement several times during a season of heavy campaigning. No summer-weight trousers were issued, but natural properties of the kersey allowed for a certain level of comfort, even in hot weather.

The color change from dark to light blue prompted numerous complaints by the Regular army. As late as January 1863, the officer in charge of the Frankfort Arsenal was still trying to obtain dark blue for the enlisted men of his command. The change, however, would last until the army abandoned the blue uniform in the latter part of the nineteenth century.

### *Confederate*

The trousers of the Confederate infantry were similar in cut and style to those of the Union army. Early Confederate regulations established the color for enlisted men's trousers as sky blue, and numerous existing examples give evidence that this color was used to some extent throughout the entire war. Far more common were the same shades of gray and brown seen in jackets issued to the Southern army. Confederate trousers were often made of the same wool-cotton jean cloth used for the jackets, though some were made entirely of cotton.[8] If the heavy wool of the Federal trousers wore out quickly, it is not surprising that the Confederate soldier was often seen marching through towns in ragged trousers. The extended campaign to Pennsylvania and back in 1863 took a heavy toll on uniforms, particularly trousers. Once the Army of Northern Virginia was back on Confederate soil, regular replacements began to arrive. A typical example is Company E of the 53rd Virginia Infantry, one of Armistead's command, which, after the campaign, between July 31 and the end of the year, received 135 pairs of replacement trousers.[9]

## FOOTWEAR

### *Union*

It is unlikely that any other single item of army issue caused as much concern and problem as the shoes worn by the infantry. The standard army shoe or bootee was made of oak-tanned leather. It had four sets of eyelets and extended over the ankle. Although some infantrymen managed to acquire and wear boots, shoes were by far the standard for dismounted men. On campaign, they were often the first items to wear out. Next to running out of ammunition, the inability to replace a soldier's shoes was the greatest potential threat to his ability to function, and poor-quality footwear was often received from contractors and issued to soldiers. In one case, the assistant inspector general of the XI Army Corps reported on July 27, 1863, that "the last issue of shoes to this Corps received . . . at Frederick, Md. [are] of an inferior quality not lasting more than two or three weeks."[10]

### *Confederate*

The supply of shoes to the Confederate army was a continuing and serious problem. Confederate footwear ranged from unavailable to barely adequate to some of the very best obtainable. A private of Company F, 53rd Virginia Infantry, served through the entire Antietam campaign in bare feet, later dying from a resulting infection.[11] At times, soldiers with skill as shoemakers were detailed from regiments in the field to make shoes from hides that had been secured by brigade or division quartermasters. Some shoes issued had cloth uppers attached to leather soles.

By 1863, some fortunate Southern soldiers received English shoes that had been run through the Federal naval blockade. These were described by a Union quartermaster as "the best I have seen for Army use." These shoes, which fastened with a strap and buckle instead of string, were well sewn and reinforced with nails, with a thin band of iron nailed to the bottom of the heel to prevent wear.[12]

*Issued by the hundreds of thousands, there are few surviving examples of the Union army soldier's standard brogans today. This pair was worn by Sgt. Gilbert Bentley of the 37th Massachusetts Volunteer Infantry during the Appomattox, Virginia, campaign of 1865.* TROIANI COLLECTION.

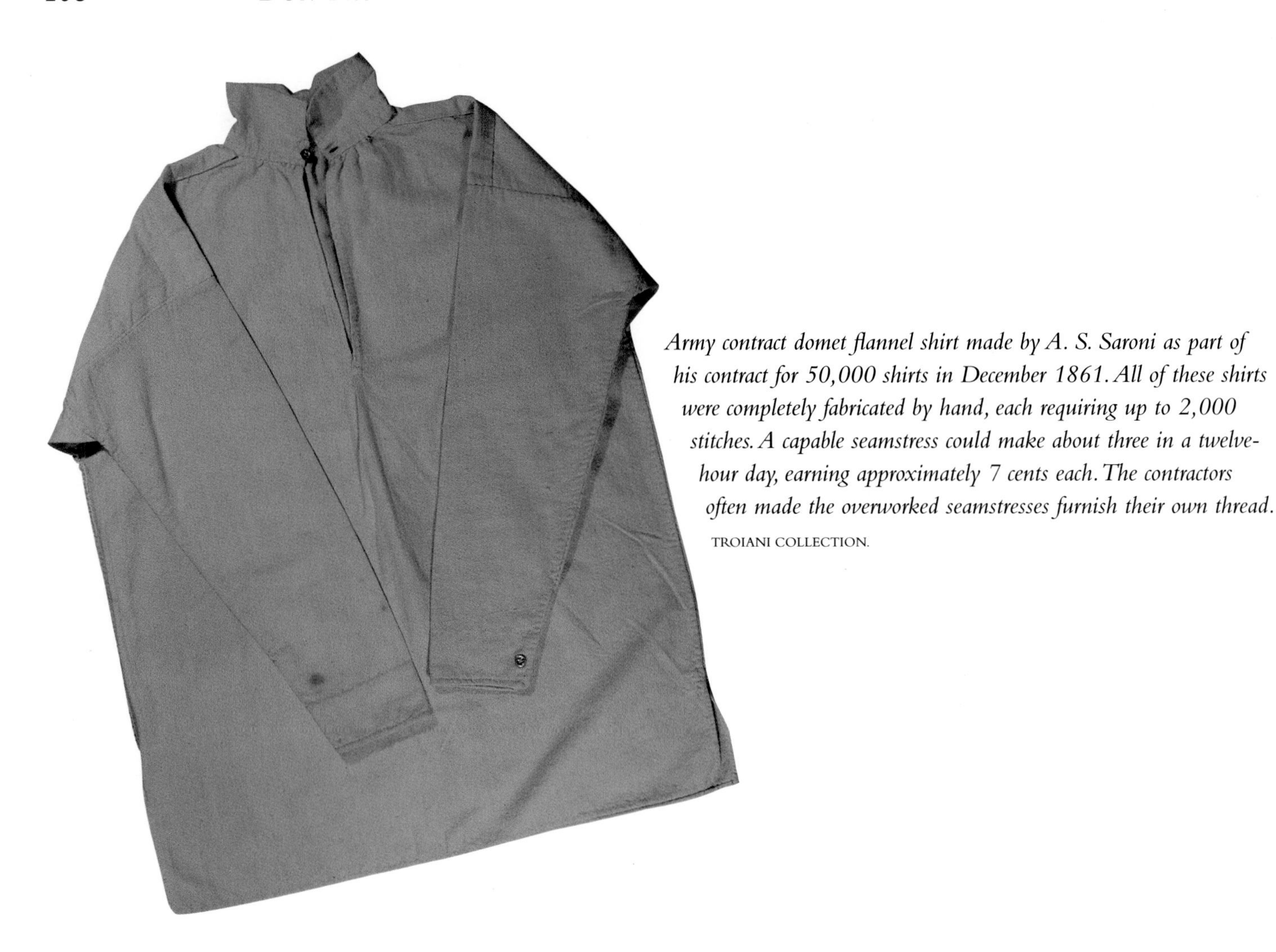

*Army contract domet flannel shirt made by A. S. Saroni as part of his contract for 50,000 shirts in December 1861. All of these shirts were completely fabricated by hand, each requiring up to 2,000 stitches. A capable seamstress could make about three in a twelve-hour day, earning approximately 7 cents each. The contractors often made the overworked seamstresses furnish their own thread.*
TROIANI COLLECTION.

## SHIRTS

### *Union*

The shirt issued by the U.S. government before and during the war was made of white domet flannel, a cotton and wool material. This pullover shirt was issued in a single size, with a single button at the neck and one at each cuff. The design made for ease of construction and certainly made requisition a simple matter of ordering enough to fill the need without regard to fit. During 1863, gray material was ordered as a secondary standard. From that date on, both were distributed on about an equal basis. Union soldiers are seen in numerous photographs in various styles and patterns of civilian shirts that were privately obtained; however, the use of civilian clothing by soldiers was discouraged and at times strictly forbidden.

### *Confederate*

Confederate shirts can best be described as nondescript, as many, if not most, were privately obtained. Regimental records do, however, show regular issue of shirts of wool as well as cotton from the Quartermaster Department. An issue to the 4th Georgia Infantry in February 1863 shows both, with wool shirts charged to the soldier at $2 and cotton at $1.[13] Among the best received by the Confederate soldier were the blue-striped British Army issue, which came through the blockade.[14] The shirts, which likely accompanied the large purchase of jackets and other items from Peter Tait in 1864, were described in the original letter sent to the secretary of war as "strong gray flannel."[15]

## DESIGNATING INSIGNIA

### *Union*

The Union infantry soldier, with few exceptions, was required to wear some manner of insignia, usually on his cap or hat, to allow quick and ready identification of the command to which he belonged. This insignia took the form of brass numbers to show his regiment, along with a brass letter to indicate the company within a regiment. In addition, some regiments also issued and required the soldier to wear a brass device shaped like a hunting horn, which was the U.S. Army designating device for infantry. Regiments that wore the model 1858 army hat usually used all three; those wearing the cap often dispensed with the horn. Photographs indicate that the wearing of designating insignia in the Western armies was not as strictly enforced as in the East.

### *Corps Badges*

One of the most enduring insignia to emerge from the Civil War was the distinctive badges intended to designate each army corps. These corps badges were first used by the Army of the Potomac in the spring of 1863. Indifferently received by the soldiers when first issued, they soon became a symbol

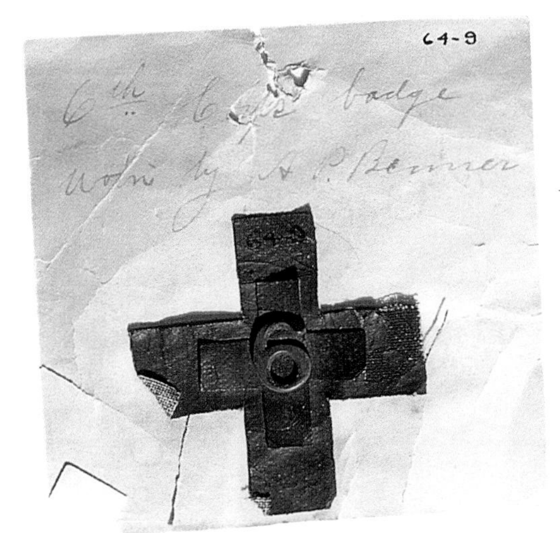


*Unusual soldier field-made VI Army Corps badge of painted oilcloth, worn by Cpl. Arthur P. Benner of Company I, 6th Maine Volunteer Infantry.* TROIANI COLLECTION.

*This folding Federal officer's slouch hat, worn by Maj. Ethan A. Jenks of the 7th Rhode Island Volunteers, has a maker's label in the lining reading, "Warburton's/Army Hat/Patented Dec. 16—1862—Made Expressly for/CL Lockwood, Washington, D.C."* JOHN OCKERBLOOM COLLECTION.

of pride that carried over into the era of veterans' reunions and monument erection in the postwar years.

The original order for corps badges came from headquarters, Army of the Potomac, on March 21, 1863:[16]

> For the purposes of ready recognition of Corps and Divisions in this Army & to prevent injustice by reports of straggling & misconduct through mistake as to the organizations, the Chief Quartermaster will furnish without delay the following badges to be worn by the officers & enlisted men of all the Regiments of the various Corps mentioned.
>
> They will be securely fastened upon the centre of the top of the cap. Inspecting Officers will at all inspections see that these badges are worn as designated.
>
> 1st Corps . . . A Sphere (Red for 1st Division, White for 2nd Div., Blue for 3rd Div.)
> 2nd " a Trefoil " " "
> 3rd " a Lozenge " " "
> 5th " a Maltese Cross " " "
> 6th " a Cross " " "
> (Light Div. Green)
> 11th " a Crescent " " "
> 12th " a Star " " "
>
> The sizes and colors will be according to pattern.
> By command of Maj. Gen. Hooker

Over the course of the war, corps badges were adopted by the entire Union army, although some corps did not adopt or use them until the final months of the conflict.

An order issued by the 1st Brigade, 2nd Division, XII Corps, on April 25, 1863, was repeated many times by other commands in the Army of the Potomac: "Hats will not be worn by the men when caps can be procured. Sutlers must be required to keep on hand letters and figures that each man may have the letter of his Company and number of his Regiment on the top of his cap, the White Star must also be worn on top of the cap."[17]

***Confederate***

Confederate soldiers received no designating insignia from the army. Some photographs show various devices affixed to the headgear of Southern soldiers. These were either privately obtained or purchased by a few Confederate regiments.

# CORPORAL, 16TH NEW YORK INFANTRY, JUNE 1862

The 16th New York Infantry was raised in the far northern counties of the state in the weeks following the firing on Fort Sumter. Like many early regiments, it took the field under a regimental designation that reflected local pride, as well as the belief that this would be a short war—the 1st Northern New York Infantry. On May 15, 1861, the volunteers were mustered into U.S. service for two years as the 16th New York Infantry.

One month later, the regiment received its first issue of uniforms. Like other New York regiments, the 16th was outfitted by the state with the dark blue jacket adopted by New York in 1861, along with sky blue trousers and a fatigue cap of dark blue. Unlike other regiments that fought at First Bull Run or other early battles, there was no mistake that these were Union soldiers. But less than a year later, the 16th suffered heavy casualties, inflicted in part because of a change to this uniform.

TIM OSTERHELD

As with numerous early war regiments, both Union and Confederate, many of the officers were local men of wealth and influence. On June 13, 1862, a letter written from the camp of the 16th New York near New Bridge, Virginia, read as follows: "I send you a photograph of Major Joel J. Seaver, of the 16th, he is a splendid fellow and all like him socially. He has just presented to each member of the regiment a nice straw hat, with a ribbon round it, on which is printed the number of the regiment in gilt letters and figures. The officers hats are bound with black, the others have no binding. He has given to the regiment rubber and woolen blankets, leggings, hats, flags and new instruments for the regimental band." Although the straw hats doubtless were a good deal more comfortable than the army-issue cap, they also proved to have a major disadvantage. The author of the regimental history of the 20th New York recalled of the 16th: "Before the Seven Days Battle the entire regiment [had received] white straw hats with wide brims. They wore these in the battle and were so conspicuous that the Rebels deliberately trained their cannons on them." Despite this, the 16th continued to wear the hats during the retreat to Harrison's Landing.

The 16th had initially been armed with M1840 smoothbore muskets. These, however, were replaced in July 1861 by Enfield rifle muskets supplied by the state of New York.

The 16th New York remained in service until May 22, 1863, serving with both the I and VI Corps in the Army of the Potomac. Following their losses on the Peninsula, the New Yorkers also suffered heavily at Crampton's Gap during the Antietam campaign and at Salem Church in the Chancellorsville campaign.

*Low-crowned straw hat worn by James J. Lampton of Company K (Columbus Riflemen), 13th Mississippi Regiment. Accustomed to wearing such hats during civilian life in the steamy climes, Southerners frequently employed this ample headgear in military service.* CONFEDERATE MEMORIAL HALL, CLAUDE LEVET PHOTOGRAPH.

*Leather leggings such as this pair worn by a soldier of the 26th Massachusetts Volunteers often proved hot and uncomfortable on campaign. By the summer of 1862, few were seen in either army.* TROIANI COLLECTION.

*New York State uniform jacket worn by Sgt. Rollin B. Truesdell of the 27th Regiment. With an exterior breast pocket, state seal buttons, and simple light blue piping around the collar and shoulder straps, these jackets were widely issued from 1861 until about mid-1863.* TROIANI COLLECTION.

*Early-war-style officer's frock coat worn by Capt. J. B. Turner of Mile's Legion (Louisiana) when mortally wounded at Plain's Store on May 20, 1863, during the opening of the Port Hudson campaign. The coat is adorned with black herringbone braid on the front and gold on the black collar and cuffs. It was brought back by a Union officer and became part of the celebrated A. E. Brooks's Collection in 1899.* WILLIAM BRAYTON COLLECTION.

*ILLUSTRATED CATALOGUE: A. E. BROOKS'S COLLECTION OF ANTIQUE GUNS, PISTOLS, ETC. HARTFORD, CONN.* (HARTFORD: CASE, LOCKWOOD & BRAINARD, 1899), 180–82.

*One of the soldier's most vital necessities on the march was the haversack in which he carried rations. Although many types were used, the standard tarred Federal-issue version shown here was by far the most prevalent.* TROIANI COLLECTION.

# 19TH TENNESSEE INFANTRY, C.S.A., APRIL 1862

The 19th Tennessee Infantry was composed of companies from all over eastern Tennessee. Although Union sentiment was strong in this part of the state, this Confederate regiment was raised and organized with little trouble in May and June 1861. The various companies were assembled at Knoxville and entered Confederate service on August 15. Although the regiment received ample supplies of uniforms and equipment in September and October, the armament left something to be desired, with most of the men receiving obsolete flintlock muskets.

As luck would have it, the regiment's first major engagement at Fishing Creek, Kentucky, on January 19, 1862, was under conditions that were unsuited to the arms they carried. One officer remembered that "the rain poured down so they [the flintlocks] would not fire at all. Several of the men after trying repeatedly to fire, just broke their guns over a fence or around a tree, and went off in disgust." The battle was a disaster for the Confederates. A night retreat forced them to abandon a large amount of equipment and supplies. The command, which included the 19th Tennessee, fell back to Nashville.

During the next two months, the 19th was reissued needed uniform items, including frock coats and caps, from the Nashville Quartermaster Depot. Many of the flintlock muskets were exchanged for percussion muskets and a few for Mississippi rifles. Within a few weeks, those who still carried the flintlocks had ample opportunity to exchange them for more modern arms on the bloody field of Shiloh.

On the morning of April 6, 1862, the Tennesseans were in the ranks of the Confederate army commanded by Albert Sidney Johnston near Shiloh Church as part of Gen. John C. Breckinridge's Division. Before the attack on the unsuspecting Union camps, the 19th was detached and moved to the extreme right of the Confederate line. From here, they became part of the afternoon attack on the Union left. Casualties were high, possibly as many as 25 percent killed and wounded, but the men of the 19th Tennessee showed clearly the courage that would carry them through the remainder of the war. Those that remained in 1865 surrendered with Gen. Joseph E. Johnston's Confederate army in North Carolina.

WILLIAM RODEN

# FIRE ON CAROLINE STREET

The men of the 20th Massachusetts, known as the "Harvard Regiment" for the number of Harvard students and graduates in its ranks, engaged in a vicious house-to-house fight as they cleared Confederate soldiers from Fredericksburg, Virginia, on December 11, 1862. The 20th had crossed the Rappahannock River as one of the regiments of Hall's Brigade, Howard's Division, in makeshift "assault" boats in the first bridgehead landing under fire in American history.

Their struggle in the streets of the old colonial town was vicious. As they pushed into Fredericksburg, the men of the 20th found Confederates lodged in its shell-battered and partially wrecked homes and stores. It took the remainder of the day to push the stubborn defenders out of the town and into what proved to be even stronger defenses. The next day, the Harvard Regiment participated in the assault on Marye's Heights. On that day, the 20th could not drive the Southern soldiers from their position, and in two days of fighting, its total casualties numbered 200 killed or wounded.

The 20th was a smart regiment. The men kept their issue uniforms in good order, and on this cold day, they covered their flannel sack coats and sky blue kersey trousers with distinctive gray overcoats. They wore these state-issued overcoats with pride, for their governor, John Andrews, had procured them especially for his state's troops. The regiment was also distinguished by red blankets rolled atop their knapsacks, adding a touch of color, unlike the drab, gray Federal blankets. As a show of regimental pride, many men placed the numeral 20 and the abbreviation "MASS" on the tops of their forage caps. The regiment's Enfield rifle muskets were clean and in good order, and the men of the 20th put them to good use in Fredericksburg on December 11 and 12, 1862.

PRIVATE COLLECTION

*Federal officer's McDowell pattern forage cap, with downward cast visor and scarlet diamond badge of the III Army Corps. Also ornamented with small, false-embroidered stamped silver-plated numbers, which designate it as having belonged to an officer of the 17th Maine Volunteers.* TROIANI COLLECTION.

*Black Federal overcoat worn by Pvt. David Dazell of the 49th Massachusetts Volunteers. Early in the war, Northern contractors were allowed to supply overcoats of other than the regulation sky blue. They were not liked in the 49th, as reported in the November 22, 1862,* Boston Daily Advertiser: *"Through the efforts of Col. Bartlett, the miserable black overcoats have been exchanged, and the regiment will soon receive the serviceable light blue overcoats similar to those of the 51st."* TROIANI COLLECTION.

*Advertised as "Canvass Zouave Army Shoes!" in a Hartford, Connecticut, newspaper during the summer of 1862, these distinctive shoes proved popular with Union troops in both the Eastern and Western Theaters of war. The Allyn House Boot and Shoe Store pronounced, "For marching; they are the best Shoe made, combining comfort and economy. . . . Volunteers attended to first. Drafted men can call after the 15th inst." Volunteer Edgar S. Yergason of the 22nd Connecticut, original owner of the pictured pair, was among those not obliged to wait until the fifteenth to purchase his Zouave shoes.* TROIANI COLLECTION.

*HARTFORD DAILY COURANT,* AUGUST 2 AND 18, 1862.

# 12TH TENNESSEE REGIMENT

DAVID RANKIN, JR.

The 12th Tennessee Infantry Regiment, the majority of its companies recruited in Gibson County, was organized into state service on June 3, 1861, at Jackson, Tennessee. In September, the regiment was ordered to Columbus, Kentucky, on the Mississippi River, as part of the garrison. Surviving quartermaster documents for the 12th Tennessee show that substantial amounts of clothing were issued during October and November 1861, including overcoats, both flannel and cotton shirts, socks, blankets, boots and shoes, pants, hats, caps, and frock coats.

A description from Columbus, Kentucky, printed in the October 30, 1861, *New York Herald* said of the Confederate soldiers that "half were uniformed . . . while balance had an Army cap, coat, pants with a stripe or military mark of some kind, and the rest simply some ordinary [civilian] costume."

Several photographs of soldiers from the 12th Tennessee, as well as the 3rd, 6th, 22nd, 29th, 31st, and 55th Tennessee Battalions, show frock coats of similar style and cut. These are eight- or nine-button single-breasted frocks, with distinctive pointed cuffs that have three buttons. The fabrics and facings are of several different colors, the coats of a dark blue-gray or gray satinette or jean cloth, with facings of light blue, black, or red.

An August 31, 1861 article, in the *Nashville Union and American* stated that the Quartermaster Department was making 2,000 garments per day and had on hand 14,000 suits of clothing. In Memphis, a similar manufacturing depot employed 300 women making up piecework clothing for the Tennessee soldiers. In April and May 1861, to provide uniforms for the Tennessee Volunteers, the Tennessee State and Financial Board had purchased some 30,000 yards of gray satinette material; 25,000 yards of mixed red, gray, and blue flannel cloth; Kentucky jean cloth; 25,000 yards of red flannel; and metal coat buttons.

Ads were run in the Nashville papers for six or eight practical tailors to cut volunteer uniforms by pattern. In September 1861, the operations and supplies of the Tennessee State Quartermaster Department were transferred to the Confederate government. In addition to Tennessee soldiers, the Memphis and Nashville Depots were to also supply clothing to the troops from Kentucky, Missouri, and Arkansas. By the fall of 1861, Nashville was the primary supply center for the Confederate armies in the Western Department No. 2 and those in faraway Virginia.

Nashville was evacuated in February 1862, following the battle and capture of Fort Donelson. Some $5 million of much-needed quartermaster goods were abandoned or destroyed in what has been called the Nashville Panic. It appears that the Tennessee pattern frock coat was also lost to the enemy. Instead, the less expensive jacket was now manufactured and issued to the soldiers of the Confederacy.

The 12th Tennessee was consolidated with the 22nd Tennessee Infantry in June 1862 and with the 47th Tennessee Infantry in October of that year. The regiment's proud history began with the battle of Belmont, where it, along with the rest of Col. Robert Russell's Brigade, bore the first shock of the Federal attack. Battle honors include some of the bloodiest fighting of the war—Shiloh, Richmond (Kentucky), and Murfreesboro, where the 12th suffered 164 casualties out of 322 engaged, a staggering 50 percent casualty rate.

The 12th Tennessee served on in the Western Theater of the war until paroled at Greensboro, North Carolina, in May 1865. At the surrender, there remained a total of only fifty officers and men of the consolidated 12th, 22nd, and 47th Tennessee Regiments.

*Confederate enlisted man's double-breasted frock coat made of gray-brown jean cloth. The inscription "L.S. 2nd Ala Vols" is marked inside the sleeve. The buttons are covered with black cloth and probably were added after the war's end when Confederate insignia were banned from public display.* MIDDLESEX COUNTY HISTORICAL SOCIETY.

*Gray satinette frock coat with black binding worn by Pvt. Joseph Ellison Adger, a member of Company A (Washington Light Infantry), 25th Regiment of South Carolina Infantry. Adger frugally retained this coat when promoted to captain in April 1862, adding the appropriate gold tape to the collar.* COLLECTION OF THE CHARLESTON (SOUTH CAROLINA) MUSEUM.

*Pair of woven cotton butternut trousers worn by Pvt. James A. McKinstry of Company D, 42nd Alabama. According to family tradition, they were worn by him at the assault on Battery Robinett, Corinth, Mississippi, on October 3, 1862.* COURTESY JAMES VANCE.

# BURNSIDE'S BRIDGE

On September 17, 1862, two Union infantry regiments forced the crossing of a narrow stone bridge that spanned Antietam Creek. These regiments, one from New York and one from Pennsylvania, both bore the regimental number 51. First to cross were the Pennsylvanians, their three regimental colors leading the way. Facing them were 400 Confederates of the 2nd and 20th Georgia Regiments, determined to exact a high toll in Yankee blood as the price of passage. There was no unique color or flash to the uniform of the 51st Pennsylvania. Brigade quartermaster records show issue of the standard fatigue blouse and forage cap. They were armed with the Enfield rifle musket.

The men had seen action just a month before at Second Manassas, where they had the misfortune of having left their knapsacks stacked under guard, only to lose them when forced to leave the field by a different route. Except for a small amount of clothing intended for another regiment, which they found at Centerville, Virginia, they would have no new issue until late September. On September 28, the regiment received a new stand of colors from friends in Norristown, Pennsylvania, and on October 5, a new individual button-together shelter tent known officially as the *tente d'abri,* which would soon become well known to Union soldiers.

As part of the IX Army Corps, commanded by Maj. Gen. Ambrose Burnside, the 51st Pennsylvania saw service in both theaters of the war. Its men fought on until the end, sustaining a total of 177 killed and mortally wounded. But despite all the hard fighting and campaigns, they would forever be linked to the few brave minutes of their desperate charge across the stone bridge at Antietam, ever after known as Burnside's Bridge.

NATIONAL CIVIL WAR MUSEUM, HARRISBURG, PENNSYLVANIA

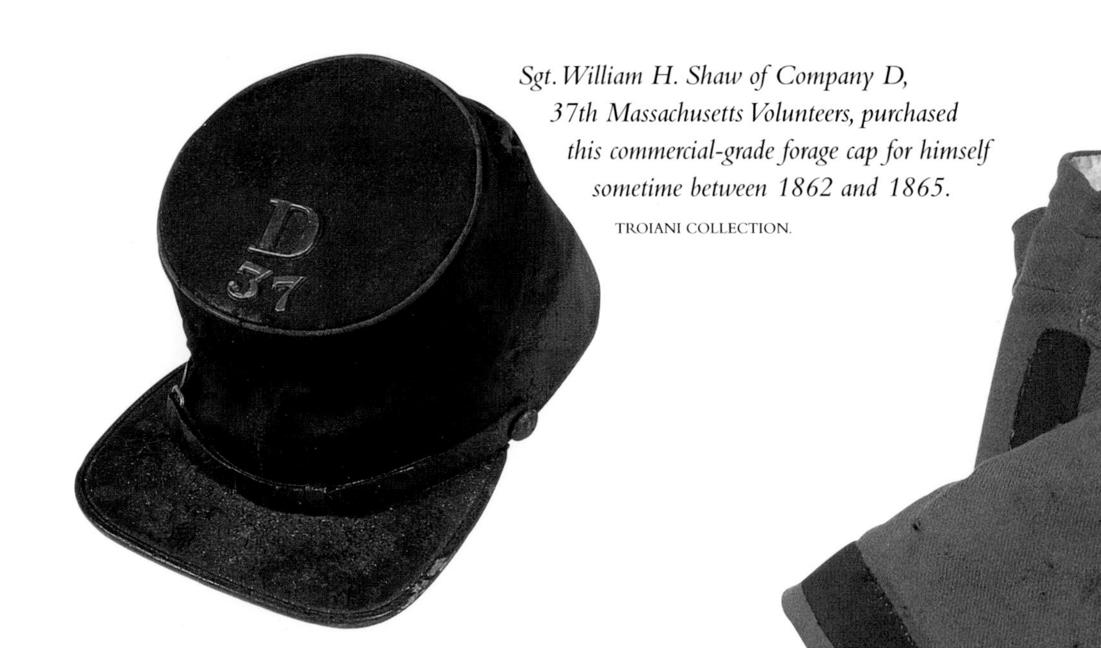


*Sgt. William H. Shaw of Company D, 37th Massachusetts Volunteers, purchased this commercial-grade forage cap for himself sometime between 1862 and 1865.* TROIANI COLLECTION.

*A pair of manufactured Federal sky blue kersey enlisted man's trousers. These were made by the hundreds of thousands by the government and private contractors throughout the war. This pair has a one-and-a-half-inch-wide dark blue stripe denoting a sergeant of infantry, which was added by the soldier himself.* TROIANI COLLECTION.

*The men of Congressman (Col.) Charles H. Van Wyck's 56th New York Volunteer Infantry had a unique description—Xth Legion—to display on their Model 1853/1855 knapsacks. The regiment was considered a legion because when it was formed, it had infantry, artillery, rifle, and cavalry companies in one unit. The name derived from the fact that Van Wyck represented the Tenth District of New York.* WEST POINT MUSEUM.

# PRIVATE, 5TH NEW JERSEY INFANTRY, MAY 1863

In the spring of 1863, as the Army of the Potomac began to prepare for the coming campaign, each regiment was ordered to box surplus clothing for storage until needed again the following winter. Because of their weight, blankets and greatcoats were generally included in the items stored. Brigade commanders often decided which uniform items would be worn and which stored. Although most regiments of the army elected to wear the four-button fatigue blouse, the men of the 3rd Brigade, 2nd Division, III Corps, consisting of the 5th, 6th, 7th, and 8th New Jersey, as well as the 115th Pennsylvania and 2nd New Hampshire commanded by Col. George C. Burling, either elected to or were ordered to wear the dress frock coat. During this same period, on February 19, 1863, the III Corps received a general order that the infantry would be issued white canvas or leather leggings by the Quartermaster Department. Also during this time of preparation for battle, the famous corps identifying badges were adopted by the Army of the Potomac. The 2nd Division, III Corps, would wear a white diamond attached to the forage cap.

The soldier illustrated here represents the 5th New Jersey as it appeared just before the battle of Chancellorsville. He is armed with a .54-caliber Austrian Lorenz rifle musket. His uniform is army regulation, and he will wear it throughout the coming campaign, which will include the battle at Chancellorsville and the march to and battle of Gettysburg. At Gettysburg, the 5th New Jersey would be sent forward as skirmishers west of the Emmitsburg Road and on July 2 would find themselves temporarily trapped between the Union and Confederate lines, where they would take numerous casualties.

JOSEPH STAHL

The regiment served in the III Corps until March 1864, when they were assigned to the 3rd Division of the II Corps. Those who did not reenlist were mustered out the following November. During its service, the 5th New Jersey lost 12 officers and 126 enlisted men, killed and mortally wounded.

*First Sgt. Enoch Whittemore of Company I, 5th Maine Volunteers, may have worn this jacket when he received his third gunshot wound of the war at Spotsylvania, Virginia, on May 10, 1864. Whittemore had sported an officers'-quality 1st Division, VI Corps, badge on the breast of his jacket, a common practice of the time, as evidenced in contemporary photographs.* TROIANI COLLECTION.

*Although enlisted men were not authorized to wear a vest, many did so during their term of service. This example was made from the same rough sky blue kersey used for trousers and overcoats.* NELSONIAN INSTITUTE.

*In early 1862, many units of the Army of the Potomac received canvas leggings of this pattern, including the regiments composing the famed Iron Brigade. The leggings were heavily used at first, but they quickly became unpopular and were not widely worn after early 1863, although they continued to be issued sporadically through 1864. This pair was issued to Pvt. James Boisbrun of Company A, 115th Pennsylvania Volunteers.* TROIANI COLLECTION.

## 14TH MISSISSIPPI INFANTRY, FORT DONELSON, TENNESSEE, FEBRUARY 18, 1863

DAVID RANKIN, JR.

As the officers and men of the 14th Mississippi began their two-mile walk from the train station to the Camp Douglas Prison Camp in Chicago, a soldier in Company B of that regiment remarked that his comrades made for a "motley looking set." As he described it, "We had all our cooking utensils with us, camp kettles, skillets, ovens, frying pans, coffee pots, tin pans, tin cups and plates. We had them on our heads, on our backs, swinging from our sides, and in our hands. Some of the boys were bareheaded, some had hats and caps with no brims . . . we were quite a show!" According to a reporter for the *Chicago Tribune* who witnessed the arrival of this first group of Confederate prisoners:

> Such a thing as uniformity in dress was impossible to find, as there were no two dressed alike. Butternut colored breeches, walnut dyed jeans greatly predominated. Most of the pants were ornamented by a broad, black stripe down the outer seam, sometimes of velvet, but mostly of cloth or serge. Shirts and drawers are all of the coarsest description. Hats and caps were diversified, yet they had a uniform cap—gray with black band. For protection against the chilling wind, the soldiers used a conglomeration of overcoats, blankets, quilts, buffalo robes, and pieces of carpeting of all colors and figures. The carpet coats are made by putting a puckering string in the edge of a piece of carpeting, and gathering it around the edge. Their officers could not be distinguished from the privates, although some had a regular gray uniform and others the Army blue, the only difference a great profusion of gold lace. Many of the soldiers carried bags [carpet sacks] of all colors, and were dressed in butternut jeans and white cotton [osnaburg] overcoats. All appeared rough and hard.

The nonuniform appearance of the early- to midwar Confederate soldiers was a direct result of goods being collected and distributed in two clothing drives, as the Quartermaster Department was unable to provide clothing for an army of 200,000 men until later in the war. In a show of unequaled patriotism by the fair women of the South, their tender hands spun and dyed the jean cloth for uniforms and sewed and collected most of the garments worn by the Fort Donelson garrison. This they accomplished under two "great appeals" for warm winter clothing, blankets, and shoes. The appeals were officially government sponsored, with the full support of the Quartermaster Department, which promised to provide transportation of the goods. These drives were the primary source of clothing for all the armies of the South during the fall and winter of 1861–62 and 1862–63. The bulk of the uniforms collected were homespun jeans, gathered up and sent to state collection points as donations or traded for Confederate bonds.

During the four-day siege and battles of Fort Donelson, February 12–16, 1862, the 14th Mississippi Infantry lost 17 killed, 85 wounded, and 10 missing out of 650 engaged. On February 15, the 14th Mississippi was part of the Confederate counterattack to open the way for a retreat or a Federal rout. Twice that day, the 14th Mississippi was ordered to make a bayonet charge to break the Yankee line. It succeeded, only to be ordered back to its trenches and surrendered.

The 14th was exchanged on August 27, 1862, after spending six long months in a prisoner-of-war camp in Chicago. The regiment went on to fight in some of the bloodiest battles of the Western Theater, serving gallantly at Vicksburg, and in the Atlanta campaign and Hood's Nashville campaign, finally ending its service in North Carolina in April 1865.

*Light-colored jean cloth Confederate trousers typical of those produced in penitentiary workshops. This pair was used by Nathan Tisdale of Company A, 30th Louisiana Infantry, who served at Meridian, Mississippi, from early 1862 until his parole on May 14, 1865.* CONFEDERATE MEMORIAL HALL, CLAUDE LEVET PHOTOGRAPH.

*Confederate soldier's rubberized rain hat, taken as a trophy by a Union soldier from the battlefield of Corinth, Mississippi, in May 1862. Products of the India Rubber Company, waterproof garments such as this were used by both sides.* TROIANI COLLECTION.

*Typical Confederate tin drum canteen, with a Federal musket sling as a shoulder strap. This specimen was captured at Gettysburg by George H. Sunderlin from Vermont, who survived the fighting to bring home this memento.* TROIANI COLLECTION.

# 13TH PENNSYLVANIA RESERVES

In early April 1861, Thomas L. Kane, an active abolitionist, applied to Pennsylvania governor Andrew G. Curtin for permission to raise companies of cavalry for the war. Since no cavalry was wanted, Kane decided instead to raise a regiment of riflemen from rural Pennsylvanians "accustomed to handling guns . . . and possessed of strong and dogged physiques through their outdoor experiences." Kane got exactly what he wanted, and the volunteers rushed to service, armed with their own rifles. While Kane's recruits were signing up, James Landregan of the Macon County Rifles spied a deer's hide hanging in a butcher shop opposite the recruiting office. He cut off the tail and placed it on his cap, thus giving birth to the regimental insignia and nickname of Bucktails.

NATHAN EDELSTEIN

The Bucktails were not at all happy to find the government offering them flintlock conversion smoothbore muskets to replace their personal rifles, but in August 1861, they received Enfield and Springfield rifle muskets, which somewhat placated the men. Known also as the 42nd Regiment, Pennsylvania Volunteer Infantry, the Bucktails never wore a special uniform. Initially they were issued standard uniforms of blouses, caps, and dark blue trousers. In Harrisburg, late in July, "Letters to be placed on the men's caps were obtained, as were also blue overcoats, cotton-flannel drawers and other necessary clothing." Thus equipped, the men of the 13th Reserves went to war. They were, however, immediately identifiable by the bucktails and strips of deerhide that they continued to wear on their caps, hats, and even their flagstaffs throughout the war.

By the summer of 1862, the Bucktails had established their reputation but had suffered losses. Two new regiments of Bucktails were raised—the 149th and 150th Pennsylvania—to create a Bucktail Brigade. Much to the initial chagrin of the 13th, the new, unproven regiments were allowed to wear the cherished fur emblem of the original regiment. The original Bucktails, however, were recognized in August 1862 with the issuance of double-set trigger Sharps M1859 breech-loading rifles. They used these new weapons with great effect at Gettysburg, in a hot struggle in the woods near that battle's famed Wheatfield. There the regiment's new twenty-three-year-old colonel, Charles Frederick Taylor, was killed while in the front lines with his men. A Medal of Honor was awarded to Sgt. James B. Thompson for capturing the flag of the 15th Georgia at this battle.

The 13th fought on, greatly reduced in numbers, if not in spirit, through the first campaigns with Grant in 1864. In June 1864, the original regiment of Bucktails was mustered out of service. They left an indelible record of valor.

*Pair of forage caps worn by Federal soldiers of the 5th Maine and 119th Pennsylvania Volunteers. Both bear the Greek cross of the 1st Division, VI Army Corps.* TROIANI COLLECTION.

*Working with precious little at hand, Silas B. Warren of Company F, 17th Illinois Volunteers, fashioned this shirt from a tent fly while a prisoner of war at Andersonville, Georgia, in December 1864. He unraveled sections of fabric to make the thread to stitch with.* M. CUNNINGHAM COLLECTION.

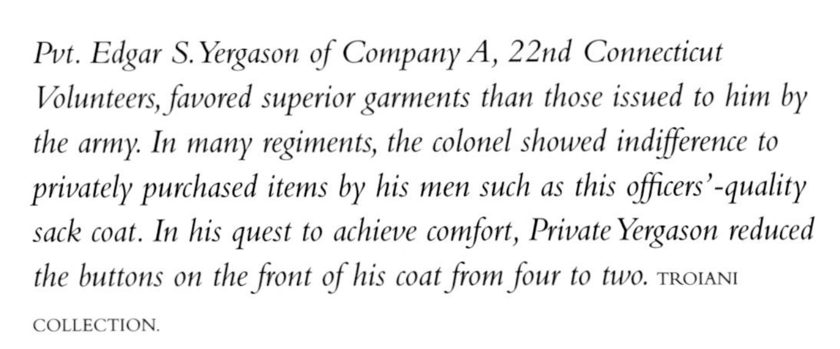

*Pvt. Edgar S. Yergason of Company A, 22nd Connecticut Volunteers, favored superior garments than those issued to him by the army. In many regiments, the colonel showed indifference to privately purchased items by his men such as this officers'-quality sack coat. In his quest to achieve comfort, Private Yergason reduced the buttons on the front of his coat from four to two.* TROIANI COLLECTION.

*Pvt. Edwin Goulding of the 15th Massachusetts was possibly wearing this forage cap when he was struck in the back by a shell fragment at Gettysburg. Goulding's cap sports the earliest pattern of the II Army Corps's trefoil badge, and the metallic edging suggests it was a private purchase. The white color denoted the 2nd Division, to which his regiment belonged.* M. CUNNINGHAM COLLECTION.

# THE IRON BRIGADE

As the Union I Army Corps fell back toward the town of Gettysburg on July 1, 1863, the 24th Michigan Infantry turned to fight a desperate rearguard action near the Lutheran Seminary. The regiment had arrived on the field early in the day with the rest of the famed Iron Brigade and had been heavily engaged ever since. Now, with several color-bearers down, the regiment's colonel, Henry A. Morrow, defiantly raised the regimental colors.

The 24th Michigan Infantry had been the last regiment to join the Army of the Potomac's famed Iron Brigade, arriving in October 1862. It was also the last to trade its forage caps for the black army dress hats that had become the symbol of the rest of the brigade, not receiving them until May 27, 1863. These hats now bore the recently adopted corps badge of the 1st Division, I Corps, a red cloth disk, along with the brass numerals and letters dictated by army regulations. Although the men of the 24th had sent their greatcoats and excess clothing to storage before the summer campaign, most had elected to retain and wear their infantry dress coats. Wearing these, along with knapsacks or bedrolls—which experience had shown must be worn into battle, as few such items that were removed and stacked were ever recovered—made hot work even hotter.

WALTER WALPIN COLLECTION

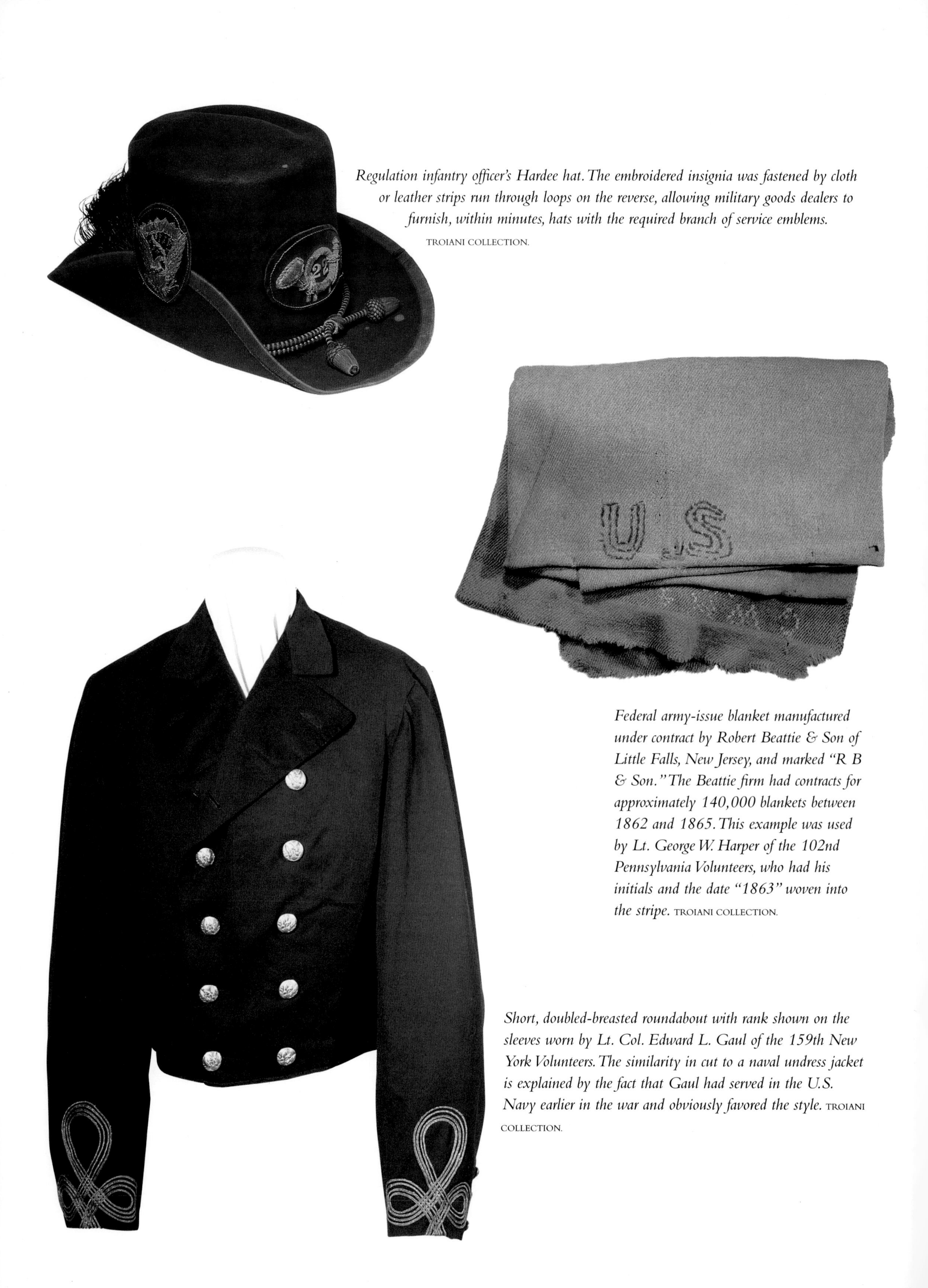


*Regulation infantry officer's Hardee hat. The embroidered insignia was fastened by cloth or leather strips run through loops on the reverse, allowing military goods dealers to furnish, within minutes, hats with the required branch of service emblems.* TROIANI COLLECTION.

*Federal army-issue blanket manufactured under contract by Robert Beattie & Son of Little Falls, New Jersey, and marked "R B & Son." The Beattie firm had contracts for approximately 140,000 blankets between 1862 and 1865. This example was used by Lt. George W. Harper of the 102nd Pennsylvania Volunteers, who had his initials and the date "1863" woven into the stripe.* TROIANI COLLECTION.

*Short, doubled-breasted roundabout with rank shown on the sleeves worn by Lt. Col. Edward L. Gaul of the 159th New York Volunteers. The similarity in cut to a naval undress jacket is explained by the fact that Gaul had served in the U.S. Navy earlier in the war and obviously favored the style.* TROIANI COLLECTION.

# 21ST OHIO VOLUNTEER INFANTRY, CORPORAL, COMPANY C, SEPTEMBER 1863

The uniform of the 21st Ohio in 1863 was typical of that worn by Federal troops serving in the Western Theater of the war. The campaigns of the winter and early spring had taken their toll on the uniforms of the regiment, and it was issued new ones in August. This uniform had none of the flash or color of the Zouave. Every item from head to toe had a practical value and was standard issue, as received from one of the two Western quartermaster depots. This soldier's hat is unadorned, and his coat is the plain fatigue blouse of a fighting man ready for action. The only bit of regulation flash present is the round brass plate bearing a U.S. eagle on the sling holding his cartridge box at his side. Even this eventually was dispensed with as the men moved in combat.

PRIVATE COLLECTION

If the uniform of the 21st can be considered typical, the arms they carried were anything but commonplace. Company C, like most of the 21st Ohio, was armed with the deadly .56-caliber, five-shot Colt revolving rifle, which it received in a shipment from Washington on May 26, 1863. Many, if not most, of the rifles carried by the regiment had been turned in by the famed 2nd Regiment U. S. Sharpshooters serving in Virginia, who disliked the complicated mechanism. As with other Eastern discards, the rifles were sent west where, in the hands of the farm boys and mechanics of the Buckeye State, they soon proved their worth. On September 20, at the bloody battle of Chickamauga, the men of the 21st were ordered to hold a position on Horseshoe Ridge, and hold it they did. Their rapid-firing Colts repulsed repeated Confederate charges and inflicted heavy losses on the enemy. Finally, when the special ammunition required to load the rifles was exhausted, they fixed bayonets and continued to fight. During this single day's fight, the 21st Ohio, with their rapid-firing Colts, expended over 43,000 rounds of ammunition.

Not withstanding their heroic stand, the regiment lost a number of men captured by Confederate troops of Gen. James Longstreet's command, who, according to the regimental historian of the 21st, "were wearing new uniforms which at a distance in the smoke and dusk of the evening, looked very much as our own."

The remaining men of the 21st Ohio continued to serve and fight with the XIV Corps and the Army of the Cumberland in the Atlanta campaign and through the Carolinas. They were mustered out on July 25, 1865.

# TOWARD THE ANGLE

The battle of Gettysburg will forever be remembered as one of the defining engagements of the Civil War. On July 3, 1863, with two days of indecisive battle behind him, Gen. Robert E. Lee, commanding the Confederate army, attempted to break the Federal line in its center. To accomplish this, he ordered an assault by three divisions of infantry totaling nearly 12,000 men, under the overall command of Gen. George E. Pickett. It was a fateful decision that gained the Southern army nothing but glory and cost the lives of many of its finest officers and men.

Among those who would lead and not return were Brig. Gen. Richard Brooke Garnett, commanding one brigade of five Virginia regiments, and Brig. Gen. Lewis Addison Armistead, in command of another five regiments of Virginians. As they moved forward, the men of these regiments presented a picture that sharply contrasted with the image of the poorly uniformed and supplied Confederate soldier. Garnett was wearing a fine new gray uniform. In May and June 1863, prior to leaving Virginia, the men of the Army of Northern Virginia who needed new uniform items had received replacements. For the infantry, these replacements included jackets and caps, many trimmed in infantry blue, as well as trousers, shirts, and underwear from the Richmond Depot, and the vital commodity of shoes. Although the depot-produced uniforms were of a high quality, the character of the shoes varied depending on the source and materials available. The fortunate received footwear of English manufacture, which buckled rather than tied. In the opinion of one Federal officer who saw them, they were "the best I have seen for Army use."

Although some Confederates were issued and carried knapsacks, many preferred what the army termed "light marching order"—a rolled blanket containing a few personal items and a change of underwear, slung over the shoulder. Like their Yankee counterparts, the Southern soldiers had learned by experience that stacking or leaving their belongings behind when going into battle usually meant they would never see them again.

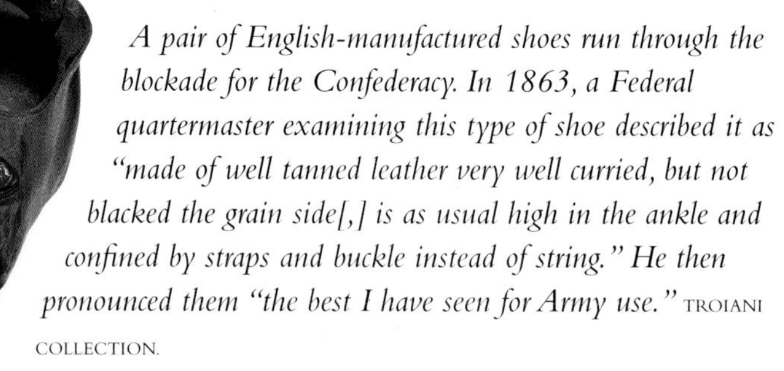

*A pair of English-manufactured shoes run through the blockade for the Confederacy. In 1863, a Federal quartermaster examining this type of shoe described it as "made of well tanned leather very well curried, but not blacked the grain side[,] is as usual high in the ankle and confined by straps and buckle instead of string." He then pronounced them "the best I have seen for Army use."* TROIANI COLLECTION.

NATIONAL ARCHIVES, RECORD GROUP 92, ENTRY 999, LE DUC LETTER, LIEUTENANT COLONEL AND CHIEF QUARTERMASTER, XI CORPS.

DR. COYLE S. CONNOLLY

*This cadet gray Confederate kepi of the style produced at the Richmond Depot, with painted fabric visor, was brought home as a war trophy by a Union soldier.* COLLECTION OF NEW YORK STATE DIVISION OF MILITARY AND NAVAL AFFAIRS.

# The Texas Brigade, 1863

PRIVATE COLLECTION

One of the fabled units of the Confederate army of Northern Virginia, the Texas Brigade, lived up to the hard-fighting reputation it gained on battlefields from Virginia to Pennsylvania. This brigade consisted of the 1st, 4th, and 5th Texas Infantry, along with the 3rd Arkansas Infantry. By 1863, after two years of campaigning, the uniforms worn by the brigade were much the same as those in general use in the Eastern Confederate army. To assure as ample a supply as possible, each of the regiments of this brigade maintained its own depot in Richmond, where surplus clothing was stored until needed. Prior to the summer campaign of 1863, each regiment had all needed clothing items supplied. The campaign that led to the monumental battle at Gettysburg, Pennsylvania, took its toll on both uniforms and equipment for the Texas Brigade. Most, if not all, items were resupplied after the brigade returned to Virginia, before it left again with the Confederate First Corps to temporarily bolster the sagging fortunes of the Confederate Army of Tennessee.

The four soldiers on the previous page represent, from left to right, the 1st, 5th, and 4th Texas, as well as a musician of the 3rd Arkansas. They stand together just prior to the attack on the Federal left flank at Devil's Den on July 2, 1863. During the first months of 1863, the 4th Texas had received an extensive issue of clothing, which included caps with rain covers. The soldier of the 1st Regiment has removed the frock coat he was issued earlier in the year. The noncommissioned officer of the 5th carries the short Enfield rifle with saber bayonet that he received in 1861. The arms carried by the brigade varied, but with the exception of the 1st Texas, they consisted mainly of .57- or .58-caliber rifle muskets. The men of the 1st received and carried a mixture of .69-caliber smoothbore muskets and rifle muskets, with the smoothbores continuing in service well into 1864.

While the brigade was in the Department of Tennessee in early 1864, and away from its clothing supply from the regimental depots in Richmond, it was necessary to detail several shoemakers from the 4th Texas to manufacture shoes and boots from leather obtained by the regimental quartermaster. During this time, for the 4th Texas alone, the detailed men manufactured 259 pairs of shoes and 22 pairs of boots. Along with its corps, the Texas Brigade returned east in time for the fateful campaigns of 1864 and the spring of 1865.

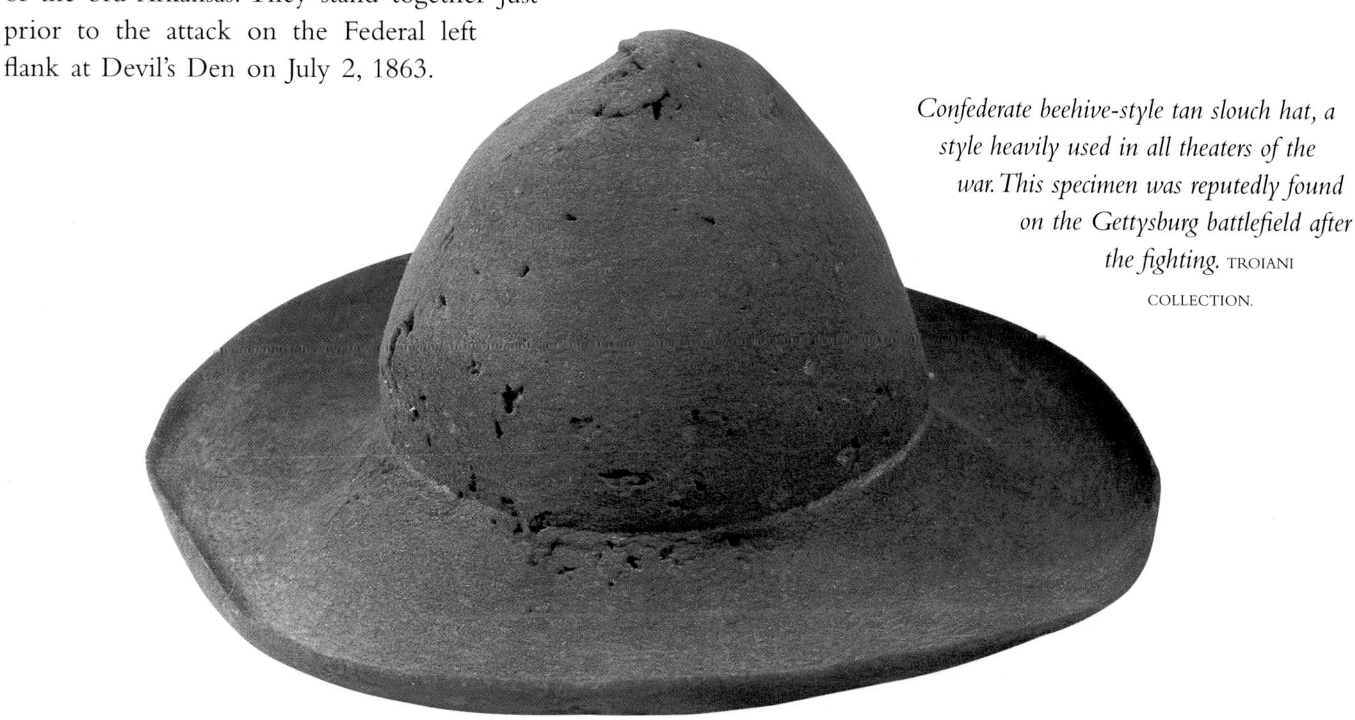

*Confederate beehive-style tan slouch hat, a style heavily used in all theaters of the war. This specimen was reputedly found on the Gettysburg battlefield after the fighting.* TROIANI COLLECTION.

# BARKSDALE'S CHARGE

On July 2, 1863, Confederate general William Barksdale and his four Mississippi regiments of infantry—the 13th, 17th, 18th, and 21st—advanced upon Federal artillery and infantry along Emmitsburg Road near the Peach Orchard. Barksdale's men were part of the overall assault of Longstreet's Corps on that hot and sunny afternoon. It was an attack that Robert E. Lee hoped would sweep the opposing Army of the Potomac from Gettysburg. If successful, it could decide the course of the war.

The 1,500 men of Barksdale's units were noted as "well shod and efficiently clothed" by Lt. Col. Arthur Fremantle, a British Army observer accompanying Lee's army. Their accoutrements included Union army knapsacks captured at the battles of Second Manassas and Chancellorsville, many of which still bore the names of the regiments to whom they had belonged. Uniformed in gray jackets, often worn with captured Federal blue trousers, Barksdale's men had a variety of headgear, from civilian brimmed hats to jaunty regulation kepis of gray and blue.

On the other side, however, there was greater uniformity, and as the advance neared the Sherfy farmhouse and barn just west of the Emmitsburg Road, the distinctive uniforms of the 114th Pennsylvania Volunteer Infantry became apparent. A Zouave unit, the 114th wore uniforms of dark blue and red with red fezzes, some wrapped in white turbans, but all with yellow tassels. The haughty Englishman, Fremantle, described them as "poor imitations" of the French Zouave garb, but the 114th uniforms were actually well made and attractive, with light blue cuffs adorning the red-trimmed jackets.

Barksdale's gray smashed into the blue-and-red lines and sent them reeling, forcing the Rhode Island artillerymen to limber their guns in hasty withdrawal. Pennsylvania regiments in standard blue were also forced back, and the Mississippi regiments plunged forward through the Peach Orchard, pushing on to further combat that would see hundreds of soldiers, as well as the valiant Barksdale, fall as the Union lines ultimately held to fight another day.

*Painted infantry drum used by Edwin S. Sutch, drummer of Company C, 138th Pennsylvania Volunteers. This example is unusual in having a large VI Corps badge incorporated within a striking motif on its front.* C. PAUL LOANE COLLECTION.

WALTER WALPIN COLLECTION

# 1ST SOUTH CAROLINA VOLUNTEER INFANTRY, U.S. COLORED TROOPS

Aside from its status as one of the first regiments of African-American troops formed, the 1st South Carolina was also one of the only regiments, black or white, to see service before being officially recognized as a military unit. The 1st had been on an expedition along the coasts of Georgia and Florida in November 1862. Its first real service as a regiment came in a weeklong expedition up the St. Mary's River on the Georgia-Florida border in January 1863. It was here, at Township, Florida, that the 1st saw its first action in a skirmish with Confederate cavalry. The men of the new black regiment fought well and received praise in the Northern press. In February 1864, the regiment was redesigned the 33rd Regiment U.S. Colored Infantry. It continued to serve in the area of South Carolina, Georgia, and Florida until mustered out on January 31, 1866.

WILLIAM GLADSTONE

The soldiers depicted here wear the first uniform issued to the 1st South Carolina. Except for the red trousers, it is the regulation U.S. Army pattern. The trousers were similar to those worn by the French Army and were probably felt to be an inducement to enlist. Such inducement was not needed, and the different color made the men of the regiment feel that they were being set apart from the white regiments, who all wore the regulation sky blue. Col. Thomas Wentworth Higginson petitioned Gen. David Hunter to have a second issue of trousers, and by mid-February 1863, the blue trousers had been received. Throughout 1863, at least five types of firearms were carried by the 1st South Carolina. These were a mixed lot of Springfields and Enfields, as well as .69-caliber foreign-made arms of different types. By January 1864, these had all been replaced with the latest Springfield rifle muskets. At last the physical hurdles had been overcome. There were many more social hurdles, however, some of which would far outlive the men of the 1st South Carolina Infantry.

# 27TH VIRGINIA INFANTRY, COLOR SERGEANT, DECEMBER 1862

By the winter of 1862, supply problems for the Confederate Army of Northern Virginia were beginning to stabilize. Although still relying on state issue and home supply, the Confederate Quartermaster Department in Richmond was now procuring uniforms in adequate numbers to clothe the army. Despite the fact that the quality and color of uniform items varied with the source of supply, the soldiers of this army were much better off than they had been just one year previously. At the same time, the Confederate arsenal, also in Richmond, was coming into full production of arms and ammunition. The Federal naval blockade of Southern ports, though an annoyance, was not yet a serious problem, and shortfalls in domestic production of both uniforms and arms were, to a great extent, compensated for by goods from Europe brought in by daring blockade runners. Regimental records of units such as the 27th Virginia Infantry show a slow but steady supply of all matériel needed to sustain a military organization on active campaign.

In many ways, the 27th Virginia was typical of the first regiments raised for Confederate service in the early months of the war. The regiment was raised in May 1861 and, along with the 2nd, 4th, 5th, and 33rd Virginia Infantry Regiments, formed a brigade that was initially commanded by Brig. Gen. Thomas J. "Stonewall" Jackson. Although Jackson soon went on to higher command, the regiments remained together to gain fame and glory as the hard-fighting Stonewall Brigade.

The color sergeant shown here holds one of the flags carried by the 27th Virginia during its years of service. This flag, along with its Confederate-issue octagonal staff, was received by the regiment on August 4, 1862. The soldier's overcoat is of English manufacture. Along with English shirts, these overcoats were welcome additions to the men's uniforms as the cold Virginia winter approached. Several pairs of black trousers made of the wool-cotton material known as cassimere were issued to every company of the 27th Virginia in October 1862. Similar trousers were issued on a periodic basis to Confederate troops throughout the war. The color sergeant's woolen jacket is a product of the Richmond Depot, as are his shoes. The brass frame buckle on his belt is typical of those commonly issued to the Army of Northern Virginia. Hats and caps both appear in the records of issue to the 27th. The chevrons to indicate the rank of this sergeant are hidden under the coat he wears, but the stature of those chosen to carry the regimental colors in Civil War regiments was such that all who served in the ranks would have known who he was. The fact that by the second winter of the war the regiments serving with this army were generally well supplied stands as a tribute to the ability and determination of the Confederacy to exist as a nation.

DAVID RANKIN, JR.

*Regulation Federal infantry dress coat with light blue cord piping and worsted corporals' chevrons. This is only one of two known extant examples made by the firm of Rudensill & Lind of Lewistown, Pennsylvania, which had a government contract for 1,000 coats in 1862. This specimen was owned by Lemuel F. Liscom of Company A, 14th New Hampshire Volunteers.* JOHN OCKERBLOOM COLLECTION.

*Brass drum presented to Henry Galloway by the men of the 55th Massachusetts Volunteer Infantry, which was the second African-American regiment raised by the state. The band and drum corps was presented with instruments on Folly Island, South Carolina, in October 1864. "Nearly eleven hundred dollars were raised by the men, without aid or suggestion from the officers, to supply the Band and Drum Corps with Instruments."* JOHN OCKERBLOOM COLLECTION.

CHARLES B. FOX, *RECORD OF SERVICE OF THE 55TH REGIMENT OF MASSACHUSETTS VOLUNTEERS* (1868; REPRINT, SALEM, N.H.: AYER, 1991), 3–4.

*This splendid beige slouch hat was worn by Capt. Henry Martin Kellogg, a schoolteacher serving in the 33rd Illinois Volunteers. At Vicksburg, Mississippi, on May 20, 1863, after shouting to his men, "Follow me to victory or death," he was struck in the head by a projectile and killed instantly. His colonel remarked, "Strange enough a rifle ball through the head took his life at the time mentioned, and as I remember no one else in the regiment even received a scratch that day." Light-colored and straw hats were occasionally favored in the oppressively hot Southern climate. The striped lining of this hat is marked "Chapeau de Paris."* M. CUNNINGHAM COLLECTION.

*BOSTON CONGREGATIONALIST,* AUGUST 14, 1863; ISAAC H. ELLIOT AND VIRGIL G. WAY, *HISTORY OF THE THIRTY-THIRD ILLINOIS VETERAN VOLUNTEER INFANTRY, 1861 TO 1865* (GIBSON CITY, ILL., 1902), 16.

# COLONEL OF THE CONFEDERACY

When the first shots were fired in April 1861, little had been done to establish a regulation uniform for the Confederate army. A letter to the secretary of war dated April 30 asking what uniform had been adopted received the following reply: "Uniform is not yet established but that usually worn by our soldiers is a brave heart and steady arm." By June, uniform regulations had been published, with the uniform of officers bearing a strong resemblance to that of the Austrian Army. Rank would be indicated both on the collar of the coat and on the sleeve. Branch of service would be shown by the color of trim. Although numerous variations existed throughout the war, most officers followed at least the spirit of the regulations. Even with no indication of rank, however, the poise and dignity of the man depicted here could leave no doubt to any who saw him that he was in command. But battle authority must be instantly apparent to all. Three stars on the collar of his sky blue–trimmed coat, as well as a triple row of gold braid on each sleeve, would tell any soldier he was a colonel of infantry.

PRIVATE COLLECTION

*Confederate officer's brown leather waist belt with interlocking buckle and the letters "CS" in Old English. The original color was probably black.* TROIANI COLLECTION.

*Gold-taped Confederate officer's forage cap, with painted linen visor and sweatband. Layers of painted cloth provided a serviceable leather substitute for the hard-pressed Southern equipage producers.*
M. CUNNINGHAM COLLECTION.

# PRIVATE, 20TH TENNESSEE INFANTRY, C.S.A., SUMMER 1863

The 20th Tennessee Infantry was raised in the northern part of the state in the summer of 1861. The regiment saw its first real action at the battle of Shiloh in April 1862 and fought as part of the Confederate Army of Tennessee for the remainder of the war. In May 1863, the regiment was on the receiving end of the first real use of repeating rifles in battle. At Hoover's Gap, southeast of Murfreesboro, Tennessee, the 20th was part of the force attacking the Union Lightning Brigade, which had recently been armed with Spencer rifles.

Regimental records show a steady supply of uniform items to the 20th, including jackets and, unlike many Confederate regiments, always hats. Also unlike most Southern units, this regiment wore a small brass badge on the hat or coat bearing the regimental designation. As a general rule, the Army of Tennessee received clothing and ordnance from depots in the Deep South such as Columbus and Macon, Georgia. The soldier shown here wears a jacket of the type manufactured at the Columbus facility and is armed with an Enfield rifle. The regiment had been initially armed with flintlock muskets, which were replaced by more modern weapons during 1862. The recorded personal effects of a private of Company E who died on March 4, 1863, were probably typical of those of this regiment:

1 knapsack
2 coverlets
2 hats
3 pair drawers
2 shirts
1 pair pants
1 pair boots
1 pair socks
1 silver watch
1 pocket book, containing $71.00 paper money

PAUL SCHIERL

# UNION INFANTRY DRUMMER, WINTER 1863–64

Despite the cold, winter for the Civil War soldier meant at least some rest from marching and the constant threat of battle. Entire armies moved into winter quarters, and picket duty, drill, and parades became the order of the day. Because of the necessity for quick audible communications, the skills of the drummer were required on a daily basis. One particular duty was the beating of reveille each morning. On a cold winter morning, the warmth given by the single-breasted, heavy woolen overcoat with its stand-up collar was more than welcome. The coat for infantry use had an elbow-length cape that added an extra layer of protection to the shoulders and could be pulled over the head to protect the wearer from wind and snow. As gloves were not an item of issue, the extralarge cuffs on the coat could be turned down to cover the hands. Regulations called for the overcoats, or greatcoats, to be made of blue-gray material. Those made for general issue during the war were of sky blue kersey, the same material used for trousers. In some cases, material that was judged too dark in color for trousers was directed to be used for overcoats.

The red cloth corps badge on this drummer's forage cap identifies him as a member of a regiment attached to the 1st Division, III Corps, Army of the Potomac. The men of this division had sent their overcoats to Washington for storage prior to the spring campaign and did not receive them back until late November.

PRIVATE COLLECTION

The miracle accomplished by the Confederate Ordnance and Quartermaster Departments in building an adequate and efficient system of manufacture and supply was a major factor in keeping Southern armies in the field and fighting for four years. Overcoming initial problems, the Confederate government from mid-1862 to late 1864 was able to produce or import in quantity nearly every item needed by its armies. Once the Union naval blockade of Southern ports, combined with the disruption of rail service by advancing Federal armies, began to take its toll, the Confederate soldier began to feel true want. The Army of Tennessee was without a doubt the hardest hit. Following Hood's disastrous advance on Nashville in December 1864, this army found itself lacking in nearly every area of supply. Uniforms, which had been an item of regular issue from depots in Georgia and Alabama, could not now reach the Southern soldiers. Wearing captured Federal items and a mixture of Confederate issue, they continued to make up in courage and determination what they now lacked in matériel. For the Army of Tennessee, as well as the Confederacy, the days were numbered.

*This light gray-brown jean cloth Confederate jacket, with locally manufactured Louisiana buttons, was worn by an Englishman who served in the Confederate army. In 1905, he donated his jacket to the Royal Artillery Museum in Woolwich, England, where it remained until the late 1990s, when it returned to this country.* TROIANI COLLECTION.

*According to a newspaper obituary clipping, John M. Mitchell of Company F, 79th Illinois Volunteer Infantry, was a fortunate soldier when the bullet that passed through his hat at the battle of Liberty Gap, Tennessee, on June 25, 1863, only wounded him. Mitchell's black slouch hat is actually a regulation Hardee hat, but wetting and telescoping the crown had made it into a respectable campaign hat.* WEST POINT MUSEUM.

# 1ST AND 2ND MARYLAND

PRIVATE COLLECTION

Although most Confederate soldiers were supposedly ragged and unkempt by 1863, the men of the Maryland Infantry of Robert E. Lee's Army of Northern Virginia were noted for their uniformity. On the road to Gettysburg, a Northern civilian remarked, "They have been telling us you rebs were a ragged set, but you seem to have pretty good clothes; and that you were badly armed . . . but you have good guns, and what's funny to me, all of them have U.S. on them." The Marylander who recorded this quote summed it up by stating, "Our regiment was better clothed than most and all our guns had been captured on battlefields."

From the very start of the war, the Marylanders were characterized by their short gray jackets and caps, or kepis, rather than the common butternut clothes and slouch hats. In 1861, when six companies of Marylanders, raised at Harpers Ferry, marched into Winchester, Virginia, to join companies from Richmond, the shout went up, "Lookout [*sic*] for you[r] baggage, boys, the Plug-Uglies are coming." The hastily

*Confederate forage cap of light-colored or butternut jean cloth material, with a thin leather visor.* COLLECTION OF NEW YORK STATE DIVISION OF MILITARY AND NAVAL AFFAIRS.

*Confederate sergeant's jacket made of gray-brown jean cloth material. The facings on the cuff are unusual in that they are only on the outside of the sleeve. Instead of the more familiar brass buttons, this coat has wooden buttons, which, though equally functional, were somewhat less martial in character.* NELSONIAN INSTITUTE.

equipped men from Harpers Ferry were described as "poorly clad and . . . unkempt and unwashed." Jane Claudia Johnson, wife of Maj. Bradley T. Johnson of the newly formed Maryland battalion, would not have her husband's men present such an appearance, so she raised $10,000 to clothe and equip the men herself. Thereafter the men of the 1st Maryland—and as they became later, the 2nd Maryland—were noted for the quality of their dress, arms, and military bearing.

By 1864, with Confederate resources stretched to nearly the breaking point, the Maryland battalion still drew and wore issue clothing, including Richmond Depot jackets and occasionally clothing from North Carolina, or clothes sent from home and smuggled through Union lines. In August 1864, one Union officer noted Maryland prisoners wearing "little kepis, half grey and half sky-blue," of the regulation style. The men of the Maryland battalion fought notably at Gettysburg and through the battles of 1864, being reduced to an effective strength of 100 men in 1865, 32 of whom were captured when Petersburg was abandoned, leaving only 63 officers and men to surrender at Appomattox.

# GEN. PATRICK R. CLEBURNE

November 30, 1864, can be counted as one of the darkest days in the military history of the Confederacy. It was on this day, near the town of Franklin, Tennessee, that the Army of Tennessee lost one of its most dynamic and aggressive leaders, Gen. Patrick R. Cleburne. In a desperate attack, with the regimental battle flags of his division held high behind him, Cleburne fell as he crossed the last line of Union breastworks.

The uniform he wore on this fateful day befitted a man of action. Rather than the conventional dress of high command, he preferred the less formal, looser-fitting officer's sack coat, suitably adorned with the emblems of his rank. He wore his gold-braided general's kepi, securely held by the chinstrap, pushed back on his head. The men of his division, most uniformed in jackets fashioned by the depots in Georgia and Alabama, followed their gallant commander, showing the same brave determination. Only darkness ended the desperate struggle, which saw some of the most savage hand-to-hand fighting of the war.

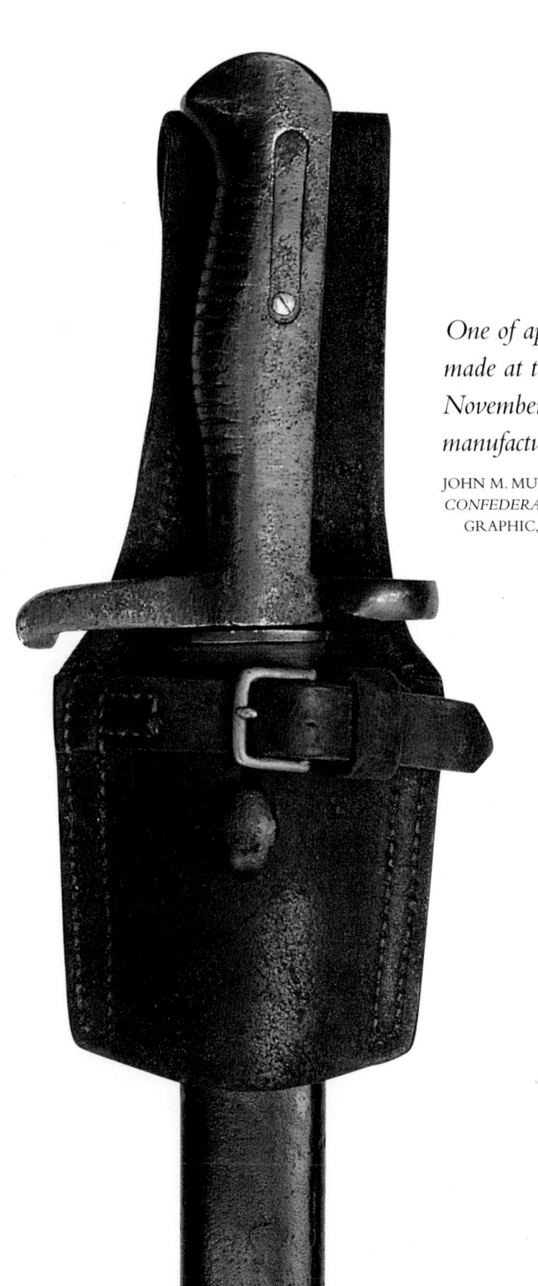

*One of approximately 331 all-iron saber bayonets made at the Tyler (Texas) Ordnance Works between November 1863 and May 1864. With English-manufactured belt frog.* A. H. SIEBEL, JR., COLLECTION.

JOHN M. MURPHY AND HOWARD MICHAEL MADAUS, *CONFEDERATE RIFLES AND MUSKETS* (NEWPORT BEACH, CALIF.: GRAPHIC, 1996), 706–7.

BOOTH WESTERN ART MUSEUM, CARTERSVILLE, GEORGIA

# PRIVATE, 29TH ALABAMA INFANTRY, SPRING 1864

In the spring of 1864, the 29th Alabama Infantry was one of the best of the veteran regiments of the Confederate Army of the Mississippi. Ahead of it lay transfer to the Army of Tennessee and the fateful campaigns of the summer. By the end of the year, names of battles such as Peach Tree Creek and Franklin would forever be burned into the memory of those lucky enough to survive.

The uniform of the regiment was typical of those issued to Confederate troops serving in the Western armies. The soldier shown here wears a jacket and trousers received from the Columbus, Georgia, Depot, one of the main supply sources for troops in this theater of the war. The 29th had received several issues of clothing in late 1863 and early 1864, including jackets, caps, and a few hats. The regiment was armed with the Enfield rifle musket and carried both English and Confederate-made accoutrements. By midwar, the Confederate supply system, including items of domestic manufacture and imports from both England and Austria, was able to sustain the soldiers to a remarkable degree. The cedar canteen carried by this soldier is likely a product of the Montgomery Arsenal, which produced large numbers of this essential item for the Western armies. While in the West, shoes remained a problem; almost everything else, though at times not abundant, was supplied in quantities adequate to meet the need.

A statement of ordnance and ordnance stores lost and expended in battle by the 29th Alabama from May 9 to June 30, 1864, attests to the hard fighting that lay ahead:

| | |
|---|---|
| 220 Enfield rifles | 256 cap pouches |
| 586 bayonets | 562 knapsacks |
| 261 cartridge boxes | 276 haversacks |
| 270 shoulder belts | 388 canteens |
| 250 waist belts | 81,453 cartridges cal. .577 |
| 307 bayonet scabbards | 74,452 musket caps |

DAVID RANKIN, JR.

# LONGSTREET'S CORPS, SEPTEMBER 1863

"They Are Certainly Superior to the Troops of the Army of Tennessee in Dress"

The retreat of Robert E. Lee's army from Gettysburg and the surrender of the Rebel stronghold at Vicksburg, Mississippi, both in early July 1863, left the Confederates looking for an opportunity to strike back at the Federal army. Confederate president Jefferson Davis decided that the place would be southern Tennessee. The plan was to reinforce Gen. Braxton Bragg's Army of Tennessee and force a rout of the Union Army of the Cumberland under Maj. Gen. William S. Rosecrans. Rosecrans's brilliant Tallahoma campaign from June to August 1863 had succeeded in flanking Bragg out of middle Tennessee. Federal forces were now in possession of Chattanooga, the door to the Deep South.

Included in these Confederate reinforcements were two divisions of Gen. James Longstreet's Corps of the Army of Northern Virginia, those of John Bell Hood and Lafayette McLaws. Before leaving Virginia, Longstreet promised his commander, Robert E. Lee, that he would defeat Rosecrans or die. Longstreet and his veterans were going west looking for a battle, and they found one at Chickamauga Creek.

Descriptions of Longstreet's Corps upon their arrival and during the battle of Chickamauga, September 19–20, 1863, found them to be uniformed differently and in sharp contrast to the Western army soldiers under General Bragg. One of Bragg's artillerymen took special notice of the Easterners' uniformity in appearance: "Our first impression was partly caused by the color of their uniform [dark blue-gray jackets, light blue pants] . . . the superior style of their equipments, in haversacks, canteens, and knapsacks. The contrast between them and General Bragg's motley, ragged

PRIVATE COLLECTION

*An oval, embossed brass Confederate enlisted man's waist belt buckle of a type favored mostly in the Western Theater.* NELSONIAN INSTITUTE.

*Butternut-colored jean cloth frock coat with Confederate block "I" buttons, worn 1861–62 by Charles Herbest, Company I, 2nd Kentucky Volunteers, of the famed Orphan Brigade. Herbest was captured at Fort Donelson. After being exchanged, he fought with the Army of Tennessee until its surrender in 1865.* M. CUNNINGHAM COLLECTION.

troops was striking in the extreme!" Bragg's soldiers, lamented one Western officer, "never looked worse. Three weeks of maneuvering in the densest dust [during the Tullahoma campaign] without washing, had conferred the same color upon everything!" Bragg's Westerners were described as generally "greasy, dirty, raggedy, barefooted, and wearing go-as-you please . . . with every imaginable variety of garments and head coverings," wearing practically "no uniform at all." Bragg's soldiers preferred to wear clothing sent from home rather than that issued by the Confederate Quartermaster Department.

A member of Kershaw's Brigade of Longstreet's Corps remembered his uniform as a "dark blue round jacket, closely fitting, with light blue trousers: [it] closely resembled those worn by the enemy." The jacket, from several accounts, was a dark bluish gray. It is believed that the jackets, trousers, and caps were produced in Richmond and issued through the Confederate Quartermaster Department. The dark blue and light blue cloth had possibly come through on blockade runners from England, some of it arriving as early as February 1863.

A soldier in the 2nd Georgia Infantry, Benning's Brigade, Longstreet's Corps, wrote, "Sometimes the government would get a supply . . . of fine English cloth, and we would get good uniforms, almost to blue." This same soldier was fired upon by his own friends in Tennessee, "So blue [like Yankees] did we appear." Even the Federals had trouble distinguishing Longstreet's men from their own. Lt. Charles Clark of the 125th Ohio Volunteer Infantry, awaiting the attack of Kershaw's Brigade, heard the order, "Cease fire! . . . they are McCooks [Union] troops!" He noted that Kershaw's Confederates "appeared at a distance to wear blue, dusty blue. We had never seen a Confederate soldier clothed otherwise

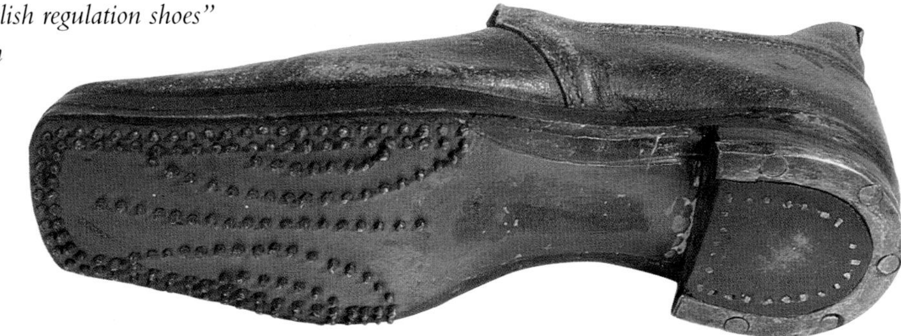

*This superbly made British Army style shoe never made it to the Confederacy, where it was so desperately needed. Captured from a blockade runner, it was preserved as a trophy of war. Note the iron heel plate and hobnailed sole. "English regulation shoes" were advertised at auction in Augusta, Georgia, in the May 14, 1863,* Augusta Chronicle and Sentinel, *selling at $6 per pair.* COLLECTION OF NEW YORK STATE DIVISION OF MILITARY AND NAVAL AFFAIRS.

*These rugged Confederate soldier's shoes were recovered after fighting near the Southside Railroad, Petersburg, Virginia. Although patterned on the Federal brogan, they are strictly of Southern manufacture, being made of undyed leather with crude pegging on the soles. Although not attractive, they were sturdy enough to get the soldier where he needed to go.* COLLECTION OF NEW YORK STATE DIVISION OF MILITARY AND NAVAL AFFAIRS.

than in butternut or gray." A volley by the Confederates ended the debate, but many a Federal soldier, and Rebel as well, seemed confused by the appearance of Longstreet's men.

Gen. Ulysses S. Grant made the same mistake. Grant had been ordered to Chattanooga to help reverse the fortunes of the Federal army, which now found itself under siege after Chickamauga. He described a confusing encounter on an inspection tour of the picket lines surrounding Chattanooga:

> [T]he most friendly relations seemed to exist between the pickets of the two armies. At one place a tree which had fallen across the stream was used by the soldiers of both armies in drawing water for their camps. General Longstreet's Corps was stationed there at the time, and wore the blue of a little different shade from our uniform. Seeing a soldier in blue on the log, I rode up to him, commenced conversing with him, and asked whose Corps he belonged to. He was very polite, touching his hat to me, said he belonged to Longstreet's Corps. I asked him a few questions, but not with a view of gaining any particular information—all of which he answered, and I rode off.

Longstreet left the Army of Tennessee in early November and marched east toward Knoxville. In what became known as the Knoxville campaign, Longstreet's men were in bare feet and rags when they returned to Lee's army in the early spring of 1864. The quartermaster general of the Confederacy wanted no more light blue pants, stating that "gray makes up better." Perhaps it was better not to be shot at by one's own men.

# 76TH OHIO VOLUNTEER INFANTRY

It is often assumed that all Confederate soldiers were ragged and in need of uniforms and that, conversely, all Union soldiers were well clothed with luxurious uniforms. The truth is that the rigors of campaigning wreaked havoc on North and South alike. One soldier of the 76th Ohio wrote, during the Vicksburg campaign, that he was indeed ragged: "The shirt I had on was gone all but the front and one sleeve . . . my blouse all rags, and my only respectable covering a forage cap." By the time his knapsack with spare clothing caught up to him, he reported, "My pants had lost all covering qualities and I had thrown them away, compelled for a day or two to serve my country garbed in underwear only."

The 76th Ohio Volunteer Infantry was organized and mustered in at Camp Sherman, Newark, Ohio, from October 1861 to February 1862. The regiment was uniformed in standard Federal uniforms for much of its service. The uniform was remembered as "a dark blue blouse, light blue pants, forage caps, low, broad soled shoes ('bootees' the government styled them) and blue overcoat with cape. Each soldier carried a gray woolen blanket and a rubber blanket." After two years of hard campaigning in the West, the 76th became a veteran regiment in January 1864. To celebrate this status, the veterans of the 76th bought themselves a new and colorful uniform:

RON TUNISON

> On the 27th [of January] the officers held a meeting to discuss the adoption of a new uniform for the Regiment. It was deemed desirable that the veterans be all clothed alike with some kind of a zouave jacket that they might make a fine appearance on their return to Ohio. A Regimental fund of about seven hundred dollars had been created which it was considered best to expend for this purpose. The officers decided on the style most appropriate to be a short dark blue jacket with rounded corners, no collar and trimmed in sky-blue binding.

The new uniform was contracted for in Cincinnati and was ready when the regiment arrived at that city prior to its veteran furlough.

The 76th was originally armed with "old second-hand Belgian rifles, a short, heavy, clumsy arm with a vicious recoil." In December 1862, however, the men received Springfield rifle muskets, which they retained through the rest of their service. Armed with Springfields and standard accoutrements, even noncommissioned officers' swords with shoulder belts in Company G, only the veterans' furlough jackets distinguished the 76th from other regiments of the XV Corps.

*Federal forage cap of the 10th Vermont, with insignia of the 3rd Division, VI Army Corps.* TROIANI COLLECTION.

*Although referred to as a Burnside hat in a period military goods catalog, there seems to be no evidence that famed Gen. Ambrose E. Burnside ever wore one. This low-crowned officer's slouch hat is done up with insignia for an unknown officer of a 4th Regiment of Infantry.* TROIANI COLLECTION.

*Infantry uniform jacket of Sgt. George H. Snell of the 121st New York Volunteers. The Federal government furnished several hundred thousand of these during the latter part of the war. They were also worn by the men of the Signal Corps.* TROIANI COLLECTION.

# 12TH INDIANA VOLUNTEER INFANTRY, 1864

In December 1863, the 12th Indiana Infantry, in dire need of uniforms after a hard campaign, received an issue of new uniforms made in Indianapolis by a merchant tailor named Joseph Staub. The uniform had a collarless, dark blue wool jacket with a nine-button front, made with a false panel to give the appearance of a Zouave jacket worn over a buttoned vest. The panel was of sky blue kersey edged with white cotton tape. Miniature trefoils of light blue cord on each breast added to the illusion of a Zouave uniform. The regiment's colonel, Reuben Williams, wrote, "We have received our new uniforms manufactured by Staub . . . and present as gay an appearance as any regiment that ever left the State."

Not everyone in the regiment was as appreciative of the new jackets, however. Sgt. John Shultz wrote home: "Our jackets have arrived. The boys pronounce them a *Grand Bore* for they are not worth half the price 6.25 and are more style and show than worth." Indeed, they must have been very unpopular, for Lt. Col. James Goodenow published the following order: "Commanders of companies will see that the *New Uniform*[s] recently issued to the men of this Regiment are not to be disposed of under any circumstances whatever. The different companies will be made acquainted with the purport of this order at the first subsequent roll call after which any violations will be reported to this Headquarters."

But the men wore the uniforms, however unpopular they may have been. A surviving jacket was worn at the battle of Resaca, Georgia, where its owner, Sgt. John Shultz, was wounded. Photographs show that the officers also wore the jacket with shoulder straps.

DICK AND M. E. CLOW

# HOOD'S TENNESSEE CAMPAIGN, SEPTEMBER TO DECEMBER 1864

DAVID RANKIN, JR.

The date was September 29, 1864. Confederate general John Bell Hood and 42,000 Confederate soldiers of the Army of Tennessee set off to begin what has become known as Hood's Tennessee campaign, the last great campaign in the Western Theater of the Civil War. It was Hood's plan to draw the Federal forces commanded by William Tecumseh Sherman away from Atlanta by threatening Sherman's lines of supply. General Sherman did follow Hood for a time, but

*Confederate cast pewter buckle with iron wire hooks soldered to the back, found on the battlefield of Knoxville, Tennessee, by a Michigan soldier.* TROIANI COLLECTION.

then he turned South to begin his famous March to the Sea. That left Maj. Gen. George H. Thomas and his Union troops in Nashville to deal with Hood.

Descriptions of Hood's Army of Tennessee for late 1864 are many. Because Hood continually changed directions as he moved North, few supplies reached his army. By necessity, the Confederates were forced to use the food and captured clothing of their enemies. They had bare feet and ragged uniforms for much of the campaign. A Union private of the 14th Illinois Infantry captured near Moon's Station, Georgia, made note that the Confederates "made all kinds of one-sided trades for our clothing, hats, boots, and shoes." From Big Shanty, this same Union prisoner watched as Hood's entire army marched past him on their way to Dalton, Georgia. He described the Confederates as "poorly clad in brown and gray cotton suits, and but for the flags they carried, might have been a section of the old Continental Army."

A Union captain captured at Dalton also remarked as Hood's entire army marched by. "They were ragged and thinly clad, having as a general thing, only pantaloons, shirt, and hat in their inventory of clothing. Their pantaloons were greasy and tattered, the shirts, shocking affairs in multitudinous variety. As a general thing they were liberally shod, though in Stewart's Division . . . over three hundred were without shoes. Not more than one in ten had blankets."

By the time Hood's Confederates reached Tuscumbia, Alabama, on October 31, an artilleryman in Guibor's Battery found his comrades to be "rather ragged, and many . . . barefooted." To cover their feet, some soldiers began to make moccasins out of rawhide from slaughtered cattle. To add to their discomfort, a cold, chilly rain began to fall, turning the roads to slippery mud. "The boys who wore moccasins had a good deal of trouble keeping them on when they got wet," remembered one Alabama infantryman.

Hood and his men made contact with a sizable Union force near Columbia, Tennessee. The Confederates' pursuit resulted in the bloody battle of Franklin, Tennessee, on November 30, 1864. Many of the Confederate prisoners captured at Franklin were in Union clothing, as described by Pvt. Adam J. Weaver of the 104th Ohio. "The Rebel prisoners are nearly all wearing parts of our uniforms . . . especially our shoes [and] overcoats. . . . They still retain their droopy felt hats which gives them a hayseedy look."

Hood followed the Federals to Nashville and laid siege to the city. On December 15 and 16, the Federals attacked, breaking Hood's lines and turning the ensuing battle into a rout for many Confederates. Hood's army moved south from Nashville, ending their retreat at Tupelo, Mississippi, on January 3, 1865. Only 17,709 soldiers and officers were reported as present for duty. A Confederate officer in Walthall's Division wrote home that "the Army cannot muster 5,000 effectives [out of 17,000]. Nine-tenths of the line officers and men are barefooted and naked . . . and many go home every day never to return."

On January 13, Hood resigned. What was left of the Army of Tennessee was shipped east to fight Sherman in North Carolina. In March 1865, an official count listed only 6,745 men as present for duty. Of that number, 2,298 had no shoes. What an end for the once magnificent Army of Tennessee!

*Butternut-colored jean cloth Confederate uniform jacket worn by John C. Zehring of Company A (Shelby Grays), 4th Tennessee Regiment. Possibly a product of the Milledgeville, Georgia, Depot, Zehring's clothing issuances indicate that he probably received this jacket in the spring of 1865.* THE HORSE SOLDIER.

*Pair of unfinished soldier's wooden-soled canvas shoes taken from Confederate quartermaster stores in Atlanta, where they were found in great quantities. Because of critical leather shortages, the Southern manufacturers were reduced to such drastic measures to keep their armies shod.*
COLLECTION OF NEW YORK STATE DIVISION OF MILITARY AND NAVAL AFFAIRS.

# 203RD PENNSYLVANIA INFANTRY, PRIVATE, FALL 1864

By 1864, the inducement of special uniforms to aid in the formation of new regiments had all but disappeared. An exception was the 203rd Pennsylvania Infantry. With the backing of Maj. Gen. David B. Birney, this regiment would be known as Birney's Sharpshooters and would wear the uniform of the famous Berdan's Sharpshooters. The new regiment began enlistment in September 1864, at a time when the original Sharpshooters had all but passed out of existence. Since 1862, the Union army Quartermaster Department had supplied the distinctive green uniform that, along with their legendary shooting skills, had been the hallmark of Berdan's regiments. Now, in the fall of 1864, there were more green uniforms on hand than there were men to wear them.

WILLIAM RODEN

The 203rd received the remaining stock of green frock coats and trousers, along with a few caps. This issue was supplemented by newly made items, just as had been the practice for the past three years. Unlike the Sharpshooters of 1861, who had received the Sharps breech-loading rifle, the men of the 203rd were issued the Springfield rifle musket, most likely the improved model of 1864. Their accoutrements included the 1864 model cartridge box with an embossed "US" within an oval pattern, reminiscent of the brass plate previously issued. This box was suspended from a black leather cross belt, but unlike that issued to Berdan's men, it was no longer adorned with the familiar round brass plate with the raised eagle. Both brass plates had been discontinued by the Ordnance Department as serving no purpose. These plates had been disliked by Berdan's men, who would have been more than happy to see them go.

Other than these variations, the enlisted men of the 203rd, from their leather leggings to their green caps, appeared as nearly exact copies of the original Sharpshooters. Only the badges of the X Army Corps, along with the brass letters and numbers adorning their caps, served to set them apart. The officers of the 203rd, as those in Berdan's regiments, wore regulation blue with the badges of rank, such as trouser stripes, of green. The famous uniforms brought with them an image that belied their inexperience. It was up to the officers and men of the new regiment to prove themselves.

Their chance came in January of the new year. Serving not as sharpshooters, but as line infantry, the 203rd made up part of the force designated to assault the Confederate stronghold at the mouth of North Carolina's Cape Fear River, known as Fort Fisher. On January 15, 1865, during this attack, the regiment suffered heavy losses, including both its colonel and lieutenant colonel, who were killed inside the Confederate works.

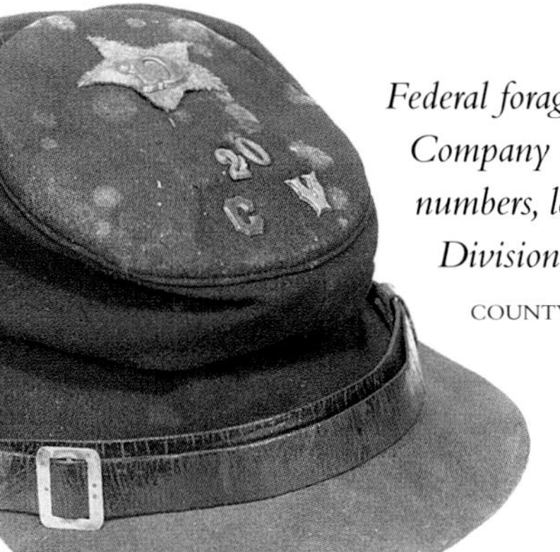


*Federal forage cap of Cpl. Henry Cornwall, Company D, 20th Connecticut Volunteers, with numbers, letters, and star badge of the 1st Division, XX Army Corps.* MIDDLESEX COUNTY HISTORICAL SOCIETY.

*One of several plaid flannel shirts made by the mother of Pvt. Edgar S. Yergason of Company A, 22nd Connecticut Volunteers, and sent to him during his term of active service. Because of the roughness of government undergarments, soldiers often preferred to provide their own whenever possible. As one soldier explained: "[T]he shirt [Army issue] was—well, a revelation to most of us both as to size and shape and material. It was so rough, that no living mortal, probably could wear it, except perhaps one who wished to do penance by wearing a hair shirt. Mine was promptly sent home . . . with the request that it be kept as a sort of heirloom in the family for future generations to wonder at."* TROIANI COLLECTION.

HARRY M. KIEFFER, *THE RECOLLECTIONS OF A DRUMMER-BOY* (BOSTON: JAMES R. OSGOOD, 1883), 40–41.

*Presumably, Sgt. Stephen H. Parker of Company D, 59th Massachusetts Volunteers, had left this custom-made dress coat behind in camp or storage when he was killed in the disastrous assault on the Crater at Petersburg on July 30, 1864. The coat bears service stripes on the lower sleeves, as Parker was a veteran of prior service in another regiment.* TROIANI COLLECTION.

# APPOMATTOX COURTHOUSE, APRIL 12, 1865

DAVID RANKIN, JR.

The formal surrender of Robert E. Lee's Confederate Army of Northern Virginia took place on April 12, 1865, at Appomattox Courthouse, Virginia. As the marching columns of gray-clad soldiers ceremoniously turned to face the Federals, the Confederates were ordered to fix bayonets, stack arms, undo and hang up their accoutrements, and lean their battle flags on the stacked guns. All was quiet during the ceremony. One Confederate soldier remembered, "We said nothing . . . neither did they say anything to us."

The prevailing mood of the Confederate officers supervising the surrender was one of sad disappointment and humiliation. Finally, when the last Confederate unit passed in line, a Union soldier cried out from the ranks, "Three cheers for the last Brigade!" "This soldierly generosity was more than we could bear," recalled a Southern officer, "Many of the grizzled veterans wept like children, and my own eyes were as blind, as my voice was dumb."

Descriptions of the appearance of the Confederates in the closing days of the Civil War are many. A Union soldier remarked that the Rebel soldiers he saw "were mostly in homespun butternut colored jean cloth, with no semblance of uniform. [It was] hard to distinguish betwixt the officers and the privates as they are all dressed alike." Another Federal remembered the soldiers of the Army of Northern Virginia as a collection of "dirty, battered, ranks of soldiers, none of them well clad, and nearly all the officers in fatigue dress."

The change in dress for the Confederate officers from a fine gray frock trimmed with gold lace to the uniform of a private went back two years, to the fall of 1863. Higher costs for uniforms and the materials needed to produce them had risen to the point of being unaffordable to many. The schedule of prices that accompanied a resolution for assistance by the staff of Bates Brigade, Army of Tennessee, to the Confederate Congress, showed that in late 1863, the average charge for a tailored officer's frock was $350; boots, $250; pants, $125; hat, $80 to $125; shirt, $50; underdrawers, $15; and socks, $10. This meant that a new officer's uniform cost over $980, when the monthly pay for a new second lieutenant was just $80 a month!

On March 6, 1864, as a remedy, General Orders No. 28 was issued out of Richmond. It stated that all commissioned officers would now be allowed to purchase privates' clothing, and cloth for clothing, from any quartermaster at the price it cost the government. Confederate officers were also entitled to one food ration in kind, the same as privates, for their mess.

A special congressional committee looking into the issue of officers' clothing found that for the latter half of 1864, 31,940 yards of fine-grade cloth for uniforms was purchased through the Quartermaster Department. Only a small portion of it, however, actually went to the line officers. The

*This type of rectangular "C.S.A." belt plate was believed to have been a product of the Atlanta Arsenal. Although widely issued to the Army of Tennessee, some were issued to Longstreet's Corps, which was serving in the Western Theater in 1863–64.* WILLIAM ERQUITT COLLECTION.

*Pvt. John A. Dolan of Austin's Battalion of Louisiana Sharphooters wore this jacket in 1865. A simple five-button jean cloth jacket with exterior pocket and blue collar, it is one of those believed made for Richard Taylor's Department of Alabama, Mississippi, and East Louisiana.* CONFEDERATE MEMORIAL HALL, CLAUDE LEVET PHOTOGRAPH.

*Confederate officer's waist belt constructed of unpainted canvas with remains of russet leather sword straps. As leather became scarce in the South, substitute materials became more prevalent.* TROIANI COLLECTION.

largest portion went to those serving in the rear echelon areas. No provisions were made by the Quartermaster Department to get the higher-grade cloth to those officers serving near the front lines.

Quartermaster General Alexander Robert Lawton informed the special committee that affordable officers' uniforms, 1,000 in number, were now being made up in Montgomery, Alabama, for Lee's command. Provision for 6,000 other officers was accomplished for the second half of 1864. Officers' uniforms were now to be supplied from the Quartermaster Department.

Many did not or could not procure the regulation dress frock, trousers, boots, and cap appropriate for their rank. By necessity, the uniform of a private, consisting of short jeans jacket and trousers, hat or cap, and a good pair of shoes, made a cheap and durable outfit. The only sign of rank was a sword, pistol, and maybe some lace on the collar denoting the grade of lieutenant or captain.

A Confederate staffer described their dress toward the end of the war: "My equipment was a blanket rolled up and carried across my shoulder, and it contained a change of underclothes. . . . Towards the last days we were almost barefoot. . . . As to hats, their variety and material was marvelous. . . . When it came to jackets and trousers, the least said is the easiest understood. They were conspicuous by their fluttering raggedness."

# PRIVATE, 2ND MARYLAND INFANTRY C.S.A., 1864

By 1864, the style of dress within the ranks of the Army of Northern Virginia had, by necessity if not by design, reached a high degree of standardization. The waist length jacket was worn by nearly all of those who marched in Lee's army. The kepi was widely used and even the arms and accoutrements, though still mixed in type and design, had taken on a sameness that was a far contrast from the early days of the war. Contributing to this was the successful importation of clothing from England and Ireland. This Marylander has been uniformed in one of the thousands of jackets received on the contract with Peter Tait of Limerick, Ireland. He has maintained a degree of individuality by replacing the issued buttons with those of his home state. His kepi shows the blue infantry trim. Overall he stands in sharp contrast to the traditional image of Confederate soldiers dressed in rags during the final months of the war.

The 2nd Maryland was part of the proud Second Corps of the Army of Northern Virginia. In February 1865, the Second Corps Quartermaster, Maj. George D. Mercer made the following report to Col. James L. Corley, Chief Quartermaster of the Army:

> Office Chief Q.M. 2nd Corps
> February 2, 1865
>
> Colonel:
>
> From an examination of the Inspection Report, I find that the troops of this Corps are represented as still requiring a large amount of clothing. This is an error, which I have corrected upon the report, by an endorsement. With the exception of a few pants and shirts the estimates forwarded on the 1st of January 65 have been very nearly filled.
>
> From the quantity of clothing issued during the past two months the troops ought to be well clothed.
>
> D. Mercer
> Maj. and Acting Corps Q.M.

DICK AND M. E. CLOW

*Pair of Union soldier's mittens of blue and white mixed yarn, with extra trigger finger. These were produced by women at home for contractors, using printed government patterns and specifications.* TROIANI COLLECTION.

*Exquisite silver VI Army Corps badges taken from the body of Lt. Col. John Wilson of the 43rd New York Volunteers on the Spotsylvania battlefield by a Confederate soldier. They were returned to his family after the war.* COLLECTION OF NEW YORK STATE DIVISION OF MILITARY AND NAVAL AFFAIRS.

*Lt. Col. Edward L. Gaul wore this black braided kepi during his service with the 159th New York Volunteers until his discharge at Morganza, Louisiana, due to illness. It bears the regulation gold-embroidered infantry horn with silver numeral 159.* TROIANI COLLECTION.

*Federal officers serving with mounted troops were allowed by regulation a short, dark blue jacket. Many officers of all branches chose this option, and the range of variations is boundless. This example, worn by Col. Ezra Carmen of the 13th New Jersey Volunteers, is buttoned with a congested row of twenty-one small eagle buttons.* TROIANI COLLECTION.

# CHAPTER 4: THE INFANTRY


### INTRODUCTION

1. National Archives, Record Group 393, entry 202, III Army Corps, Letters, Orders, and Reports, 1862–64.
2. Ibid., Record Group 94, Regimental Books, 53rd Pennsylvania Infantry.
3. Ibid., Record Group 109, M-374 and M-269, Service Records of the 19th Alabama and 17th Mississippi Infantry Regiments.
4. Ibid., M-331, Compiled Service Records of Confederate General and Staff Officers, Maj. John F. Lay, Assistant Inspector General.
5. Ibid., Record Group 94, Regimental Papers, 5th Michigan Infantry.
6. Ibid., Record Group 109, M-437, Letters Received by the Confederate Secretary of War.
7. Ibid., Record Group 92, entry 2182, January 2, 1862, Letter from Quartermaster General in re General Orders 101.
8. Editors of Time-Life Books, *Echoes of Glory: Arms and Equipment of the Confederate Army* (Alexandria, Va.: Time-Life Books, 1991).
9. National Archives, Record Group 109, M-324, Compiled Service Records of Confederate Soldiers from Virginia, Papers of 53rd Virginia Infantry.
10. Ibid., Record Group 92, entry 999, Letters Sent Relating to Clothing and Equipage, Volume 22, Letter Sent by Wm. G. LeDuc, Lieutenant Colonel and Chief Quartermaster, 11th Corps.
11. Ibid. Record Group 109, M-324, Papers of the 53rd Virginia Infantry.
12. Ibid. Record Group 92, entry 999, Letters Sent Relating to Clothing and Equipage, Volume 22, Le Duc Letter.
13. Ibid., Record Group 109, M-226, Compiled Service Records of Confederate Soldiers from Georgia, 4th Georgia Infantry.
14. Editors of Time-Life Books, *Echoes of Glory*.
15. National Archives, Record Group 109, M-437, Tait Letter.
16 Ibid., Record Group 92, Quartermaster Consolidated Correspondence File, B. G. Badger to Joseph Baggot, Headquarters, Army of the Potomac, March 21, 1863.
17. Ibid., Record Group 94, Regimental Order Book, 147th Pennsylvania Infantry, Order from 1st Brigade, 2nd Division, XII Corps.

### CORPORAL, 16TH NEW YORK INFANTRY, JUNE 1862

Eugene Miller and Forrest F. Steinlage, *Der Turner Soldat: Diary of Erland Futter* (Louisville, Ky.: Calmar Publications, 1988), 91.

Newton Martin Curtis, *From Bull Run to Chancellorsville* (New York: G. P. Putnam's Sons, 1906) 114–15.

### 19TH TENNESSEE INFANTRY, C.S.A., APRIL 1862

Civil War Centennial Commission of Tennessee, *Tennesseans in the Civil War* (Nashville: Civil War Centennial Commission, 1964).

David Sullins, *Recollections of an Old Man* (Bristol, Tenn.: King Printing Co., 1910), 212, 214.

National Archives, Record Group 109, M-268, Military Service Records Various Officers, 19th Tennessee Infantry.

### FIRE ON CAROLINE STREET

George A. Bruce, *The Twentieth Regiment of Massachusetts Volunteer Infantry, 1861–1865* (Boston: Houghton, Mifflin, 1906), 49.

Charles F. Walcott, *History of the Twenty-First Regiment Massachusetts Volunteers in the War for the Preservation of the Union, 1861–1865* (Boston: Houghton, Mifflin, 1882), 240.

Photograph of Cpl. Robert Weston, Company A., 20th Massachusetts Volunteers, formerly in the Michael J. McAfee Collection.

### 12TH TENNESSEE REGIMENT

*New York Herald,* October 30, 1831.

*Nashville Union and American,* August 31, 1861.

### BURNSIDE'S BRIDGE

Stephen W. Sears, *Landscape Turned Red* (New York: Ticknor & Fields, 1983).

National Archives, Record Group 94, Regimental Papers, 51st Pennsylvania Infantry.

Ibid., Record Group 156, Quarterly Returns of Ordnance and Ordnance Stores on Hand in Regular and Volunteer Army Organizations.

Thomas H. Parker, *Regimental History of the 51st Pennsylvania Infantry* (Philadelphia: King and Baird, 1869).

Frederick H. Dyer, *A Compendium of the War of the Rebellion* (New York: Thomas Yoseloff, 1959).

**PRIVATE, 5TH NEW JERSEY INFANTRY, MAY 1863**

National Archives, Record Group 94, Regimental Books of the 5th New Jersey Infantry.

Ibid., Record Group 156, Quarterly Returns of Ordnance.

Earl J. Coates and Dean S. Thomas, *An Introduction to Civil War Small Arms* (Gettysburg, Pa.: Thomas Publications, 1990), 91.

*The War of the Rebellion: The Official Records of the Union and Confederate Armies,* vol. 27, part 1, 575.

Frederick H. Dyer, *A Compendium of the War of the Rebellion* (New York: Thomas Yoseloff, 1959), 1358.

**14TH MISSISSIPPI INFANTRY, FORT DONELSON, TENNESSEE, FEBRUARY 18, 1863**

Reminiscences of Milton Asbury Ryan, Company B, 14th Mississippi Infantry, Carter House Collection, Franklin, Tennessee.

*Memphis (Tennessee) Appeal,* February 22, 1862.

*Bloomington (Illinois) Pantagraph,* February 25, 1862.

*Caryle (Illinois) Weekly Reveille,* February 23, 1862.

*Watertown (Wisconsin) Democrat,* March 6, 1862.

**13TH PENNSYLVANIA RESERVES**

O. E. Howard Thomson and William H. Rauch, *History of the "Bucktails"* (Philadelphia: Electric, 1906).

Edwin A. Glover, *Bucktailed Wildcats* (New York: Thomas Yoseloff, 1960).

**THE IRON BRIGADE**

O. B. Curtis, *Story of the Twenty-fourth Michigan of the Iron Brigade: Known as the Detroit and Wayne County Regiment* (Detroit: Winn & Hammond, 1891).

**21ST OHIO VOLUNTEER INFANTRY, CORPORAL, COMPANY C, SEPTEMBER 1863**

National Archives, Record Group 393, part 2, entry 5784, Inspection Reports of the 3rd Brigade, 2nd Division, XIV Corps.

Capt. Silas S. Canfield, *History of the 21st Regiment Ohio Volunteer Infantry* (Toledo: Vrooman, Anderson and Bateman, 1893), 95.

National Archives, Record Group 94, Regimental Books, 21st Ohio Infantry.

**TOWARD THE ANGLE**

Kathy Georg Harrison and John W. Busey, *Nothing but Glory* (Gettysburg, Pa.: Thomas Publications, 1987), 49.

National Archives, Record Group 92, entry 999, LeDuc Letter, Lieutenant Colonel and Chief, XI Corps Quartermaster.

**THE TEXAS BRIGADE, 1863**

National Archives, Record Group 109, M-323, Service Records of Soldiers from State of Texas, 1st, 4th, and 5th Texas.

**1ST SOUTH CAROLINA VOLUNTEER INFANTRY, U.S. COLORED TROOPS**

Frederick H. Dyer, *A Compendium of the War of the Rebellion* (New York: Thomas Yoseloff, 1959), 1636.

Frederick P. Todd, *American Military Equipage, 1851–1872,* vol. 2 (n.p.: Chatham Square, 1983).

National Archives, Record Group 156, M-1281, Summary Statements of Quarterly Returns of Ordnance and Ordnance Stores on Hand in Regular and Volunteer Army Organizations.

**27TH VIRGINIA INFANTRY, COLOR SERGEANT, DECEMBER 1862**

National Archives, Record Group 109, M-324, Compiled Service Records of Confederate Soldiers Who Served in Organizations from the State of Virginia, 27th Virginia Infantry.

**COLONEL OF THE CONFEDERACY**

National Archives, Record Group 109, M-437, Letters Received by the Confederate States Secretary of War.

**PRIVATE, 53RD GEORGIA INFANTRY, JULY 1863**

National Archives, Record Group 109, M-266, Compiled Service Records of Confederate Soldiers Who Served from Georgia, 53rd Georgia.

Editors of Time-Life Books, *Echoes of Glory,* Confederate volume (Alexandria, Va.: Time-Life Books, 1991), 185.

**1ST MINNESOTA**

National Archives, Record Group 393, part 2, entry 70.

Harry W. Pfanz, *Gettysburg: The Second Day* (Chapel Hill: University of North Carolina Press, 1987), 410.

**PRIVATE, 20TH TENNESSEE INFANTRY, C.S.A., SUMMER 1863**

National Archives, Record Group 109, M-268, Compiled Service Records of Confederate Soldiers, Tennessee.

Ibid. Service file of Pvt. John A. Sanders, Company E, 20th Tennessee Infantry.

**UNION INFANTRY DRUMMER, WINTER 1863–64**

National Archives, Record Group 393, part 2, entry 205, Weekly Reports of the Assistant Inspector General to the Headquarters, Army of the Potomac.

**1ST AND 2ND MARYLAND**

Ross Kimmel, "Enlisted Uniforms of the Maryland Confederate Infantry," parts l and 2, *Military Collector and Historian* 41, no. 3 (fall 1989): 98–108; no. 4 (winter 1989): 183–88.

**GEN. PATRICK R. CLEBURNE**

*Richmond Examiner,* November 1, 1864.

**PRIVATE, 29TH ALABAMA INFANTRY, SPRING 1864**

National Archives, Record Group 109, M-311, Compiled Service Records of Confederate Soldiers That Served from Alabama, 29th Alabama.

Ibid., M-331, Compiled Service Records of General and Staff Officers, File of John Ansley, MSK.

Ibid., M-311, Alabama Service Records, File of Samuel Abernathy, Captain, Company E, 29th Alabama.

**LONGSTREET'S CORPS, SEPTEMBER 1863**

Larry J. Daniel, *Soldier in the Army of Tennessee* (Chapel Hill: University of North Carolina Press, 1991), 11.

John B. Lindsley, *Millitary Annals of Tennessee: Confederate* (Nashville: J. M. Lindsley, 1886), 820–23.

Glenn Tucker, *Bloody Battle in the West* (Dayton, Ohio: Bobbs-Merrill, 1976), 172.

Augustus Dickert, *History of Kershaw's Brigade* (n.p.: Elbert E. Aull, 1899), 268.

W. R. Houghton, *War Record of W. R. Houghton While Serving in Confederate States Army* (Montgomery, Ala.: Paragon Press, 1912), 62.

Charles Clark, *Opdycks Tigers, 125th O. V.I.* (Columbus, Ohio: Spahr & Glenn, 1895), 107.

Ulysses S. Grant, *Personal Memoirs of U. S. Grant* (New York: Charles Webster, 1885) 320–21.

**76TH OHIO VOLUNTEER INFANTRY**

Charles A. Willison, *A Boy's Service with the 76th Ohio* (Huntington, W. V.: Blue Acorn Press, 1995).

Ordnance Report.

**12TH INDIANA VOLUNTEER INFANTRY, 1864**

James Spears, "The Zouave Jacket," *Indiana History Bulletin* 40, no. 3 (March 1963): 35–37.

**HOOD'S TENNESSEE CAMPAIGN, SEPTEMBER TO DECEMBER 1864**

Aaron Smith, *On Wheels and How I Came There* (New York: Eaton and Mains, 1892), 194–95, 200–201.

*Richmond Examiner,* November 2, 1864.

Samuel B. Dunlap Diary, October 28–November 1, 1864, State Historical Society of Missouri.

T. E. Matthems, 33rd Alabama Memoir, Alabama State Archives.

Wiley Sword, notes sent to author.

*The War of the Rebellion: A Compilation of the Official Records of the Union and Confederate Armies* (Washington, D.C.: Government Printing Office, 1880–1901), ser. 1, vol. 45, part 1, 733–39.

**203RD PENNSYLVANIA INFANTRY, PRIVATE, FALL 1864**

National Archives, Record Group 94, Regimental Books, 203rd Pennsylvania Infantry.

Ibid., Record Group 92, entry 2182, Washington Depot to Schuylkill Arsenal, September 23, 1864.

*The War of the Rebellion: The Official Records of the Union and Confederate Armies,* series I, vol. 46, part 1, 414–21.

**APPOMATTOX COURTHOUSE, APRIL 12, 1865**

Chris Calkins, *The Final Bivouac: The Surrender Parade at Appomattox and the Disbanding of the Armies, April 10–May 20, 1865* (Lynchburg, Va.: H. E. Howard, 1988), 36, 39, 56, 73.

*The War of the Rebellion: A Compilation of the Official Records of the Union and Confederate Armies* (Washington, D.C.: Government Printing Office, 1880–1901), vol. 22, pt. 1, 651–67.

S. A. Miller, *Report: Special Committee on Pay and Clothing,* February 11, 1865.

James H. M'Neilly, "Going Out and Coming Back," *Confederate Veteran* 29, no. 8 (August 1921): 288.

**PRIVATE, 2ND MARYLAND INFANTRY, C.S.A., 1864**

Based on an example in the collection of the Maryland Historical Society.

National Archives, Record Group 109, M-331, Compiled Service Records of Confederate General and Staff Officers, file of George D. Mercer.

# CHAPTER 5

# *The Cavalry*

PRIOR TO THE OUTBREAK OF WAR, THE U.S. ARMY mounted force was composed of five regiments: two regiments of dragoons, one of mounted rifles, and two of cavalry. For the most part, these troopers were scattered over the Western frontier, dealing with the problems presented by a white population who wished to settle lands loosely held for centuries by the Native Americans. On August 10, 1861, the adjutant general's office issued General Orders No. 55, which, to the chagrin of the dragoons and rifles, did away with the separate divisions and designated all as cavalry.[1] Once the shooting started, most of the Regular enlisted men of these regiments remained loyal to the Union, but several key officers with cavalry experience elected to join the Confederate cause.[2] In fact, Company A, 1st Confederate Regular Cavalry, was made up of men who deserted from the U.S. Army as they were leaving the Department of Texas. In essence, however, both armies, starting the war with a limited number of men with real cavalry experience, soon found themselves overshadowed by the influx of volunteers with little or no training in mounted service beyond what some had gained in the militia. Nevertheless, the daring exploits of these volunteers, both Union and Confederate, would rival those of any cavalry the world had ever seen. Together these Americans would write a new chapter in the use of mounted troops in warfare.

The prewar uniform worn by the U.S. mounted regiments had been adopted in part in 1854, with changes in 1858 adding the final touches. The facings on these uniforms—orange for dragoons, green for mounted rifles, and yellow for cavalry—were a point of honor that, at a glance, distinguished the service of the trooper. General Orders No. 55 added insult to injury by eliminating the orange and green. Both dragoons and mounted rifles resisted receiving new uniforms trimmed in cavalry yellow until necessity overcame pride. War would certainly make such concerns seem trivial, although it was noted by Theophilus F. Rodenbough, by the historian of the 2nd Dragoons, that the regiment was able to stretch out the change for nearly two years.[3]

In the Federal army, the uniforms for both Regulars and volunteers of cavalry were manufactured or purchased by the Quartermaster Department, operating from Philadelphia's Schuylkill Arsenal and new depots established to meet the emergency. The supply procedures, as well as the methods of procurement, were the same as for the other branches. For the Confederacy, the Richmond Depot and other facilities across the South met the needs of the Southern troopers. With identical sources of procurement and supply for the cavalry,

*Prewar dress epaulets of Capt. Alfred Pleasonton of the 2nd U.S. Dragoons. In 1851, the branch color of the two regiments of dragoons was changed to orange, which is represented in the circlets bearing the numeral 2 shown here.* WEST POINT MUSEUM.

infantry, and artillery, it is not surprising that their basic garments, such as shirts and other undergarments, were identical. The uniforms of the cavalry, although distinct in some details, did not differ greatly from those issued to the rest of the army. The greatest distinctions were the bright yellow trim, at first scorned by the old-line Regular dragoons and rifles, and the air of superiority that seemed to set the trooper apart from those who must campaign on foot.

### HEADGEAR

#### *Union*

The Federal trooper was authorized two types of headgear, a hat and a forage cap, both originally adopted by the army in November 1858.[4] Except for the trim and insignia, both of these were identical to those issued to the infantry. The hat was looped up on the right side and held by a brass eagle; brass crossed sabers (for dragoons and cavalry) and the company letter along with the regimental number were worn on the front of the crown. The enlisted men of the mounted rifles wore only the company letter on the front of the hat. The ornamentation was completed by a worsted wool cord, with tassels, the color of the branch, around the base of the crown, and a black feather attached in front and lying around the side opposite the looped-up brim. The pattern 1858 forage cap was made of a dark blue cloth, with a welt around the crown the color of the arm of service and the company letter on the front.

Both of these hats remained in service throughout the Civil War. The most significant change was the elimination of the colored welt on the forage cap early in the war, an economic measure that eliminated the need to supply separate caps for each branch of service. Many Federal cavalry regiments received an initial issue of both types of headgear. As the war progressed, the type of issue headgear actually worn varied, depending on the wishes of the commanding officer. Existing orders make it apparent that many enlisted men attempted to express their individuality by adopting hats of varying types and colors. This practice usually resulted in orders condemning the practice, although at any given time a Federal trooper may have been seen sporting a hat that set him apart from his comrades. Orders and circulars from various regimental order books show clearly that headgear certainly attracted the attention of those in command.[5]

> Orders no. 20 — H.Q. 1st Vt. Cavalry
> Camp near Harrisonville, Va.
> July 11, 1862
>
> Commanders of companies will see that the enlisted men of their companies wear the uniform cap, recently issued by the Quartermasters and will see that none of their men wear slouch or straw hats in the ranks.

> Orders no. 28 — H.Q. 6th U.S. Cavalry
> Jan. 23, 1863
>
> The Commanding officer has noticed the irregular and unmilitary appearance of many of the men, an evil increased by their being permitted to wear felt and white hats and in fact whatever they choose—Hereafter every man will be required to wear the regulation uniform cap. They are on hand and can and must be drawn today.[6]

> Regimental Order no. 18 — H.Q. 9th New York Cavalry
> near Culpeper C.H. March 4, 1864
>
> After April 1, 1864 and during the summer months no Forage caps will be worn by any trooper of this command. The U.S. Army hat (black) will be the style until further orders.
>
> By order of
> Wm. Sackett
> Col. Cmdg. 9th N.Y. Cav.

*Officer's forage cap believed to have been worn by Col. William Stedman of the 6th Ohio Volunteer Cavalry. With richly embroidered crossed sabers surmounted by a silver bullion numeral 6, this cap is an excellent example of high-quality officers' field headgear. It bears the maker's imprint, "US Akron."* JAMES C. FRASCA COLLECTION.

*Model 1858 Federal cavalryman's uniform hat, marked in the crown "Manufactured by James H. Prentice, Brooklyn, New York," who contracted for 50,000 such hats in October 1861. It was worn by John W. McClain of the 6th Ohio Volunteer Cavalry. Misshapen, with its top field-crushed down and soldier-made ventilation holes punched through, it vividly illustrates how these hats often appeared in the field.* JAMES C. FRASCA COLLECTION.

E. J. COATES AND F. C. GAEDE, COMPS., "U.S. ARMY QUARTERMASTER CONTRACTS, 1861–1865" (UNPUBLISHED MANUSCRIPT, 1993), 234.

Circular H.Q. 1st N. J. Cavalry
Oct. 21, 1864

Notwithstanding the orders that have been issued the Maj. Commanding has noticed with astonishment and regret, that several of the 1st Sgts. of companies continue to appear in slouch, unsoldierly hats. Hereafter any such will be ordered off the Parade, and a second offense will be followed by a reduction to the ranks.

Regimental Order no. 93 1st Maryland Cavalry
November 1864

. . . enlisted men found wearing a hat while on duty after he shall have been supplied with a cap . . . will be severely punished."

General Orders no. 37 H.Q. 3rd Michigan Cavalry
Brownsville, Ark. Dec. 27, 1864

. . . The black felt hat issued by the Government will be worn without trimmings, the crown being folded in the "Continental Style." The forage cap may be worn as undress or on fatigue and stable duty.

***Confederate***

Confederate uniform regulations initially called for a gray forage cap with a band around the lower edge the color of the branch of service. This was changed in January 1862 to require the cap body itself to be the branch color, with a dark blue band.[7] Since Confederate regimental procurement records rarely give anything but the cost of caps issued, the number of regulation caps actually reaching the field is difficult to establish. Confederate troopers, unlike their Northern counterparts, received either caps or hats, but rarely both. Regimental records, particularly in the Army of Northern Virginia, clearly show a regular issue of military caps. Whereas hats also often appear on receipts for clothing, the number of caps in nearly all cases is greater. This fact is substantiated by a report from the manufacturing branch of the Richmond Clothing Depot. On March 31, 1864, Capt. O. F. Weisiger reported receiving 58,442 cap fronts from Maj. W. G. Ferguson, quartermaster.[8] These may have been the caps contracted for with the firm of Peter Tait of Ireland, who was to send in "50,000 caps ready cut (grey cloth) with peak" during the first three months of 1864.[9] Whatever the case, the combined manufacturing and issue records speak loudly that the typical Confederate trooper in the East, like his Yankee foe, was probably more often than not dressed in the military cap. Records of manufacture in the depots supplying the Confederate armies in the Western Theater of the war often list hats and caps under the same accounting, making it more difficult to determine the actual issue. The fact that caps were easier and cheaper to produce makes it likely that the issue of caps to the armies serving west of the Allegheny Mountains was a common occurrence.

With all of this said, the only factor that is impossible to analyze is the Confederate trooper himself. It is well known that Confederate enlisted men often obtained headgear from unorthodox sources. Since there seems to have been much less attention to what the Confederate cavalryman was wearing to cover his head than is evident in the Union army, the actual percentage of hats versus caps will remain unknown.

## JACKETS, BLOUSES, AND APPENDAGES

### *Union*

Most of the enlisted men serving in the Union cavalry received both a uniform jacket and a fatigue blouse. The blouse was identical in all respects to that issued to all other branches of the army. The jacket, with its twelve-button front and high-standing collar, was identical to that issued to the light artillery except for the color of trim, which was cavalry yellow. It was a common practice for cavalrymen to have their jackets altered to a closer, more tailored fit than the standard issue. This tailoring often included lowering the collar, removing the pillows (belt supports), and shortening the length. At some point, apparently beginning in early 1863, the practice of removing the yellow trim from the jacket became a fad in both the Eastern and Western Theaters. As the fad spread, so too did the negative responses from commanding officers.

Regimental Order no. 25 9th Michigan Cavalry
May 12, 1863

The Commanding officer notices that it is becoming a general custom for the Non-Commissioned officers and privates to rip off the braid on their uniform jackets thereby defacing and otherwise mutilating them. Such practices are positively forbidden . . . officers will see that it is immediately replaced.

Special Order no. 65 H.Q. 9th Penn.
Veteran Cavalry
Whiteside, Tenn.
Oct. 11, 1864

. . . No enlisted man will be allowed to disfigure his uniform jacket by tearing off the regulation stripes, and for such offense will be stopped one months pay and if a non-commissioned officer reduced to the ranks.

Department of W. Va. H.Q. 2nd Brigade,
Cavalry Division
Martinsburg, March 23, 1864

. . . The stripping of braid from the dress jacket . . . is expressly forbidden.

It is difficult to determine the extent to which the jacket was worn in the field. Along with the cap, it is evident that the wearing of the jacket by enlisted men while on campaign was often left to the discretion of those in command.

Circular H.Q. 3rd Division
Warrenton Junction Aug. 1, 1863

Brigade Commanders will see that their commands will be furnished with Blouses in place of Jackets.

By Order
G. A. Custer Cmd. Division[10]

Regimental Order no. 69 H.Q. 13th
New York Cavalry
Vienna, Va. Nov. 14, 1863

Commanders will see that their men wear the blouse except on Dress Parade, Guard, Inspection and such occasions as may be proper when they shall wear the uniform jacket. The jacket when not worn must be folded and always kept in perfect repair.

Circular [extract] H.Q. 1st Vermont Cavalry
May 2, 1864

Sergeants and Corporals can if they desire, wear the uniform jacket. All others will wear the blouse.

General Orders no. 7 H.Q. Cavalry
[part] Middle Military Division
Dec. 2, 1864

The use of jackets and hats by the men will be at once discontinued and the Blouse and cap with cross sabres and the letter of the Company attached will be instituted.

An immediate inspection will be made to ascertain the number of Blouses, caps, cross sabres and letters required by each regiment and the requisition for the same sent in and filled at once.

Commanding officers will hereafter approve no requisition for jackets and hats and compel the men of their command to habitually wear the Blouses and Caps.

By Command
Bvt. Maj. Gen. Torbert[11]

#### *Shoulder Scales*

Federal cavalrymen were one of the major recipients of brass shoulder scales, which had been universally issued to the prewar mounted regiments. The scales, when received, were worn generally on dress parade and were considered an unnecessary nuisance by most troopers.

***Confederate***

The jacket of the Confederate cavalryman was manufactured by the same depots that made the nine-button uniform jacket that became the unofficial standard for the Confederate army. As a general rule, the only difference was yellow trim, which could be found on many depot-manufactured jackets for cavalry at least until the last year of the war. In addition, many Confederate cavalry jackets used a brass button with the single letter "C" for cavalry. Unlike the Federal trooper, the Confederate did not have a choice between fatigue and dress coats. What he was issued was what he wore. With very few exceptions, Confederate regimental records show receipts for jackets. It is rare that color is mentioned; however, when prices per garment are noted, they often vary slightly. A requisition for the 1st Virginia Cavalry filled on December 31, 1862, shows receipt of five jackets costing $12 each and four jackets priced at $12.50. No explanation is given, but since 50 cents was a sum to be considered at the time, there was obviously some variation in quality.[12] A similar receipt for items received by Company D of the 12th Virginia Cavalry, dated August 31, 1863, shows an even wider disparity, listing sixteen jackets at $14 each and twenty-two jackets at $12. On several occasions, this same regiment did note the actual color of jackets received. On April 15, 1863, Company K received twenty English gray jackets at $12 each. The following summer, Company G received both black and gray jackets, with no price given.[13]

## DESIGNATING INSIGNIA

***Union***

*Regimental Designation*

Cavalry designating insignia consisted of stamped brass crossed sabers, with each saber measuring 3 3/4 inches, crossed in the middle; the regimental number, also of stamped brass, 5/8 inch in height; and the company letter, 1 inch long. These were originally designed to be placed on the cavalry hat, but during the war they were also universally worn on the top of the forage cap. The order issued to the 1st New Jersey Cavalry on November 29, 1864, was repeated in the order books of the majority of Federal cavalry regiments: "The attention of Company Commanders is again called to the manner in which the cap ornaments are placed on the cap. In all cases the sabres must be evenly adjusted[,] the Company letter above the sabres and the number of the regiment below."

*Corps Badges*

Although detachments were often assigned to infantry headquarters, the Federal cavalry functioned as a separate corps in both the Eastern and Western Theaters of the war. No badge was officially adopted, and no order has been found specifying that any badge be worn by either Eastern or Western cavalry regiments. The badge represented on some cavalry monuments commemorating actions of the Army of the Potomac Cavalry was worn by only a few officers.

*Chevrons*

Chevrons to designate noncommissioned officer rank were the same configuration for cavalry as for infantry or artillery, but their color was yellow. Although army regulations called for the chevrons to be worn above the elbow on each sleeve of the jacket or blouse, numerous entries in regimental order books attest to the fact that sergeants and corporals were often negligent when it came to sewing them on. Several reasons may account for this, not the least of which is that they had to pay for them. It may also be that the bright yellow stripes of command offered an inviting target for enemy sharpshooters. Whatever the reason, orders are abundant instructing those who failed in this regard to adhere to regulations:

> General Orders no. 11 [part] H.Q. 2nd Penn.
> Cavalry
> Dec. 3rd, 1862
>
> . . . Hereby all non-commissioned officers must wear the proper badge of rank at all times.

> Special Orders no. 65 H.Q. 9th Penn.
> Veteran Cavalry
> Whiteside, Tenn. Oct. 11, 1864
>
> All non-commissioned officers of this Regiment are hereby ordered to wear the stripes and chevrons belonging to their respective grades.

> Orders no. 29 H.Q. 6th U.S. Cavalry
> Feb. 2, 1865
>
> Non-commissioned officers are again instructed to wear the chevrons of their rank according to Regulations.

## TROUSERS

***Union***

The trousers for mounted men in the Federal army were, with only a few exceptions, made of sky blue kersey wool, with an extra layer of this material in the seat and legs as reinforcement. Noncommissioned officers were required to wear trouser stripes of a width appropriate to their rank: 1 1/2 inches for sergeants and 1/2 inch for corporals. For the cavalry, these stripes were made of yellow worsted wool. Most regiments had a man with sewing ability designated as a tailor, who was paid a nominal sum by newly promoted noncommissioned officers to apply the stripes to the trousers.

*Black woolen overcoat worn by Maj. Hugh Mortimer Nelson of the 6th Virginia Cavalry, C.S.A. This coat features a red lining on the cape and oddly enough is fitted with South Carolina and U.S. ordnance buttons. Nelson served as an aide-de-camp to General Ewell and died of disease a few months after the battle of Gaines' Mill in 1862.* TROIANI COLLECTION.

***Confederate***

Confederate troopers were issued the same trousers as the other branches of service. Regulations called for sky blue, which made captured Federal trousers a legitimate part of the uniform. Regimental records indicate that, as with the jackets, the trousers varied in quality and color. This fact is made evident in the prices, charged for trousers, that appear on receipts. The 12th Virginia Cavalry, on requisitions received in 1863, listed pants at $8, $11, $12, and $12.25. The same regiment received and issued trousers of light blue, dark blue, and gray. It can be safely assumed that those described as gray ran the complete range of shades of that color.[14]

## OVERCOATS AND PONCHOS

***Union***

For comfort in cold and inclement weather, the Federal cavalryman was issued both an overcoat, or greatcoat, of sky blue kersey wool and a poncho of rubberized canvas. Quartermaster regulations described the coat as double-breasted, with a collar that could be worn turned up or folded down. The cape was long, extending to the cuff of the sleeve. The coat differed from that issued to the infantry, in both the double-breasted cut and the long cape, which were designed to give the trooper protection. When not worn, the overcoat was rolled and strapped to the pommel of the saddle.

The poncho was similar to the rubber blanket issued to the infantry, but it had a cut in the center with a fold-over flap large enough for a man's head to pass through. This arrangement allowed the trooper to wear the poncho draped over his body as a shield from the rain. If conditions warranted, both the coat and poncho could be worn.

> Special Orders no. 5 [part] — H.Q. 9th New York Cavalry<br>Acquia Church, Va.<br>February 15, 1863
>
> Hereafter upon marches, drill or inspections, Commanders of Companies will be held accountable for the dress of their respective commands[;] they will also have the men dressed according to the state of the weather; clear, moderate the dress jacket will be worn, cold the greatcoat in addition and in inclement weather the ponchos over the greatcoat.
>
> By Order;<br>S. Nichols, Maj. Commanding[15]

***Confederate***

Overcoats for Southern troopers varied in style, color, and material. Regulations called for an overcoat of gray wool cut in the same manner as that issued to the Federal army. Regimental clothing receipts show that the Confederate government made every effort to provide coats for its soldiers. The very best overcoats received by Confederate soldiers of any branch were those run through the Union naval blockade from England. Confederate prisoners observed in December 1863 by Frank Rauscher, a member of the 114th Pennsylvania Infantry, were wearing "overcoats . . . of much better material than our own. They were of English manufacture, a much darker blue than [ours]."[16] The Tait proposal given to the Confederate secretary of war in December 1863 called for 50,000 greatcoats of "stout grey cloth cut and ready for sewing" to be received from England in the first months 1864.[17]

Despite the chance for "friendly fire" incidents, the Confederate troopers did not hesitate to make full use of captured Federal overcoats. This at times worked to their advantage. On the morning of October 4, 1864, a member of Blazer's Scouts, a Federal independent mounted command, was riding alone near Cedar Creek, Virginia, when he was captured by five mounted men dressed in Federal overcoats who he had suspected were Rebels. His narrative of the event, which appeared in a veterans' newspaper, the *National Tribune,* on October 31, 1889, leaves no doubt that this was far from an unusual occurrence.

Confederate cavalry regimental clothing receipts also mention the issuance of ponchos to Southern cavalry. Since the practical design of the poncho leaves little room for variation, it can be assumed that these were similar to those issued to Federal troopers.

## FOOTWEAR

### *Union*

The Union cavalryman was invariably issued leather boots. These were of a standard pattern and varied little throughout the war. The leg of the boot was twelve inches high, and the top was wide enough to allow the trooper to tuck in his trousers. Orders relating to the trousers being worn inside or outside the boots generally are specific only for units on dress parade, dictating that the trousers then be worn outside the boot.

> General Orders no. 9 [part] 1st Brigade,
> 2nd Division
> Cavalry Corps, Army of the Potomac
> Oct. 18, 1864
> On all reviews and inspections or parades, unless in bad weather, trousers will be worn outside of the boots.
> By Command;
> Brig. Gen. Davies[18]

It can be presumed that on the march, the decision whether to tuck the trousers into the boots was left to the discretion of the individual trooper.

### *Confederate*

The shortage of leather in the Confederacy made the issue of boots to the Confederate cavalryman anything but standard. Regimental records occasionally show boots but far more often show shoes being received by the Southern trooper. Regimental records of the 1st Virginia Cavalry show mixed issues of boots and shoes until March 1864, when Company K received thirty-nine pairs of shoes and five pairs of boots. Thereafter in this regiment, only shoes are shown as items of issue.[19] As an example of the situation faced by the Confederate soldier, on September 27, 1863, Company H of the 1st North Carolina Cavalry received six pairs of cloth shoes for issue.

# 2ND U.S. CAVALRY, BUGLER, 1861

U.S. CAVALRY MUSEUM, FORT RILEY, KANSAS

In the early days of the war, the men who made up the few regiments of the Regular army were held in awe by the multitude of volunteers who filled the ranks of the U.S. Army. This was doubly true of the dragoons, who arrived in the East from posts in the Far West. Here were men who had served for years in such places as Texas, New Mexico, and California. They were the very embodiment of legends and stories that many young men who had grown up in the East had read and dreamed of.

The 2nd Dragoons joined the Army of the Potomac after service in Utah, New Mexico, and Kansas. The scattered companies arrived in Washington piecemeal, with Company K first, in July 1861, followed over the next several months by the remaining companies with the exception of Companies C, I, and G, which did not join the regiment until November 1862.

During this period, a transformation took place that was to change both the uniform and the organization of the dragoons. On August 3, 1861, the entire U.S. mounted force was consolidated into a single corps. Until then, this force had consisted of three regiments of cavalry, one of mounted rifles, and two of dragoons. Now they would collectively be known as the 1st through the 6th U.S. Cavalry. For the dragoons, this was a demoralizing blow. Not only did they lose the proud

*Double rich cavalry major's shoulder straps backed with yellow velvet. This set was worn by Maj. Edward H. Wright of the 3rd U.S. Cavalry, an aide-de-camp to Gen. George B. McClellan.* TROIANI COLLECTION.

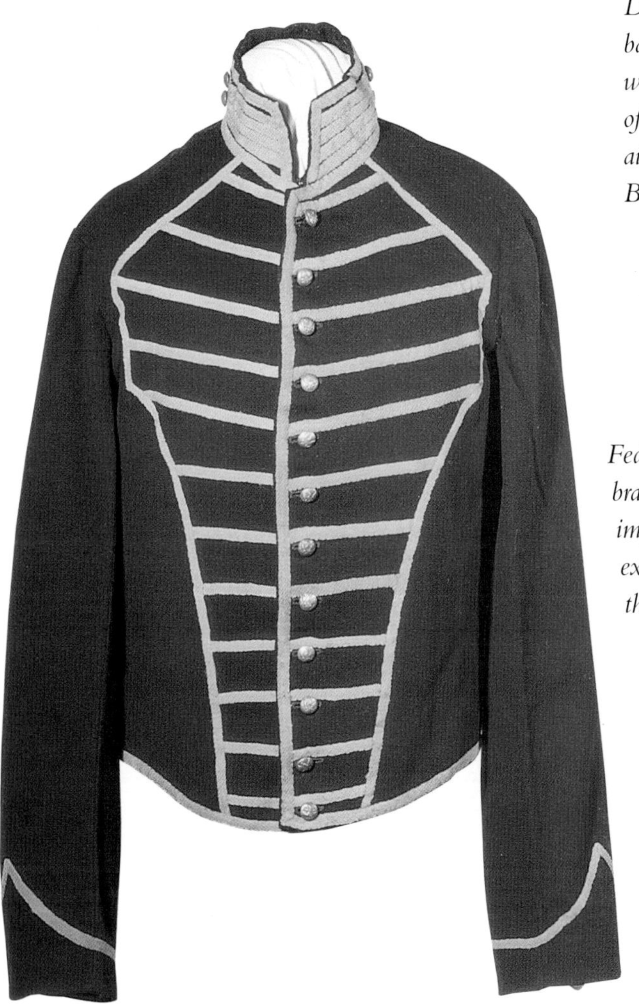

*Federal cavalry musician's uniform jacket, trimmed with yellow worsted herringbone braid across the breast. As signals in the mounted services were given by bugle, it was important for officers to be able to distinguish the trumpeters in the smoke and excitement of conflict. Trumpeters generally rode gray horses to further visually set them apart from the rank and file.* TROIANI COLLECTION.

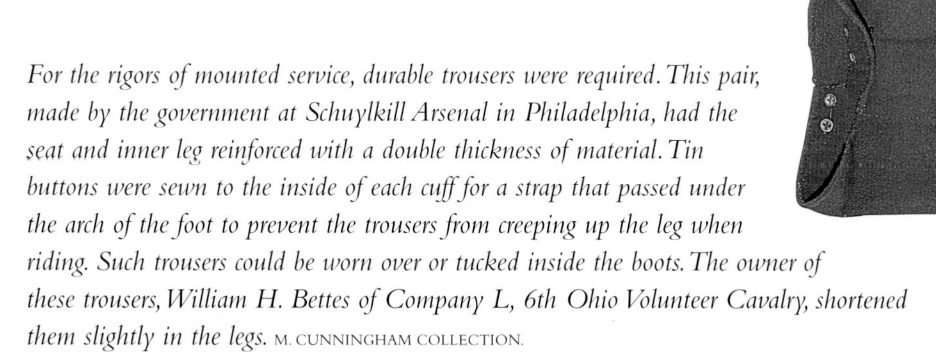

*For the rigors of mounted service, durable trousers were required. This pair, made by the government at Schuylkill Arsenal in Philadelphia, had the seat and inner leg reinforced with a double thickness of material. Tin buttons were sewn to the inside of each cuff for a strap that passed under the arch of the foot to prevent the trousers from creeping up the leg when riding. Such trousers could be worn over or tucked inside the boots. The owner of these trousers, William H. Bettes of Company L, 6th Ohio Volunteer Cavalry, shortened them slightly in the legs.* M. CUNNINGHAM COLLECTION.

title of "dragoon," but the color of their uniform trim would change from "the cherished orange . . . to the gaudy yellow" of the cavalry, as the historian of the 2nd Dragoons, Theophilus F. Rodenbough, put it. To lessen the impact, the original order allowed the dragoons to continue to wear the orange until their uniforms wore out and existing stocks of uniforms were exhausted. It was nearly two years before the last dragoon was forced by necessity to finally become amalgamated into the cavalry.

At this same time, another change in uniform that was much disliked by the Regulars was ordered. In December 1861, the secretary of war issued General Orders No. 101, directing that the color of the trousers be changed from dark blue to sky blue. For many, this change was made only after the dark blue was no longer available. Consequently, some Regulars, despite the rigors of service in the field, managed to retain the dark blue as late as January 1863.

The 2nd Cavalry served with distinction throughout the Civil War as part of the Cavalry Corps of the Army of the Potomac. In 1865, as the volunteers returned home to a heroes' welcome, the men of the 2nd U.S. left camp in Maryland and proceeded to Fort Leavenworth, Kansas, and their old stamping grounds, the Plains.

# THE BOLIVAR TROOP, COMPANY A, 1ST BATTALION MISSISSIPPI CAVALRY

WINSTON CAMERON

The Bolivar Troop was recruited in Bolivar County, Mississippi, in late 1860 in response to Lincoln's victory in the presidential election of that year and the impending threat of war. Capt. Frank Armstrong Montgomery took great pride in the fact that his company was part of the independent Army of Mississippi. Mississippi seceded from the Union on January 9, 1861, and for a period of five weeks assumed the status of a sovereign nation, until becoming part of the Confederate States of America.

The "Ordinance to Regulate the Military System of the State of Mississippi" of January 23, 1861, called for ten cavalry companies to be organized. Under this ordinance, each Bolivar Trooper was issued two Colt revolvers, a saber, and a Maynard carbine. Captain Montgomery noted in his memoirs, "My company for the time was very well-armed!" A private in the Noxubee Cavalry, which also served in Miller's Battalion, wrote that the weight of two pistols, saber, and carbine was so heavy that they had trouble mounting their horses. The pistols were afterward kept in holsters on the saddle horns.

Military equipment was scarce in Mississippi, so Captain Montgomery traveled through the South to procure provisions for his troop. While in New Orleans, he purchased for himself and his lieutenants new officers' sabers and belts,

*Quilted jean cloth hat worn by Pvt. Landon Cheek of the 1st Mississippi Cavalry. Of particularly sturdy construction, the crown has small ventilation holes to allow air to circulate.* CONFEDERATE MEMORIAL HALL, CLAUDE LEVET PHOTOGRAPH.

along with some "very handsome" cavalry saddles. Each trooper was to provide his own horse, and Montgomery found saddles for his enlisted men in Memphis. With great pride, he commented that by the time they left Memphis, they "made a very soldier-like appearance."

A description of 5th sergeant Frank A. Gayden, captured near Charleston, Missouri, in August 1861, provides some details about their uniform. Gayden, "greatly crestfallen at his capture," was dressed in a "gray shirt and had a broad yellow stripe on his pants. [He was] armed with a splendid Maynard rifle, a pair of Colt's Navy revolvers, and a cavalry sword."

The Bolivar Troop's uniform, though unique, generally followed the uniform prescribed under Mississippi's ordinance. General orders stated that each cavalryman was to wear "for fatigue . . . a blue flannel shirt with a star of white on each side of the collar." Trousers were to be "gray, with a stripe one inch wide, of the facings of their respective corps." For cavalry, the facings were yellow at first, and orange was added in May 1861. The men wore overshirts of light blue-gray, with all trim, including rank stripes, of a solid black. Their trousers were a shade of blue. The men wore hats of gray felt, pinned on the right side with a white metal star or button and a black ostrich plume, and adorned on the front with the brass letters "BT" in old script.

Captain Montgomery's overshirt was of a similar style but had large, dark, pointed cuffs, ornamented with two buttons. He wore the prescribed captain's shoulder straps of "dark blue cloth, bordered with an embroidery of gold, one quarter of an inch wide, with two embroidered bars" to denote his rank.

While at Union City, Tennessee, in June 1861, the battalion was formed from different Mississippi cavalry companies serving under Gen. Frank Cheatham of Tennessee. John Henry Miller of the Pontatoc Dragoons was elected major. The Bolivar Troop then became Company A of Miller's 1st Battalion of Mississippi Cavalry.

On April 2, 1862, just days before the battle of Shiloh, a consolidated regiment, the 1st Improvised Mississippi Cavalry, under Col. A. J. Lindsay, was formed. The Bolivar Troop became Company H of this new regiment. The regiment was reorganized at Tupelo, Mississippi, in May 1862, with the twelve-month men having now reenlisted for the duration of the war. Captain Montgomery was elected lieutenant colonel, and Capt. Richard A. Pinson was elected colonel of the Mississippi 1st Cavalry Regiment.

The soldiers of the Bolivar Troop finished the war in Gen. Frank C. Armstrong's Brigade, Chalmer's Division, Forrest's Cavalry Corps, Department of Alabama, Mississippi, and East Tennessee. Battle credits list over 100 engagements, skirmishes, or major battles—a proud military history for a "hell-roaring Battalion of Cavalry."

# 1ST NORTH CAROLINA CAVALRY, OCTOBER 1861

MICHAEL FLANAGAN

The 1st North Carolina Cavalry was raised in that state in the summer of 1861. They would serve, largely with the hard-fighting cavalry of the Army of Northern Virginia, until the final surrender at Appomattox. The regiment received its initial issue of uniforms and equipment from the state in early October. This uniform consisted of a sack coat of gray cloth from North Carolina mills. This same style was issued to nearly all early North Carolina units, with each branch of service distinguished by color of trim. Throughout the war, North Carolina made every effort to assure that her sons were well clothed and supplied. The distinctive cut of the initial issue changed from a coat to a jacket by the second major receipt of clothing in May 1862.

If the clothing issued in 1861 showed a great degree of uniformity, the Ordnance received by the 1st North Carolina did anything but. Although well armed, the Carolinians carried a diversity of weapons, including a variety of muzzle-loading pistols, revolvers, rifles, carbines, and sabers. One company received the artillery version of the Colt revolving carbine; however, by August 1862, most of these were listed as needing repair. As with the majority of Confederate cavalry regiments, this variety of arms did not improve, but the problem in fact became more pronounced as the war continued.

Included in the intriguing items of early issue to the regiment were a number of white buff saber belts, of Mexican War vintage. Also of particular interest were the saddles received. While some troopers rode on Texas Ranger–style saddles, others were issued saddles referred to as the New Orleans or Nashville style. No matter what arms or saddle they used, the troopers of the 1st North Carolina gave a good account of themselves in some of the hardest-fought cavalry battles ever waged.

# Mounted Rifle Rangers, January 1862

In September 1861, Gen. Benjamin Butler was authorized to raise a division of troops in New England. Needing cavalry, Butler in turn authorized twenty-five-year-old S. Tyler Read of Attleboro, Massachusetts, to raise two companies and H. A. Durivage to raise one. These three unattached companies of Massachusetts cavalry would be the only mounted force in Butler's New Orleans expedition.

Read's companies were recruited as the Mounted Rifle Rangers, a name that no doubt brought visions of adventure and glory to the minds of young men, while Durivage's company was known as the Light Cavalry. The uniforms for the three companies reflected the nature of the service that their names implied. A reporter for the *Boston Evening Journal* was impressed by the sight of Captain Read's men: "They carry heavy sabres and short rifles, and are to be provided with revolvers beside. The uniform, without being showy, is a very superior and imposing feature of the equipments, and reflects great credit upon Pierce Bros. & Co., of this city, by whom it was manufactured. The overcoats are of dark blue cloth, the collars being trimmed with green cord. The jackets are trimmed with green, and the shoulders mounted with brass scales." The Rifle Rangers had also been issued headgear of a pattern patented in July 1861 by John F. Whipple of New York. The "short rifles" noted were Sharps carbines. The Rifle Rangers did not receive Colt army revolvers until June 1862, after the companies arrived in New Orleans.

In June 1863, the two companies of Rifle Rangers, as well as the Light Cavalry company, were assigned to the 3rd Massachusetts Cavalry, newly organized in Louisiana from the 41st Massachusetts Infantry. It is doubtful that Read's proud troopers were happy with this change. Early inspection reports of the foot soldiers-turned-cavalrymen were anything but favorable. Two months after formation, a colonel from the inspector general's office commented, "I consider this regiment in anything but effective condition, and as having few claims to the title of 'Cavalry.'"

U. S. CAVALRY MUSEUM, FORT RILEY, KANSAS

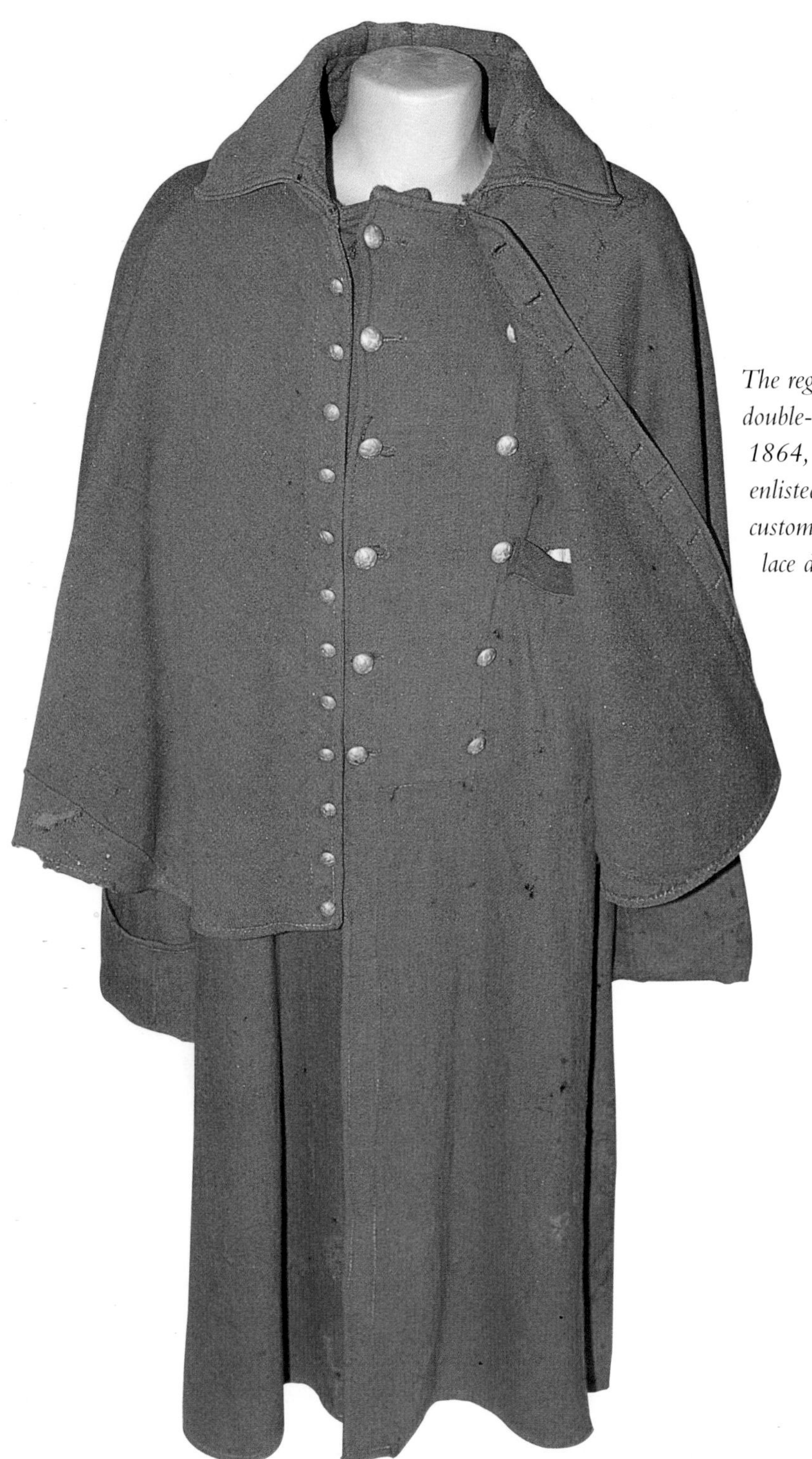

*The regulation sky blue Kersey overcoats for mounted soldiers were double-breasted and had longer capes than those of foot troops. In 1864, officers were authorized to wear the same overcoat as the enlisted men, sanctioning what had in effect already been a popular custom. This coat was worn by a colonel, as indicated by the black lace denoting rank at the cuff.* M. CUNNINGHAM COLLECTION.

*Forage cap with insignia of Company F, 15th New York Volunteer Cavalry, used by Pvt. William H. Hosford, who carved his name and unit into the underside of the visor. Hosford died of disease in September 1864 at Cumberland, Maryland.* TROIANI COLLECTION.

# 1ST ARKANSAS MOUNTED RIFLES, PRIVATE, COMPANY D, 1861

The 1st Arkansas Mounted Rifles was raised at Little Rock in June 1861. Although the men were initially mounted, by April 1862 they had turned in their horses and would serve the rest of the war as infantry. As with most Trans-Mississippi Confederate volunteers, the initial procurement of both uniforms and arms for the regiment posed challenges that would have discouraged those of weaker will and determination. A September 25, 1861, letter from the quartermaster general's office in Richmond to the assistant quartermaster at Fort Smith, Arkansas, summed up the problem and said in part, "if you can procure any articles of clothing that are fit for issue to the troops you should do so. It is not pretended to supply a uniform, it cannot be done."

DAVID RANKIN, JR.

The early uniform of the 1st Arkansas is evidenced by issues shown in the clothing account book of Company D. Prior to early 1862, issues consist mainly of overshirts, pants, and shoes. This is clearly illustrated by an existing photograph of an officer of the regiment, that shows him uniformed in a manner that would have made him indistinguishable from an enlisted man. The clothing accounts of Company D show no issue of hats well into 1862, and it can be assumed that the men supplied their own. The hat shown is similar to many found on the steamboat *Arabia*, which was excavated near the present course of the Missouri River beginning in 1989.

As with most Trans-Mississippi regiments, the arms of the 1st Arkansas varied greatly. Regimental records show a quantity of Hall rifles being delivered in November 1861. These were most certainly part of the flintlocks taken from the Little Rock Arsenal.

After being dismounted in April 1862, the regiment moved east of the Mississippi and joined the Confederate Army of Tennessee. Their fate and future would be intertwined with that of this army until its surrender near Durham, North Carolina, on April 26, 1865.

# 6TH PENNSYLVANIA CAVALRY, 1861–65

With scarlet pennants fluttering from the ends of nine-foot lances made of Norway fir, the 6th Pennsylvania Cavalry, better known as Rush's Lancers, made a splendid spectacle on the parade ground. These antique weapons, however, were not found to be as practical on the many battlefields of the war as the twelve carbines initially issued to each company for picket and scout duty. Still, it was not until May 1863, more than a year and a half after the regiment's organization in Philadelphia by Col. Richard H. Rush, that the European-inspired lances were replaced entirely with carbines. By that time, Rush's Lancers had participated in the Peninsula campaign, Antietam, and Fredericksburg. They went on to fight in every major battle of the Army of the Potomac to Appomattox. Cavalry general John Buford praised the volunteers by dubbing them the "Seventh Regulars."

Despite their exotic weaponry, the uniforms of the 6th were basically those of all Union cavalrymen. Quartermaster General Montgomery C. Meigs wrote, "Colonel Richard H. Rush of Philadelphia[,] having authority from the War Department to such effect[,] you will furnish his Regiment of Cavalry . . . with the uniforms he desires, which I believe differs from the Regular uniform only in regard to trousers[,] they being light blue instead of dark blue." Some had their uniform jackets reworked by company tailors into nonstandard forms during the war, but in general, the men of the 6th looked like any Union cavalrymen without their lances.

1ST TROOP PHILADELPHIA CITY CAVALRY MUSEUM

# 8TH TEXAS CAVALRY, TERRY'S TEXAS RANGERS

Only a very few dedicated Civil War historians would immediately recognize the numerical designation of this famous regiment. But even the casual student would immediately be familiar with the name Terry's Texas Rangers. The regiment was originally raised in September 1861 to serve in Virginia but instead was diverted to service in the Western Theater of the war. It was here that Col. Benjamin F. Terry lost his life at the battle of Woodsonville, Kentucky, on December 17, 1861, and here that the regiment began to gain a reputation worthy of the Lone Star State.

As with most Confederate regiments, the uniform of the rangers varied during the war depending on the availability of material at any particular time. They were at times supplied with red-trimmed jackets and red shirts. Pride in their state often took the form of a handmade "Lone Star" affixed to the favored slouch hat. Like other Texas regiments, they received clothing supplied by their home state for most of the war.

If their uniform varied, so did their arms. Perhaps indicative of their background, the rangers were always well supplied with revolvers, often carrying more than one per man. Early in the war, the regiment was also armed with a short double-barrel shotgun. Some of these had a bar and ring attached identical to those common to carbines such as the Sharps. A listing of ammunition required by the regiment, dated May 13, 1862, bears testimony to the variety of arms found in their ranks:

PRIVATE COLLECTION

20,160 cartridges for Navy six shooters
6,000 cartridges for Army six shooters
5,000 cartridges for shotguns
25,000 cartridges, buck and ball cal. .69
4,000 cartridges for Mississippi rifle
1,000 cartridges for Enfield rifle

Other requisitions dating as late as July 1864 show an even greater disparity in arms being carried, due largely to captures from the enemy. Of particular interest is a note found in the file of Sgt. Robert Burns, dated June 20, 1864, which states that at that time the rangers had sixty captured Spencer repeating rifles, but "the men [were] refraining from their further acquisition only because of the difficulty of procuring ammunition."

Terry's Texas Rangers continued to serve until the final days of the war.

# BRANDY STATION REVIEW

June 8, 1863, was a day of glory. When it came to cavalry operations, the horsemen of the Army of Northern Virginia, under the leadership of dashing Gen. J. E. B. Stuart, were the unchallenged masters of the field. On this day, General Stuart accompanied the army commander, Gen. Robert E. Lee, on a grand review of his proud troopers. The anticipated summer campaign was beginning, and it had started well. The army had scored a decisive victory on the field of Chancellorsville, but this had been largely an infantry fight. Now the men of the cavalry were eager to once again challenge the Federal horsemen.

Over the winter, the cavalry had received regular replacements of needed uniform items. Jackets, caps, and trousers were often requested and listed as received on requisition forms. All ordnance, including arms, ammunition, and leather goods, had also been supplied. As the commanding officers galloped by, their appearance alone was enough to instill pride and confidence in both officers and men. Both generals, uniformed in regulation gray, were the epitome of the Confederate high command—Lee the picture of authority, and Stuart the image of the Southern cavalier. Lt. Louis R. Fortescue, a Union officer captured on July 5, met and vividly remembered Stuart: "His regulation grey uniform was profusely decorated with gold braid, and was topped with a broad-brimmed black felt hat, pinned up at the side with a star from which drooped an extravagantly large ostrich feather. On his left breast was a shield, about two inches in width, which held a chain attached to the handle of a small stiletto, the blade being passed through the button holes of his coat." At this moment, the Confederate cavalry had reached its zenith. In less than twenty-four hours, Yankee cavalry would challenge them on this very field and, with a newfound fury, fight the greatest cavalry engagement ever witnessed on American soil.

*A fine-quality Confederate cavalry officer's frock coat worn by Capt. Thomas Pinckney of the 4th South Carolina Cavalry, probably in 1864–65. It is trimmed with light yellow piping, gold tape sleeve braids, and buttons with a "C" designating cavalry. Although regulations called for solid-colored collar and cuffs, many officers' coats were trimmed with less ostentatious piping.*

COLLECTION OF THE CHARLESTON (SOUTH CAROLINA) MUSEUM.

LARRY PAGE

# QUANTRILL'S GUERRILLAS

DAVID RANKIN, JR.

On October 5, 1863, some 300 to 500 splendidly mounted and heavily armed men rode south through Jasper County, Missouri. Some were clad in complete Federal blue uniforms, others in ordinary civilian garb, while many wore a peculiar kind of overshirt. A loose blouse that was cut low in the front, the slit narrowing to a point above the belt and ending in a ruffle or rosette, it was worn over a regular shirt and tie. It was usually made of homespun jean cloth of a brownish color, though some were a brilliant scarlet. It had huge pockets, one on each breast and one on each side below, like those in a coat. Many were finely embroidered or decorated with beads by wives or sweethearts; others were coarse and plain. This was the famous guerrilla shirt, and the riders were the band of Capt. William Clarke Quantrill, whom the Confederacy had officially made a captain of Partisan Rangers. He and his men had been declared outlaws by the Union forces, but to his supporters in Missouri, he was a dashing, free-spirited protector, an avenging angel.

*Uniform jacket of the 15th Pennsylvania Cavalry, trimmed with orange cording. Originally raised in 1861 as an independent company called the Anderson Troop, after Gen. Robert Anderson of Fort Sumter fame, the 15th was later expanded into a full regimental establishment.* TROIANI COLLECTION.

The guerrilla shirt adopted over time by Quantrill's men became a distinctive uniform of sorts. Some men wore them tucked neatly into their trousers; others let them fly loose in the wind. Baggy trousers tucked into high-topped boots, a broad leather belt bristling with revolvers, and a round-brimmed hat cocked at an angle adorned with a feather or metal star completed the costume. One eyewitness commented that "you could always tell a bushwhacker, because they wore feathers or bunches of ribbons, etc. in their hats."

On August 21, 1863, Quantrill's guerrilla band, led by some of his men dressed in Federal uniforms and flying the national colors, raided and sacked Lawrence, Kansas, a stronghold of Union support. Joseph Savage remembered seeing "what he thought were Union soldiers, in low-crowned, broad-brimmed hats, all alike, unshaven, stoop-shouldered, all without coats—nearly all wore red-flannel shirts, begrimed with camp grease and dirt. They had thrown away their coats, knowing they could get new ones in Lawrence." Many were tied to their saddles with straps to prevent them from falling off their horses when asleep. They were grimy and dirty from the long night's ride. Quantrill was said to have been dressed in a brown guerrilla shirt.

In four hours of murderous rampage and revenge, Quantrill's men left 180 men and boys dead in the streets, dragging some from their homes to be murdered in front of their families. They set the torch to much of the city, with 154 homes and businesses burned, the loss estimated at over $1 million. It was Quantrill's belief that it was a bushwhacker's war of no surrender and no quarter on both sides.

The Lawrence massacre led to swift retribution, as Federal forces under General Orders No. 11 drove the residents of four Missouri border counties onto the open prairie, while Jayhawkers pillaged and burned everything left behind. Quantrill and his raiders participated in the Confederate retaliation for this atrocity. Colorfully dressed and well armed, usually with two navy six-shot Colt revolvers, and two or three more on the saddle, as well as a Sharps carbine or shotgun, they were a formidable foe to the Federal soldiers in Missouri. But when Union forces drove the Confederates back, Quantrill fled to Texas. His guerrilla band split into several smaller units, including one headed by his notorious lieutenant, "Bloody Bill" Anderson, known for wearing a necklace of Yankee scalps into battle. Quantrill was eventually killed while on a raid into Kentucky in 1865.

Even in Quantrill's death, he and his followers remained folk heroes to their supporters in Missouri. Several ex-raiders—the brothers Frank and Jesse James and Cole and Jim Younger—went on to achieve their own notoriety in the late 1860s by applying Quantrill's hit-and-run tactics to bank and train robberies.

Quantrill and his guerrilla raiders were at times horribly cruel and merciless to their enemies, soldiers and civilian alike. Even to other Confederates, they remained an enigma. Protectors of freedom or outlaws, Quantrill and his men wrote their own page in the history of the American Civil War.

# Trooper, 7th Virginia Cavalry, 1863

MICHAEL FLANAGAN

*Regulation kepi for cavalry officers worn by Capt. Julian G. Pratt of the 18th Virginia Cavalry. The elegant cap body of yellow wool (slightly faded) is bedecked with a gold lace quatrefoil on the crown and is finished off with a humble oilcloth visor. Pratt had three horses shot from underneath him at the third battle of Winchester, on September 19, 1864.* GARY HENDERSHOTT.

As part of the illustrious Laurel Brigade, the 7th Virginia Cavalry helped create the legend of invincibility that surrounded the cavalry of the Army of Northern Virginia during the first two years of the war. Although raised primarily in the Shenandoah Valley, the regiment also included a number of Maryland men who left their native state to fight for the Southern cause. The 7th Virginia's battle record was second to none, with Brandy Station, Gettysburg, Ream's Station, and Cedar Creek among the many engagements it was involved in, but its greatest claim to fame was the fact that it was commanded by the dashing and legendary Turner Ashby. Although Ashby commanded the 7th for only a short time before his promotion to brigadier and subsequent death in a rearguard action near Harrisonburg, Virginia, the regiment was often referred to as Ashby's Cavalry.

The uniform and equipment of the 7th Virginia was typical of the cavalry of the Army of Northern Virginia. By the later months of 1862, overcoats and other items of clothing, arms, and equipment of British origin were making their appearance in the ranks of the Confederate army. In addition, Confederate arms-making facilities had begun to approach their full potential. On March 13, 1863, the 7th received the first of a number of Confederate-made Robinson carbines that would be issued to them. These carbines, manufactured in Richmond, were direct copies of the renowned Sharps carbines and rifles, but they were plagued with problems and often had to be turned in for repair.

*Capt. Julian G. Pratt's frock coat is piped in yellow and has regulation rank insignia, but lacks the authorized solid yellow collar and cuffs. Plain officers' coats without facings were commonplace in the Confederate army.* GARY HENDERSHOTT.

# 2ND MISSOURI CAVALRY, MERRILL'S HORSE

It is doubtful that any volunteer cavalry regiment had a more competent commanding officer than the 2nd Missouri Cavalry did in Col. Lewis Merrill. He had been appointed to command by Gen. John C. Frémont and the regiment was dubbed Merrill's Horse. Merrill had been a captain in the 2nd U.S. Cavalry and had extensive experience on the prewar frontier. He knew well how to train a cavalry regiment and how to instill both pride and efficiency in his men. One method was to adopt a distinctive uniform, and to strictly enforce how it was worn and maintained.

The uniform included a jacket trimmed in the regulation yellow, but with a distinctive pattern on its paneled front, and a sky blue forage cap with an orange welt around the crown as a tribute to Merrill's service in the 2nd Dragoons. "All additions to or alterations of this uniform as prescribed are positively prohibited," Merrill ordered, "and will not be tolerated under any circumstances." Early armament of the regiment included an M1843 Hall carbine, an M1860 Colt army revolver, and an 1840-pattern saber.

The service of the 2nd Missouri was hard and dirty, and lacked the glory of the cavalry that served with the major armies east of the Mississippi River. The regiment spent most of its existence fighting guerrillas in Missouri and Arkansas. To the troopers' credit, they did it well. Merrill remained in command of the 2nd until the end of the war. He continued to serve in the U.S. Army until his retirement in 1886. A part of this service included the destruction of the Ku Klux Klan in various parts of the postwar South.

EARL J. COATES

*Medium blue forage cap worn by Pvt. Darius Seely of Company H, 2nd Missouri Cavalry, Merrill's Horse. Manufactured expressly for all the enlisted men of Merrill's command, this cap of officers'-quality materials has a distinguishing orange welt around the crown. Seely served throughout the war and prided himself on being a proficient forager and skirmisher.*

TROIANI COLLECTION.

# RANGER MOSBY

MICHAEL FLANAGAN

John Singleton Mosby and his command wrote a chapter in Civil War history that is as fascinating to historians today as it was to those young men who chose to follow him. Operating behind Union lines in Northern Virginia, he and his men employed tactics that caused much larger numbers of Federal troops to be diverted to protect vital supply lines.

Although small in stature, Mosby looked every inch the cavalier. Photographic records and published recollections never fail to show or mention the ostrich-plumed hat worn by Mosby and many of his command. Even when dressed in an officer's sack coat with a lieutenant colonel's rank on the lay-back collar, instead of the short double-breasted jacket he often wore, Mosby's bearing left no doubt as to his ability to command.

# TROOPER, 12TH VIRGINIA CAVALRY, 1864

PRIVATE COLLECTION

As part of the famed Laurel Brigade, the 12th Virginia Cavalry saw more than its share of war. The men who rode in the ranks of the regiment had been recruited in Virginia's Shenandoah Valley. For them, much of the war took on special meaning, as they were not only fighting for the Confederacy, but also defending the Valley, their home.

As with most Confederate regiments, the 12th received a variety of uniform pieces during the war. Although the general style of uniform remained constant, the material from which the various parts of the regimental garb were made varied greatly. As a result, the color and quality of the items were never consistent, as evidenced in the regimental personnel files. On June 6, 1864, Company F received "25 pairs of trousers of which 14 were gray, 7 light blue and 4 dark blue. Also received were 26 Jackets, 14 gray and 12 black."

*Privately purchased royal blue woolen trousers with wide yellow stripe, worn by Maj. Hugh Mortimer Nelson of the 6th Virginia Cavalry until his death in late 1862. The lower sections of the leg are sheathed in leather to protect the trouser bottoms against wear, a common practice for mounted troops.* TROIANI COLLECTION.

*Tall Confederate officer's forage cap, worn by Maj. Hugh Mortimer Nelson of the 6th Virginia Cavalry between 1861 and 1862. Maj. Gen. Thomas J. "Stonewall" Jackson wore a cap virtually identical to this one, complete with the civilian small brass flower buttons.* TROIANI COLLECTION.

Other companies received similar assortments. Also prevalent was a mixed issue of headgear, which on occasion included a few "military caps." And though it may seem strange, by far the largest issue of footwear was not boots, but shoes.

Ordnance returns in various officers' files show a wide variety of arms used by the regiment, with several different makes and calibers of both carbines and revolvers often used within the same company. The regimental ordnance return for March 31, 1863, lists ammunition received for Enfield rifles, Colt army and navy revolvers, Colt revolving rifles, Sharps, Robinson, Merrill, and Smiths carbines. Later, a number of English Kerr revolvers were added, as well as other arms that the fortunes of war brought their way.

# GEN. NATHAN BEDFORD FORREST

Confederate cavalry gained a solid reputation as an efficient and hard-fighting body in both the Eastern and Western Theaters of the war. In the West, such leaders as Gen. Nathan Bedford Forrest became famous for hard-hitting tactics that often led to victory over superior Union commands. From the beginning, the soldiers under Forrest's command were armed with a wide variety of sidearms, which included everything from shotguns to Colt revolvers. Uniforms also showed a wide diversity in style and color.

By mid-1863, Confederate clothing manufacture had reached a high degree of efficiency. Western commands such as Forrest's received much of their clothing from the facilities at Atlanta, Augusta, and Columbus, Georgia, as well as factories in such places as Montgomery, Alabama. Because these facilities received cloth from a number of diverse sources, uniforms were made in a variety of hues ranging from dark gray to shades of brown. Overcoats manufactured and supplied to Confederate forces were similar in cut to those worn by Union troops, but they generally had large, plain buttons in a variety of materials and colors. For the men who rode with Forrest, numerous encounters with their Federal opponents often supplemented the supply of uniforms they received from the South.

*Tan British Army–issue saddle blanket bearing a black, stenciled, "broad arrow" and "WD" (War Department) marking. Capt. Charles S. Hill, ordnance officer of Gen. Patrick Cleburne's division, wrote in December 1863, "I call to your attention the frequent application made on me by both Field and Staff officers of this Division for English saddle blankets & such necessities for officers. . . . I understand there is a large quantity at Atlanta."* TROIANI COLLECTION.

NATIONAL ARCHIVES, RECORD GROUP 109, M-331, COMPILED SERVICE RECORDS OF CONFEDERATE GENERAL AND STAFF OFFICERS.

GREENSBORO HISTORICAL MUSEUM

# ONE OF FORREST'S MEN, FIRST SERGEANT, RUCKER'S CAVALRY BRIGADE, JULY 1864

Gen. Nathan Beford Forrest was considered one of the finest cavalry generals to emerge from the war. His energy and spirit carried over to the men who rode and fought under his command. Forrest's men received uniforms from the various depots that supplied the Confederate Western armies. By 1864, most jackets produced in these depots no longer had the colored trim that indicated branch of service. Though many of these depots continued to supply forage caps, many, if not most, of the troopers preferred hats.

As with most Confederate cavalry, the arms carried by Rucker's Brigade included a mixed bag of muskets, rifles, carbines, and revolvers, though an inspection report for July 1864 shows that the brigade had no sabers. It was not uncommon for Confederate troopers to arm themselves with two revolvers.

There were many problems with the quality of saddles produced in Southern arsenals, and Yankee saddles of the McClellan pattern were prized items. A complaint from the ordnance officer of Wheeler's Cavalry Corps to the Atlanta Arsenal, referring to Confederate-made saddles, stated that "[t]he men in some cases refuse to take them, knowing that in most instances that they will last but a month or so and are certain to cause a sore back in a week or ten days." The sergeant shown here has reached beyond the normal Confederate supply system and recently acquired a new saddle compliments of Uncle Sam, complete with all the equipment of some hapless Union trooper.

ALEX DEQUESADA

*Small, silver star badge lost on the battlefield of Utoy Creek, Georgia, on August 6, 1864, by an unknown soldier from the 3rd Texas Cavalry of Gen. Sol Ross's Brigade. Star emblems were favored by many other states in addition to Texas, including Mississippi and North Carolina.* WILLIAM ERQUITT COLLECTION.

# 3RD NEW JERSEY CAVALRY, 1ST U.S. HUSSARS, 1864–65

Nicknamed the Butterflies because of their gaudy hussar-style uniforms, the 3rd New Jersey Volunteer Cavalry was not a bandbox regiment. The 3rd was recruited in the winter of 1863–64, and special permission was granted for the regiment's distinctive dress as a means of encouraging recruiting, even though it cost about $3 more per uniform than the regulation Federal-pattern cavalry uniform. At the regimental headquarters near Trenton, recruits poured in from January to March 1864, and by April, the regiment was completely equipped and mounted. It went immediately to Washington, where it joined the Army of the Potomac.

The Butterflies' uniform included a dark blue jacket with yellow cords across the breast and on the front of the orange collar, sky blue trousers with yellow stripes, a visorless cap that was worn tilted to the left, and a yellow-lined sky blue talma, or cloak. Although their colonel, Andrew Morrison, wanted only sabers, the regiment was armed initially with three types of breech-loading carbines and Whitney and Colt revolvers. In November 1864, the regiment received Spencer repeating carbines, which the men put to good use. The 3rd served in such major battles as Winchester, Cedar Creek, Five Forks, Saylor's Creek and Appomattox. Mustered out in June 1865, the regiment had lost fifty officers and men in combat.

PRIVATE COLLECTION

*The uniform jacket owned by this sergeant of the 11th New York Cavalry, Scott's 900, was privately purchased and made of officers'-quality broadcloth with many elegant niceties lacking in the standard-issue garment. When this regiment was originally formed in early 1862, it was issued dark blue trousers.* TROIANI COLLECTION.

# 4TH TENNESSEE CAVALRY, BLACK TROOPER, CHICKAMAUGA, SEPTEMBER 1863

By late 1863, the U.S. Army had realized the value and fighting potential of the black man. Throughout that year, numerous regiments of African-Americans had enlisted and seen action. For the Confederate army, however, it was not until the closing days of the conflict that the government formally sanctioned the enlistment of former slaves to fight for the South. Although numerous proposals were received from Confederate officers to organize black regiments, they all came too late. How many black men would have enlisted to fight for the South will always be a matter of speculation. That some would have willingly joined, however, is certain. From the beginning of the conflict, some had followed their masters into Confederate service as noncombatants in the same servile capacity they had fulfilled in civilian life.

As servants, the men remained behind the battle line and had ample opportunity to equip themselves with gear from casualties and prisoners. The result was that these men were often better equipped than the Confederate soldiers.

At the battle of Chickamauga, the servant of the regimental commander of the 4th Tennessee Cavalry proved that, like the man he served, he too was a leader of men. Having organized the other regimental servants into a "company" of about forty men, he demanded the right to follow the regiment into battle. First detailed to hold the horses of the white soldiers, the black company moved forward to the battle line and plunged into the fight along with the regiment, suffering four killed and seven wounded. The informal organization of this "company" of black Confederates left no record of their uniform, equipment, or arms.

WILLIAM GLADSTONE

The trooper shown here is largely outfitted with pieces of Union uniforms that had come his way during the months of campaigning with his master's regiment. A Union forage cap, Union mounted trousers, and boots taken from some unfortunate Federal trooper are worn along with a Confederate infantry jacket of the style worn by Kentucky's famed Orphan Brigade. The vest may have been given the trooper by the officer he served. The checked shirt is of a style issued in large quantity to the Army of Tennessee. He carries a Federal-issue infantry overcoat and wears Federal accoutrements that were found in abundance on many battlefields. His arms, a Colt navy revolver and a Sharps carbine, were recent finds.

# CHAPTER 5: THE CAVALRY


## INTRODUCTION

1. National Archives, Record Group 94, entry 44, Adjutant General's Office Orders and Circulars.
2. Ibid., Record Group 109, Compiled Service Records of Confederate General and Staff Officers, file of Capt. John Bradley.
3. Theophilus F. Rodenbough, comp., *From Everglade to Canon with the Second Dragoons* (New York: D. Van Nostrand, 1875).
4. National Archives, Record Group 92, entry 2182, War Department General Orders no. 13, November 13, 1858.
5. Ibid., Record Group 94, Regimental Books.
6. Ibid., Record Group 391, entry 821, Orders from August 1861 to February 23, 1863.
7. Ibid., Record Group 109, chapter 1, Adjutant and Inspector General, vol. 202.
8. Ibid., M-331, Compiled Service Records of Confederate General and Staff Officers.
9. Ibid., M-437, Letters Received by the Confederate Secretary of War.
10. Ibid., Record Group 393, entry 1449, Orders, 3rd Division Cavalry Corps, Army of the Potomac.
11. Ibid., Record Group 94, Regimental Order Books, 8th New York Cavalry.
12. Ibid., Record Group 109, M-324, Compiled Service Records of Confederate Soldiers from the State of Virginia, 1st Virginia Cavalry.
13. Ibid., 12th Virginia Cavalry.
14. Ibid.
15. Ibid., Record Group 94, Regimental Books, 9th New York Cavalry.
16. Frank Rauscher, *Music on the March, 1862–65: With the Army of the Potomac, 114th Regt. P. V. Collis Zouaves* (Philadelphia: Wm. F. Bell, 1892), 134.
17. National Archives, Record Group 109, M-437, Letters Received by the Confederate Secretary of War.
18. Ibid., Record Group 94, Regimental Books, 1st Pennsylvania Cavalry.
19. Ibid., Record Group 109, M-324, Compiled Service Records of Confederate Soldiers from the State of Virginia, 1st Virginia Cavalry.

## 2ND U.S. CAVALRY, BUGLER, 1861

Theophilus F. Rodenbough, *From Everglade to Canon with the Second Dragoons* (New York: D. Van Nostrand, 1875).

National Archives, Record Group 92, entry 2182, box 17, T. T. S. Laidley to Dept. Q.M. General Geo. H. Crosman, January 27, 1863.

## THE BOLIVAR TROOP, COMPANY A, 1ST BATTALION MISSISSIPPI CAVALRY

Frank Alexander Montgomery, *Reminiscences of a Mississippian in Peace and War* (Cincinnati: Robert Clarke Company, 1901), 39, 44.

J. C. Deupree, *The Noxubee Squadron of the First Mississippi Cavalry, C.S.A., 1861–1865,* Mississippi Historical Society Publications 2 (1899): 15.

*St. Louis Democract,* August 16, 1861.

"Orders of the Military Board," in *Southern Military Manual* (Jackson, Miss.: J. L. Power, 1861), 7, 9.

Photographs, Herb Peck Collection.

## 1ST NORTH CAROLINA CAVALRY, OCTOBER 1861

Frederick P. Todd, *American Military Equipage, 1851–1872* (n.p.: Chatham Square, 1983), 2: 1060.

National Archives, Record Group 109, M-270, Compiled Service Records of Confederate Soldiers Who Served in Organizations from the State of North Carolina, Records of 1st North Carolina Cavalry; files of Capt. George W. Folk; Ordnance Sgt. Wm. D. Anthony, and Col. William C. Cheek.

## MOUNTED RIFLE RANGERS, JANUARY 1862

Rev. James K. Ewer, *Third Massachusetts Cavalry, Company C,* Historical Commission of the Regimental Association, (Maplewood, Mass.: William G. J. Perry Press, 1903), 277–82.

*Boston Evening Journal,* December 31, 1861.

National Archives, Record Group 94, Regimental Papers, 3rd Massachusetts Cavalry.

## 1ST ARKANSAS MOUNTED RIFLES, PRIVATE, COMPANY D, 1861

James L. Nichols, *The Confederate Quartermaster in the Trans-Mississippi* (Austin: University of Texas, 1964).

National Archives, M-900, roll 1, Confederate Quartermaster General Letters and Telegrams Sent; Record Group 109, chap. 8, vol. 45.

Ron Field, *Brassey's History of Uniforms: American Civil War, Confederate Army* (Herndon, Va.: Brassey's, 1998), 82.

Steamboat *Arabia* Museum, Kansas City, Missouri.

National Archives, M-376, Compiled Service Records of Confederate Soldiers, Arkansas.

Peter A. Schmidt, *Hall's Military Breechloaders* (Lincoln, R.I.: Andrew Mowbray Publishers, 1996), 121.

**6TH PENNSYLVANIA CAVALRY, 1861–65**

Samuel P. Bates, *History of the Pennsylvania Volunteers* (Philadelphia, 1868), 741–753.

National Archives, Quartermaster Group, Clothing Series, Letter Book 18.

**8TH TEXAS CAVALRY, TERRY'S TEXAS RANGERS**

Frederick P. Todd, *American Military Equipage,* 1851–1872 (n.p.: Chatham Square, 1983), 2:1218.

Correspondence with Norm Flayderman, who has a similar 8th Texas shotgun in his collection.

National Archives, Record Group 109, M-323, Compiled Service Records of Confederate Soldier Who Served from the State of Texas, file of John A. Warton, Colonel 8th Texas Cavalry.

**BRANDY STATION REVIEW**

National Archives Record Group 109, Compiled Service Records of Various Confederate Cavalry Commands.

Diary of Lt. Louis R. Fortescue, attached to the U.S. Signal Corps, captured on the Confederate retreat from Gettysburg, War Library and Museum, Military Order of the Loyal Legion of the United States, copy in Brake Collection, U.S. Military History Institute.

**QUANTRILL'S GUERRILLAS**

William Elsey, *Quantrill and the Border Wars* (New York: Connelly Pageant Book Co., 1909), 215, 317, 318, 347, 362.

**TROOPER, 7TH VIRGINIA CAVALRY, 1863**

Richard L. Armstrong, *7th Virginia Cavalry,* Virginia Regimental History Series.

National Archives, Record Group 109, M-324, roll 177, Regimental Personnel files of the 7th Virginia Cavalry, file of Lieutenant Colonel Marshall.

John M. Murphy and Howard M. Madaus, *Confederate Rifles and Muskets* (Newport Beach, Calif.: Graphic Publishers, 1996).

**2ND MISSOURI CAVALRY, MERRILL'S HORSE**

Francis B. Heitman, *Historical Register and Dictionary of the United States Army* (Washington, D.C.: Government Printing Office, 1903).

National Archives, Record Group 94, Regimental Books, 2nd Missouri Cavalry, Personal Service Record, Lewis Merrill; Record Group 156, Quarterly Ordnance Returns.

**RANGER MOSBY**

National Historical Society, *The Image of War, 1861–1865* (Garden City, N.Y.: Doubleday & Co., 1983), 4:141–42.

**TROOPER, 12TH VIRGINIA CAVALRY, 1864**

National Archives, Record Group 109, M-324, Compiled Service Records of Confederate Soldiers Who Served in Organizations from the State of Virginia, Records of the 12th Virginia Cavalry.

**GEN. NATHAN BEDFORD FORREST**

National Archives, Record Group 109, M-935, Monthly Inspection Report, Wheeler's Cavalry Corps.

**ONE OF FORREST'S MEN, FIRST SERGEANT, RUCKER'S CAVALRY BRIGADE, JULY 1864**

National Archives, Record Group 109, M-935, Monthly Inspection Report, 6th Brigade, 1st Division, Wheeler's Cavalry Corps, June 1864; M-331, file of Lt. Col. Moses H. Wright, Ordnance Officer, Atlanta Arsenal; file of Capt. S. P. Kerr, Ordnance Officer, Wheeler's Corps, from Tunnel Hill, Georgia, April 20, 1864.

**3RD NEW JERSEY CAVALRY, 1ST U.S. HUSSARS, 1864–65**

Michael J. McAfee, "3rd Regiment New Jersey Volunteer Cavalry, 1864–65," *Military Images* 21, no. 4 (January–February 2000): 6–7.

John Elting and Roger Sturcke, "1st U.S. Hussar Regiment, 1864–1865," *Military Collector and Historian* 30, no. 1 (spring 1978): 13–16.

**4TH TENNESSEE CAVALRY, BLACK TROOPER, CHICKAMAUGA, SEPTEMBER 1863**

National Archives, Record Group 109, M-251, file of A. I. Peeler, Company I, 5th Florida Infantry; M-275, Records of General and Staff Officers and Nonregimental Enlisted Men, file of Capt. C. L. Moore.

Charles Kelly Barrow, J. H. Segars, and R. B. Rosenburg, *Forgotten Confederates: An Anthology About Black Southerners,* Journal of Confederate History Series, vol. 14 (Atlanta: Southern Heritage Press, 1996), in the *Hawkinsville Georgia Dispatch,* February 5, 1885.

# CHAPTER 6

# *The Artillery*

DURING THE CIVIL WAR, ARTILLERY PLAYED A SIGnificant role in every major battle. Unlike the other combat arms, however, artillery never acted alone. Placed in its proper perspective, artillery is an important, and potentially decisive, supporting arm for both infantry and cavalry. This fact was recognized by Antoine Henri Jomini in his classic work *The Art of War,* first published in 1838, which was widely studied by Civil War officers. Jomini stated that it was "not right to say that artillery can act independently of the other arms, for it is rather an accessory."[1]

For centuries, artillery has been divided into two distinct types, heavy and light. The designation was decided by the size of guns the artillery served, which determined the role it would play in any military action. In simplest terms, heavy guns were generally confined to fortifications, whereas light guns accompanied the army into the field. The light artillery could be mounted or on foot, depending on whether it was being used in support of infantry or cavalry.

Uniforms for both the Union and Confederate artillery were manufactured and issued in the same manner as those for the cavalry and infantry. In many cases, the uniform items issued depended on the type of service to be performed by the soldier. In the North, the major depots, located in Philadelphia, New York, Cincinnati, and St. Louis, procured or manufactured most of the uniforms for the artillery. Southern artillery uniforms were obtained from the various established depots scattered from Virginia to Texas. A look at the clothing worn by the cannoneers of both armies will show the differences that distinguished Yankee from Rebel, as well as the variations that set the artillery apart from the other branches of service.

## HEAVY ARTILLERY

### UNION

The heavy artillery served guns that were, in general, too large to be taken into the field. Because they were usually confined to fortifications, which potentially could be overrun by enemy infantry, heavy artillery soldiers spent a good deal of time drilling as infantry, preparing to fight the invaders on their own terms. The service required of these soldiers dictated that the uniform they wore be nearly identical to that of the infantry.

#### *Headgear*

Initially many heavy artillery enlisted men were from the Regular army and, as prescribed by army regulations, had received both the M1858 dress hat and the forage cap. As the system of earthwork forts was built to protect Washington and other cities liable to Confederate attack, large numbers of volunteers were pressed into service to man them. Many of these volunteers had enlisted to serve as infantry but now found their regiments converted to heavy artillery. These men, who made up the vast majority of the garrison at the numerous forts in general, received only the forage cap. The brass designating insignia issued for artillery consisted of crossed cannons, along with a company letter and regimental number. These were to be worn on the army dress hat, along with a red tassel and cord, a black ostrich plume, and a brass eagle device that looped up the left side of the brim. When only the cap was issued, the brass insignia was usually worn on top of the cap.

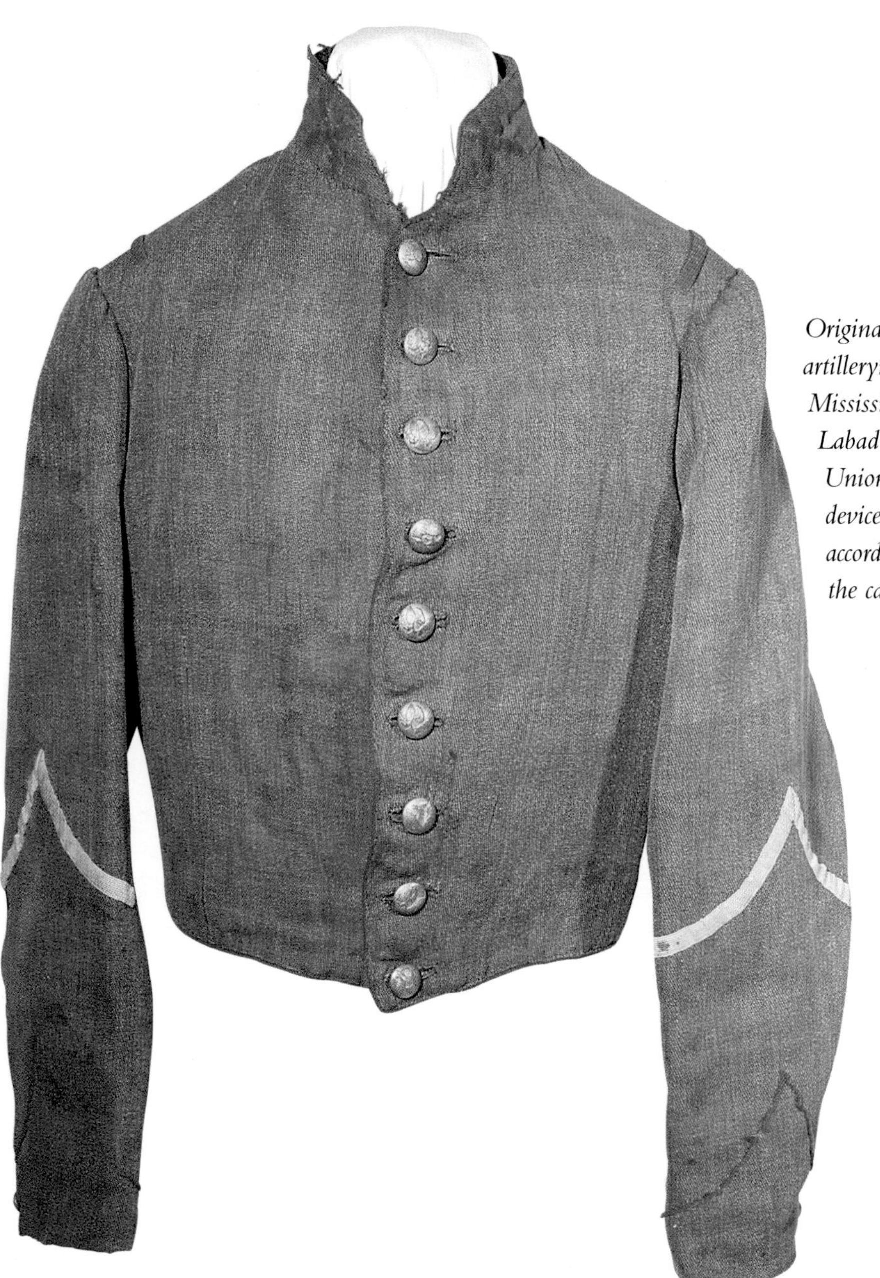

*Originally a dark blue-gray jean cloth, this Confederate artilleryman's jacket belonged to a soldier of Battery H, 1st Mississippi, and was recovered from the battlefield of Labadieville, Louisiana, on October 27, 1862, by a Union soldier. The collar displays red cutout cannon devices, and the sleeves have yellow silk chevrons, which according to Mississippi regulations signify prior service in the cavalry.* TROIANI COLLECTION.

*Federal officer's regulation hat insignia for artillery, with metallic embroidered crossed cannons with the unit number against a red center.* C. PAUL LOANE COLLECTION.

### *Coats and Blouses*

The dress coat for the heavy artillery was cut the same as that for the infantry and was identical except for the trim on the collar and cuffs, which was artillery scarlet. Most heavy artillerymen also received the same fatigue blouse worn by other army enlisted men.

### *Trousers*

Heavy artillery enlisted men wore the same trousers of sky blue kersey material issued to the infantry. The only difference was the color of the stripe, which designated a noncommissioned officer.

### *Shirts*

Shirts were standardized in the army, and no distinction was made as to branch of service.

### *Other Items*

During the time the men of the heavy artillery remained in garrison, life was measurably different than that of their comrades who served in the field with the light artillery or infantry. The personal belongings of a soldier of the 1st Maine Heavy Artillery who died on April 9, 1863, in the regimental hospital at Fort Alexander in the defenses of Washington, D.C., show a store of items that would be the envy of a combat soldier:[2]

| | | |
|---|---|---|
| 1 Colt revolver and case | 1 cap cover | 1 thimble |
| 1 bullet mold | 1 drinking tube | 1 neck tie |
| 1 powder flask | 1 knit jacket | 1 testament [Bible] |
| 1 box caps | 2 woolen blankets | 1 miniature [photograph] |
| 1 wrench | 1 knife and fork | 1 pair boots |
| 5 cartridges | 1 tin plate | 1 rubber blanket |
| 13 postage stamps | 6 steel pens | 1 pair slippers |
| 2 rings | 1 comb | 1 pair pants |
| 4 pocket handkerchiefs | 3 letters | 1 cap |
| 1 bunch letters | 3 papers | 1 dress coat |
| 1 writing case | 8 shirts | 1 over coat |
| 2 pen wipers | 2 pair drawers | |
| 9 skeins thread | 3 pair socks | |
| 2 bottles Jamaican Ginger | 2 towels | |
| 1 Nutty mixture | 1 paper of pins | |
| 1 pocket diary | 2 papers of needles | |

## CONFEDERATE

As with the Union, the Confederate soldier serving as heavy artillery received nearly the same uniform as the infantry. Jackets seem to have been a common item of issue, along with caps. When trimmed, all uniform items of Confederate artillery issue would have received the traditional artillery scarlet.

# LIGHT ARTILLERY

## UNION

The guns served by the light artillery were taken into battle pulled by a six-horse team harnessed in pairs. Artillerymen serving as drivers rode mounted on the left horse in each team to control the quick movement of the gun into battle position. A battery of Federal artillery usually consisted of six guns of the same type, as well as the caissons and wagons needed to support the guns. The gunners for the foot artillery marched with the guns or rode on the ammunition chests. The horse artillery required all cannoneers to be mounted, a necessity to follow the rapid pace set by the cavalry they were supporting. The uniform of both branches of the light artillery more closely resembled those of the cavalry.

### *Headgear*

Uniform regulations of 1861 called for the Federal light artillery soldier to be issued a cap with a scarlet horsehair plume, scarlet tassel and cord, and brass insignia that included an eagle and crossed cannons.[3] This cap closely resembled a shako, having a hard body that raised to $5\frac{3}{4}$ inches in front and $7\frac{3}{8}$ inches in the rear. It had a wide, stiff glazed visor, with the top, or crown, made of the same material. All in all, it was a handsome and very military-looking ensemble that was totally unsuitable for wear on anything but dress parade.

Some light artillery batteries were issued the M1858 army hat. Battery L, 2nd Illinois Light Artillery, received 140 "Artillery hats, complete" on April 5, 1862, with crossed cannons and an "L" and "2."[4] The battery is also listed with forage caps, but the hat apparently continued to be worn, as an order dated July 16, 1863, prohibited altering the shape of the hats.[5]

By far the most common headgear worn by the Federal light artillery was the M1858 forage cap, as shown in numerous requisitions and returns from volunteer batteries in every theater of the war, as well as numerous period photographs. An order issued to the light artillery at Camp Berry, Washington, D.C., on November 22, 1863, gave explicit instructions regarding the forage cap: "Hereafter every enlisted man of this post will wear the regulation forage cap, no caps of any other [type] will be worn by enlisted men either on or off duty, this order is not intended to prohibit noncommissioned officers from wearing caps of nicer material and manufacture provided they are of a pattern similar to the regulation Forage cap."[6]

### *Jackets and Blouses*

Light artillery enlisted men, both volunteers and Regulars, were issued both a fatigue blouse and a waist-length jacket with a high-standing collar. The jacket, with its scarlet trim and twelve-button front, was a handsome uniform worn with great pride by most cannoneers. The men of the 6th New York Independent Battery were among many who had the jacket altered to give a more tailored appearance, often having the collar lowered at the same time. One man from the battery was detailed by the commanding officer as "company tailor." An order dated January 10, 1864, set the rate to alter a jacket at 50 cents.[7]

The four-button fatigue blouse for light artillery was identical to that issued to the infantry. The records of the 13th New York show that during 1863, they received ninety-one jackets and sixty-six blouses to replace those worn out in service or to uniform new recruits.[8]

### *Trousers*

The light artillery received two types of trousers, both made of the regulation sky blue kersey material, due to the unique structure of the service that required both mounted and dismounted men. Cannoneers serving on foot received trousers that were identical to those received by the infantry. Mounted soldiers were issued trousers with an added layer of material in the seat and legs to compensate for the excessive wear caused by the saddle. A scarlet stripe designating a noncommissioned officer was worn as regulations dictated. An interesting order found in the records of Battery L, 1st Ohio Light Artillery, required all mounted men to "provide themselves with straps to hold down the legs of their trousers."[9]

### *Overcoats*

Mounted Union artillerymen received overcoats identical to those worn by the cavalry, and those issued to foot artillerymen were identical to those worn by the infantry.

### *Footwear*

Those serving in the light artillery received either boots, as issued to cavalry, or shoes, as received by the infantry, depending on whether they were mounted or dismounted.

### *Insignia and Accessories*

The prescribed insignia for artillery, dating from 1836, consisted of brass crossed cannons along with the regimental number and company (battery) letter, universally worn on the hat or cap.[10] Light artillery batteries, designated independent batteries and not assigned to an artillery regiment, would wear only the number of the battery. These items were standard issue provided by the Quartermaster Department, although soldiers sometimes purchased and wore more ornate insignia.

### *Corps Badges*

Beginning in the spring of 1863, the use of corps badges was mandated for all those serving within the ranks of the various army corps of the Army of the Potomac. Several corps within this army adopted a red, white, and blue variation of the prescribed badge for the headquarters staff. In several, this badge was authorized for the artillery attached to the corps, most notably within the I, III, and V Corps. Concerning the I Corps, Gen. Robert McAllister noted that "no special badge has been ordered for the artillery; but most of them have adopted the corps headquarters badge."[11]

The III Corps artillery's General Order No. 3, dated September 6, 1863, gave detailed drawings of a diamond-shaped badge to be worn by batteries attached to the three divisions of that corps. The badge was divided into four sections, each in the shape of a small diamond. Batteries assigned to the 1st Division had the upper and lower sections of red cloth, with the left section white and the right blue. The 2nd Division batteries wore the top and bottom sections white, with the left red and the right blue. The 3rd Division batteries had blue top and bottom sections, with the left red and the right white.[12]

At least two corps, the VI and the IX, simply ordered their artillery to wear the badge of that corps in scarlet or red. The order book of the 34th New York Independent Battery, which served with the IX Corps, contains an order dated April 10, 1864, calling for the use of the badge of that corps to be "worn on the top of the cap or front of the hat." Also acceptable was the use of a badge "of the same design, made of gold or gilt, silver or white metal, bronze or copper, to be attached to the left breast of the coat as a pin or suspended by a red, white and blue ribbon."[13] The following December 23, IX Corps General Order No. 49 in part restated the first order and, in addition, called for the men of the artillery brigade to wear the badge in red "under the regulation cross cannon."[14]

### *Shoulder Scales*

During the decade preceding the Civil War, brass shoulder scales had been issued to all mounted troops. These scales were worn in the same manner as cloth epaulets, becoming universal with all branches of the army in 1855. During the war, many were issued to volunteers, but they were seldom worn. The issue and wearing of the scales within some volunteer batteries of light artillery are well documented. An order issued to Independent Battery C, Pennsylvania Light Artillery, April 13, 1864, states in part, "Shoulder scales and caps will be worn in all parades and duties when the jacket is required." The 24th New York Independent Battery received similar orders on July 22, 1863: "At retreat every man will appear in dress jacket and scales."[15]

## CONFEDERATE

Confederate light artillery batteries were organized much the same as those in the Union army, with the exception that Confederate batteries often contained only four guns and frequently contained guns of mixed types. Unlike the Federal army, however, the Confederacy made no effort to provide a distinct style of uniform for the light artillery. It was only the color of the uniform trim, and in some cases that of the cap being worn, that set the artilleryman apart from the infantry-man or cavalryman.

### *Headgear*

The Confederate artillery enlisted man, like his comrades in the rest of the army, wore a variety of headgear. Hats were commonly issued with no description given, and the style was likely dependent upon what could be obtained at the time. Caps were issued in substantial quantity and in some cases were the most distinctive part of the Confederate artillery uniform. Regulations called for a cap with a red body, and such were indeed received and worn by some Confederate gunners. Examples exist that were worn by men in the 1st Battalion Virginia Light Artillery and Hart's South Carolina Battery.[16] On January 14, 1864, the Pee Dee Artillery of South Carolina received forty-five red caps. It is possible that these caps were a product of the Confederate quartermaster facility at Charleston, South Carolina.[17]

### *Jackets*

The Confederate light artillery received uniforms from the same facilities that provided uniforms for the rest of the army. The issue of jackets was universal throughout the war. Until the last year of the conflict, many of those manufactured in Southern depots were trimmed in red or scarlet in the fashion adopted by that facility. The jackets imported under the Tait contract in 1864 were not trimmed.

### *Trousers*

Confederate regulations called for the wearing of sky blue trousers by enlisted men, and it is likely that many were issued to the Confederate light artillery. It is equally likely that many were received courtesy of the Federal army via capture. As with the other branches of the Confederate army, the color and cloth of the trousers varied depending on availability, and gray or shades of brown were as likely to be part of any new issue received in the field. Unlike the Federal mounted soldiers, the Confederate artillerymen who rode into battle seldom, if ever, received trousers with the added layer of cloth reinforcement that was standard issue in the Union army.

### *Footwear*

More often than not, the Confederate artilleryman, whether mounted or dismounted, received army-issue shoes. As with other items, these were exactly the same as those received by the infantry, and they suffered the same variances in quality as those worn by the foot soldiers.

### *Insignia*

The Confederate Quartermaster Department made no issue of distinctive insignia, such as the crossed cannons commonly received by the Federal artillery. Chevrons and trouser stripes of scarlet were issued or fabricated in the field, and along with jacket trim, these served to distinguish the Confederate cannoneers.

### *Overcoats*

Confederate overcoats were manufactured or imported in quantity but do not appear to have been produced or issued in distinct patterns for mounted versus dismounted troops, as in the Federal army. Some were made without capes, which were always present on those issued to Federal soldiers. Federal overcoats were prized items to the Confederate soldiers and were often worn by them, sometimes with unfortunate results resulting from mistaken identification as Yankees.

# WASHINGTON ARTILLERY

In the decade prior to the outbreak of the war, the New Orleans newspapers carried numerous references to the city's premier and oldest militia organization, the Washington Artillery. Parades, rifle matches, and social functions seemed to be incomplete without members of the unit present. With their dark blue frock coats trimmed in artillery red, red kepis, white buff leather belts, and artillery sabers, the men of the Washington Artillery represented everyone's ideal of military men. Each man of the organization wore with pride the unique gold badge of the organization, crossed cannons surrounded by a belt with a gold tiger head suspended below. Upon the badge were engraved the words "Washington Artillery," along with a phrase that neatly summed up the spirit of the organization: "Try Us."

By 1861, the Washington Artillery was a battalion of four companies. On May 3, its commander, Maj. J. B. Walton, telegraphed the Confederate secretary of war stating that his battalion, numbering 300 men, was "ready and desirous to take the field." The service of the battalion was immediately accepted for the period of the war, and the men were ordered to report to Lynchburg, Virginia. From here they were ordered to Richmond and assigned to the Army of Northern Virginia. Shortly after the first battle at Manassas, the dress coats of the Washington Artillery were sent to Richmond to be used on "swell occasions," but the red kepis remained. During the next four years, the Yankees had ample opportunity to try the mettle of the men from New Orleans, which was never found wanting.

The Washington Artillery had the distinction of being represented in both theaters of the war. A fifth company was formed in New Orleans in February 1862. Rather than joining the rest of the battalion in Virginia, they made a name for themselves with the Army of Tennessee, seeing their first action at Shiloh on the morning of April 6, 1862.

DAVID RANKIN, JR.

*Artillery officer's frock coat worn by Lt. Col. William Richardson Hunt as commander of the Briarfield Mississippi Arsenal from 1862 to 1865. As typical of many Confederate officers' coats, this fine specimen is outfitted throughout with Federal staff officers' buttons.* GARY HENDERSHOTT.

*Lieutenant Colonel Hunt's trousers, with a 1-inch-wide red woolen stripe on each leg.* GARY HENDERSHOTT.

# McPHERSON'S RIDGE

Gettysburg, July 1, 1863: Two brigades of Union cavalry under the overall command of Brig. Gen. John Buford had taken position west and north of town and since early morning had been engaged with advancing Confederate infantry. Among the first to arrive to support the hard-pressed troopers was Lt. John Calef's Battery A, 2nd U.S. Artillery. The battery of six 3-inch rifle guns was met as it came onto the field by General Buford himself, dressed in an officer's sack coat and accompanied by a lone cavalry bugler. The general immediately ordered Calef to place his guns on either side of the Chambersburg Pike near the McPherson barn. Without hesitation, the battery moved forward, unlimbered, and went immediately into action.

The men of Calef's Battery, most of them proudly wearing the red-trimmed jackets of the Federal light artillery, were a familiar and welcome sight to the cavalrymen. The battery was entirely mounted and thus was able to accompany the fast-moving cavalry, giving them the extra firepower they needed. That firepower, added to the fast-firing carbines of the cavalry, enabled the troopers to hold this critical line until the Federal infantry of the I and XI Corps were able to relieve them.

*Forage cap worn by Irish cannoneer Daniel P. Doyle of the 9th Massachusetts Battery between May 1864 and June 1865, when his unit served with the Reserve Artillery Brigade of the V Army Corps. The tricolored corps badge is unusual in that Doyle painted it directly on the crown of the cap.* TROIANI COLLECTION.

*Sky blue trousers with reinforced seat, worn at Gettysburg by Lt. Edward N. Whittier of the 5th Maine Battery. The legs are taped for wear inside boots and fastened at the ankle with hard, black rubber buttons. They are piped in red cording for artillery, as per regulation.* TROIANI COLLECTION.

PRIVATE COLLECTION

# THE WATSON FLYING BATTERY, NEW ORLEANS, LOUISIANA, 1861

A New Orleans newspaper in July 1861 reported that the new Watson Flying Artillery was to be the finest company that has yet entered the field of Mars! Organized and equipped at an estimated cost of $40,000 to $60,000, the battery was raised and paid for by Augustus C. Watson, a wealthy planter and gambler from Tensas Parish, Louisiana. In its ranks were said to be the finest representatives of the old Creole families of New Orleans. Referred to as "men of wealth and high standings," they were proud to be garbed in the "resplendent uniforms" of Watson's Battery.

DAVID RANKIN, JR.

The battery's first captain was Allen Bursly, a West Point graduate touted in the papers as an experienced army officer. Bursly's first lieutenant, A. G. Gage, saw action during the Mexican War at the battle of Monterey. In a masterful coup, Watson was able to persuade Maj. Daniel Beltzhoover, chief of staff to General Twigg's Department of Alabama, Mississippi, and East Louisiana, to accept the position of battery commander. Beltzhoover was a West Point graduate as well, having served in the 1st Regiment of U.S. Artillery from 1847 to 1855. He also may have been attracted to the mystique of this rich man's company that was said to be "destined to attain a great celebrity in our [the Confederate] Army."

By the end of July 1861, the Watson Battery was complete. Four 6-pound bronze guns and two 12-pound howitzers mounted on "splendid gun carriages," with caissons and full appointments, were ready, cast and built in New Orleans by Edmund J. Ivers. Two hundred white horses, "the finest suited to the work in the State of Louisiana," would pull the guns.

At 4:00 P.M., on August 13, 1861, the men of the Watson Flying Artillery assembled in Lafayette Square. They were marched to the steamboat landing for the trip upriver to Augustus Watson's plantation. Their uniforms, equipment, horses, and guns would follow.

A very handsome uniform was chosen, with a nine-button shell jacket of steel gray, faced and piped in red crimson. The jacket sleeves sported a French cuff, piped in yellow and adorned with eight ball buttons. The trousers were steel gray as well, with a red crimson stripe. The matching cap had a red cord, crossed cannons, and the brass letters "WB." The letters were purchased by battery members in honor of their founder, Augustus Watson. The black leather belt had a two-piece buckle bearing the Louisiana pelican state seal.

Equipped and staffed as it was, Watson's Flying Artillery should have had an envious record in the Civil War. Instead, the battery was destroyed not by Federal fire, but through internal dissension. Augustus Watson, in a patriotic gesture, enlisted in the company as a private, but to many he was a private in name only. The blue bloods of New Orleans felt

*Bloodstained coat worn by Pvt. James Wiley Gibson, 1st South Carolina Artillery, when shot through the chest by a sniper while working on fortifications at Secessionville, South Carolina, on June 16, 1862. This plain seven-button frock coat was believed to be an example contracted by the state from Porter's Industrial School for Girls in Charleston. The piping was probably originally red.*
COLLECTION OF THE CHARLESTON (SOUTH CAROLINA) MUSEUM.

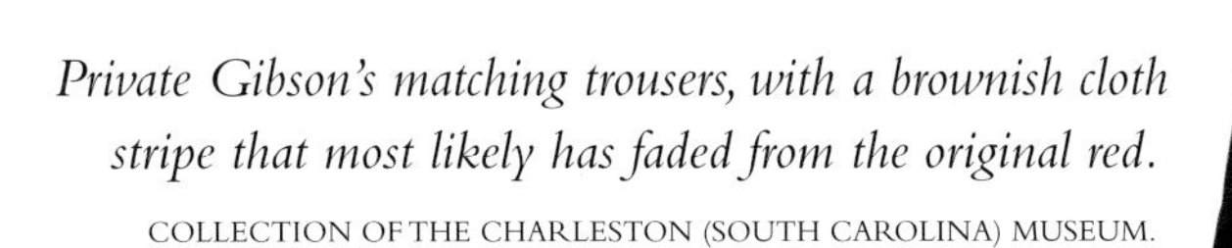

*Private Gibson's matching trousers, with a brownish cloth stripe that most likely has faded from the original red.*
COLLECTION OF THE CHARLESTON (SOUTH CAROLINA) MUSEUM.

that Beltzhoover drilled them too hard and seemed "rough and unfeeling." Arriving in Memphis on September 18, then ordered to Columbus, Kentucky, as part of the garrison, the Watson Battery began to break up. It was said that some members resigned to join the Louisiana Point Coupee Battery. A petition asking to be released from the battery and allowed to join some other unit was signed by forty of the men and sent to General Polk. With the situation unresolved, many of the men tore the "W" off their caps in protest of their dismal situation.

To make matters worse, in their first test under fire at the battle of Belmont, Missouri, on November 7, 1861, the entire battery of six guns was abandoned to the advancing Federals under U. S. Grant. Two of the guns were taken back to Cairo as trophies of war. Most of the battery horses were lost, forty-five killed outright in the battle, and all of the men's personal gear and tents were burned.

The battery continued to serve through the war until it was surrendered at Port Hudson, Louisiana, on July 9, 1863. This battery, once said to be destined for "celebrity in our Army," destroyed once at the battle of Belmont and again at the battle of Corinth, Mississippi, on October 3–4, 1862, left little in the way of records or documents to pass along their history. They were no doubt brave men, and in their "resplendent uniforms," they did indeed ride white horses into the halls of history.

# 2nd Connecticut Heavy Artillery, 1864

WARREN TICE

The 2nd Connecticut Heavy Artillery shared a similar history and fate with several other regiments of heavy artillery that garrisoned the defenses of Washington in 1863 and early 1864. All of these regiments had been recruited as infantry, but upon reaching the nation's capital, helped build and then garrison the extensive system of earthwork forts that defended the city. Although the duty they were called upon to perform kept them out of harm's way, the constant drill as infantry as well as on the heavy guns mounted in the forts never let them forget they were soldiers.

Many of the 2nd Connecticut felt likely disappointment when they read of the battles and exploits of other regiments from their state. Had they been able to foresee the future, however, those who felt cheated serving as garrison soldiers perhaps would have had an appreciation for that mundane duty. As the summer campaign of 1864 began, the 2nd Connecticut and other garrison regiments were sent from the forts they occupied into the field, not as artillery but as infantry. Within the next year, most of these regiments more than made up for the months they spent in comparative security. The heavy artillery regiments wound up with more killed and mortally wounded in battle than any of the hundreds of infantry regiments that served in the campaigns of 1861–65. The 2nd Connecticut alone mustered out in August 1865 with a total of 12 officers and 242 men on its roll of honored dead.

The 2nd Connecticut had been originally raised as that state's 19th Infantry. It retained that regimental number until November 1863, when it officially became the 2nd Heavy Artillery. The change in designation also called for a change in uniform. Regimental Order No. 1, January 1, 1864, directed that all uniform jackets and hats be turned over to the regimental quartermaster, who would issue caps and dress coats. The order further stated that "no men . . . will be allowed to wear a hat of any kind."

Many of the troops in the Washington defenses received Enfield rifle muskets. While some turned them in and received Springfields before leaving the city, men of the 2nd Connecticut retained theirs. They would put them to good use in action from Spotsylvania to Appomattox as part of the famous VI Army Corps.

*Note the exceptionally elegant tailoring and snug waistline. After serving with the 5th New York Volunteers, Duryée's Zouaves, and having been wounded at Gaines' Mill, Capt. Ralph E. Prime was commissioned lieutenant colonel of the 6th New York Heavy Artillery.* TROIANI COLLECTION.

# BATTERY LONGSTREET, BATTLE OF ANTIETAM, SEPTEMBER 17, 1862

DICK AND M. E. CLOW

For hours that must have seemed like an eternity, the Army of Northern Virginia held its own under relentless pounding by a Federal army determined to drive it from the field and back into Virginia. Casualties mounted by the minute on all quarters. Capt. M. B. Miller's 3rd Company of the famed Washington Artillery Battalion had sustained losses from Union sharpshooters, leaving him without enough cannoneers to serve all the guns in his battery.

Fully aware of the desperate conditions, Gen. James Longstreet seized the moment. Dismounting his staff to man one of Miller's Napoleon guns, and personally directing the fire, the Confederates fired double charges of case shot and canister into the ranks of Maj. Gen. Israel B. Richardson's Union Division, mortally wounding Richardson and seriously wounding Col. Francis Barlow, who commanded his right column. With their commanders down, the Federal attacks in this sector of the field slackened. The battle continued for several hours. For the Confederates, the timely arrival of reinforcements under Gen. A. P. Hill saved the day. Nowhere can the determination of the Confederates be better illustrated than here, with staff officers in full uniform manning guns to help fight a numerically superior Federal army to a standstill.

*Richmond Depot type uniform jacket, worn by Lt. Daniel O. Merwin of Moody's Louisiana Battery when his right arm was shattered in a counterbattery duel at Garnett's Farm, Virginia, on June 28, 1862. This plain jacket has red piping and a gold cord rank bar on the collar. Surviving his wounds, Merwin was promoted to major and served at the camp of instruction at Enterprise, Mississippi, in 1863.*
CONFEDERATE MEMORIAL HALL, CLAUDE LEVET PHOTOGRAPH.

*Confederate artillery officer's jean cloth sack coat with matching vest, both with red piped trim. This type of garment, with loose, easy fit and outside pockets, was favored by officers of both sides during the conflict. Some examples had branch service trimming of the appropriate color, while many had none at all.* CONFEDERATE MEMORIAL HALL, CLAUDE LEVET PHOTOGRAPH.

# 1ST COMPANY, RICHMOND HOWITZERS, 1863

VALMORE FORGETT

One of the better-known batteries of artillery to serve the Confederacy from the state of Virginia was the 1st Company of Richmond Howitzers. The company had its origin in 1859, and it was first called out in response to the perceived threat to the state following the John Brown raid on Harpers Ferry. At this time, the unit had been hastily equipped for the emergency and armed with muskets, with little in the way of uniform dress. As war clouds gathered, the company began a serious regimen of drill and ordered gray uniforms made. By the time it joined the Confederate army at Manassas, it had come a long way. Two other companies of Richmond Howitzers were formed in May 1861, but the three never served together.

The corporal shown here leaning against one of the battery's howitzers is wearing the uniform that was typical of the Army of Northern Virginia in 1863. His jacket, which is piped in artillery red, is the second pattern produced by the Richmond Quartermaster Depot. His headgear is a cap, also trimmed in red for artillery. His boots are of fine quality and may have been of English origin, as is the belt visible under his jacket. The overcoat draped over the gun barrel came to him courtesy of the Yankees.

# 8th U.S. Colored Heavy Artillery, Private, Company K, 3rd Battalion, Late Summer 1864

WILLIAM GLADSTONE

This regiment was raised in Rhode Island during the last six months of 1863 as the 14th Rhode Island Heavy Artillery. Their designation was changed to the 8th U.S. on April 4, 1864, and to the 11th U.S. Colored Heavy Artillery in May of the same year. They continued to be carried on army rolls as the 8th Regiment until the fall, however.

Unlike many other colored regiments, the ranks of the 8th contained mostly men who had never known the yoke of slavery. Nearly all had been brought up free in their native state. An inspection report dated August 10, 1864, commented on the superior nature of the regiment and made special note of the fact that "the men are almost all free, and not freed men." It also noted that the majority of the regiment could read and write, and that the men were usually well informed. For such men to go and fight in the South took a special courage, as capture left open the possibility of a permanent loss of freedom.

Though it was heavy artillery, this regiment received the uniform jacket of the light artillery. As was the regulation with all regiments of heavy artillery, they received the arms and accoutrements of infantry. During the period before and after the Civil War, heavy artillery regiments drilled both on the large guns mounted in the various forts and as infantry.

The regiment was divided by battalions, with the 3rd Battalion serving its entire enlistment in the defenses of New Orleans. They were mustered out on October 2, 1865.

*Federal artillery musician's uniform jacket, with a metallic gold thread edging in addition to the worsted regulation red piping. The original owner, William Henry Lewis of Battery G, 1st Rhode Island Light Artillery, undoubtedly felt the need for further ornamentation. An unexpected benefit of wearing a musician's heavily adorned jacket was articulated upon in a letter Lewis penned in June [1863?]: "I have got as pretty a Southeron damsel as ever you saw I went to here hous last night & had a good time there was a fiddel & other music I till you the read tape on my jacket draws gals rite to me." Bugler Lewis was mortally wounded at the battle of Cedar Creek, Virginia, in October 1864 and died shortly thereafter.* COURTESY OF PAMPLIN HISTORICAL PARK AND THE NATIONAL MUSEUM OF THE CIVIL WAR SOLDIER.

WILLIAM HENRY LEWIS, UNPUBLISHED MANUSCRIPT, PAMPLIN PARK HISTORICAL PARK AND THE NATIONAL MUSEUM OF THE CIVIL WAR SOLDIER COLLECTION.

*Uniform jacket of a New York artillery corporal. With a practical eye toward their own comfort, soldiers often modified regulation garments by lowering the collars and making various other changes. In many units, the officers turned a blind eye to such minor infractions, as this corporal's battery commander obviously did. Documents show instances where tailors were hired to customize jackets for entire units.* TROIANI COLLECTION.

# CRUTCHFIELD'S VIRGINIA, HEAVY ARTILLERY BATTALION

Like their counterparts in the Federal army, the Confederate soldiers who manned the heavy artillery batteries protecting their nation's capital spent most of their time drilling both as infantry and artillery. Serving in relative comfort, the heavy artillerymen perfected the skills of the soldier and waited. These men were described in glowing terms by Robert Stiles, who would later command them: "They were splendid soldiers in external appearance and bearing. I had never seen anything approximating to them in the field. Their dress parades, inspections, reports, salutes, bearing in the presence of officers and on guard, were wonderfully regular, accurate and according to the drill and regulations."

The true test of their soldiering ability did not come, however, until the final days of the war. With the collapse of the Petersburg line and the imminent evacuation of Richmond in April 1865, the heavy artillerymen under the command of Col. Stapleton Crutchfield spiked and abandoned their guns, and on April 2, they joined the retreating Confederate army. The men were now low on most supplies and were in light marching order. Many of the men were wearing Federal overcoats, which had served them well on duty in the defensive batteries. Now it was different. Maj. Robert Stiles warned them that in battle, the use of these coats could be dangerous. Despite this many opted for comfort over safety, with tragic results. At Sayler's Creek, Crutchfield's Brigade took up positions on the left of the Confederate line. In heavy fighting, Crutchfield was killed, and several of the men fell victim to fire from others in the brigade who, seeing the blue Yankee coats, mistook them for the enemy.

PRIVATE COLLECTION

*Rough gray wool enlisted man's frock coat, worn in the later part of the war by Sgt. Maj. Edward D. Robinson of Manly's Battalion, South Carolina Artillery. Dressed out with U.S. eagle buttons, it shows evidence of a sergeant major's chevrons (now missing) from Robinson's appointment to that rank in August 1864. This coat is similar to that described in the Confederate States' regulations for enlisted men.* COLLECTION OF THE CHARLESTON (SOUTH CAROLINA) MUSEUM.

*Regulation Federal-issue drum for artillery regiments. This example was made by C. & F. Soistman in Philadelphia, who in July 1864 had a contract for 100 three-quarter-size and 200 full-size artillery drums.*

TROIANI COLLECTION.

E. J. COATES AND F. C. GAEDE, COMP., "U.S. ARMY QUARTERMASTER CONTRACTS, 1861–1865" (UNPUBLISHED MANUSCRIPT, 1993), 267.

# CORPORAL, 4TH NEW JERSEY LIGHT ARTILLERY, DECEMBER 1864

TIM OSTERHELD

During the Civil War, U.S. Army uniforms were issued in only four sizes. This had been true before the conflict and would remain so for years afterward. Within the Regular army it was common practice for soldiers who took pride in their appearance to have the garments altered to create a more custom, tailored fit. During the war the practice was emulated by many serving as Volunteers. In some cases the practice resulted in condemnation by those in command. In others, however, it was condoned, with company or regimental tailors being designated to accommodate those wishing to enhance their military appearance. A few officers took personal pride in their units a step further by ordering certain changes in the uniforms. One of these was the captain of the 4th New Jersey Light Artillery Battery, George T. Woodbury.

The battery was organized at Trenton, New Jersey, and mustered on September 16, 1863. In February 1864 the following circular was issued to the Battery:

> 4th New Jersey Battery Camp Berry, D.C.
> February 26, 1864
> circular: The Captain Commanding has procured for the enlisted men red flannel linings for overcoats capes, at the price of $1.30 a piece. They will be put in by the Company tailor and the cost deducted from the pay of the men next pay day. The material is the same as that in the original coat furnished the Battery before leaving the state, having been procured from the firm who made the Company uniforms.
> George T. Woodbury
> 4th N. J. Battery

Two months later Captain Woodbury's strict attention to detail within his command was further evidenced by his General Orders No. 1 issued at Gloucester Point, Virginia, on April 26 following the battery's assignment to the X Corps.

> The enlisted men of this command will immediately reduce their clothing to the following allowance; viz. 2 forage caps, 2 Artillery jackets, 2 pairs trousers, 2 pairs shoes or boots, 2 shirts, 2 pairs of drawers, 3 pairs of stockings, 1 blanket, 1 overcoat and 1 rubber blanket or gum overcoat. All clothing in excess of this allowance will be immediately packed, plainly marked and turned over to the QM Sgt.

Captain Woodbury resigned due to disability, and was succeeded by 1st Lt. Charles R. Doane. When corps badges were issued to the X Corps lieutenant (now captain) Doane, he maintained the exacting tradition set by his predecessor. On October 31, 1864, he issued General Order No. 17, which allowed no room for deviation.

> Corps Badges will be furnished on application to the QM Sgt. and every enlisted man is required to provide himself at once. The figure 4 will be placed below the cross cannon [ on the cap ] and the badge above with one of its points upwards and the opposite end directed toward the centre of the cross cannon. Care will be taken that the points are well stitched down.

The 4th New Jersey Battery was certainly one of the finest dressed of any group of cannoneers outside the Regular army. The unique scarlet-lined capes on their greatcoats predated the issue of such coats by the U.S. Army by at least fifteen years.

# CHAPTER 6: THE ARTILLERY

### INTRODUCTION

1. Baron de Jomini, *The Art of War* (1838; reprint, Philadelphia: J. B. Lippincott, 1862).
2. National Archives, Record Group 94, Regimental Books, 1st Maine Heavy Artillery.
3. *Revised Regulations for the Army of the United States, 1861* (Philadelphia: George W. Childs, 1862).
4. Ibid., Battery L, 2nd Illinois Light Artillery.
5. Ibid.
6. Ibid., 1st Ohio Light Artillery.
7. Ibid., 6th New York Independent Battery.
8. Ibid., 13th New York Independent Battery.
9. Ibid., 1st Ohio Light Artillery.
10. Frederick P. Todd, *American Military Equipage, 1851–1872,* vol. 1 (Providence: Company of Military Historians, 1974).
11. James I. Robertson, Jr., ed., *The Civil War Letters of General Robert McAllister* (New Brunswick, N.J.: Rutgers University Press, 1965).
12. National Archives, Record Group 393, entry 214, III Corps Artillery Brigade Inventory and Inspection Reports.
13. Ibid., Record Group 94, Regimental Order Book, 34th New York Independent Battery.
14. *The War of the Rebellion: The Official Records of the Union and Confederate Armies,* vol. 42, (Washington, D.C.: Government Printing Office, 1901), part 3, 1066.
15. National Archives, Record Group 94, Regimental Order Book, 34th New York Independent Battery.
16. Editors of Time-Life Books, *Echoes of Glory* (Alexandria, Va.: Time-Life, 1991), Confederate vol., 163.
17. National Archives, Record Group 109, M-267, Compiled Service Records of Confederate Soldiers Who Served in Organizations from the State of South Carolina, Capt. Zimmerman's Company, Pee Dee Artillery.

### WASHINGTON ARTILLERY

William Miller Owen, *In Camp and Battle with the Washington Artillery of New Orleans* (Boston: Ticknor, 1885), 49.

National Archives, Record Group 109, M-437, Letters Received by the Confederate States Secretary of War.

### MCPHERSON'S RIDGE

*The War of the Rebellion, Official Records of the Union and Confederate Armies,* vol. 27 (Washington, D.C.: Government Printing Office, 1901) part 1, 1030.

Michael J. Winey, *Union Army Uniforms at Gettysburg* (Gettysburg, Pa.: Thomas Publications, 1998), 19–20.

### THE WATSON FLYING BATTERY, NEW ORLEANS, LOUISIANA, 1861

*New Orleans Daily Picayune,* June 20 and August 12, 1861.

### 2ND CONNECTICUT HEAVY ARTILLERY, 1864

Frederick H. Dyer, *A Compendium of the War of the Rebellion* (New York: Thomas Yoseloff, 1959), 3:1007.

National Archives, Record Group 94, Regimental Papers, 2nd Connecticut Heavy Artillery.

### BATTERY LONGSTREET, BATTLE OF ANTIETAM, SEPTEMBER 17, 1862

Stephen W. Sears, *Landscape Turned Red* (New York: Ticknor and Fields, 1983), 251.

### 1ST COMPANY, RICHMOND HOWITZERS, 1863

Lee A. Walker, Jr., *The Richmond Howitzers* (Lynchburg, Va.: H. E. Howard, 1993).

Editors of Time-Life Books, *Echoes of Glory* (Alexandria, Va.: Time-Life, 1991), Confederate vol., 135.

### 8TH U.S. COLORED HEAVY ARTILLERY, PRIVATE, COMPANY K, 3RD BATTALION, LATE SUMMER 1864

National Archives, Record Group 94, Regimental Books, 8th U.S. Colored Heavy Artillery.

Frederick H. Dyer, *A Compendium of the War of the Rebellion,* (New York: Thomas Yoseloff, 1959), 1722.

### CRUTCHFIELD'S VIRGINIA, HEAVY ARTILLERY BATTALION

Robert Stiles, *Four Years under Marse Robert* (New York: Neale Publishing Co., 1910), 333.

### CORPORAL, 4TH NEW JERSEY LIGHT ARTILLERY, DECEMBER 1864

Frederick H. Dyer, *A Compendium of the War of the Rebellion* (New York: Thomas Yoseloff, 1959), 3:1355.

National Archives, Record Group 94, Regimental Books New Jersey Light Artillery Batteries.

## CHAPTER 7

# *Special Branches and General Officers*

THE HISTORIES OF THE GREAT ARMIES OF THE CIVIL War that maneuvered and fought for four bloody years rarely mention the multitude of support personnel without whose efforts no victory would have been possible. In the U.S. Army in 1861, these included the Adjutant General's, Judge Advocate's, Inspector General's, Quartermaster, Subsistence, Pay, and Ordnance departments; Engineers and Topographical Engineers corps; and the chief signal officer. The Confederate army, as established in 1861, included the Adjutant and Inspector General's, Quartermaster, Commissary General's, and Medical departments. Also established were two bureaus, Ordnance and Signal, as well as a Corps of Engineers. To a great extent, the officers and men of the staff departments and corps were some of the most dedicated and professional soldiers to serve either the Union or the Confederacy. So, too, were the men who marched with the army as pioneers; filled a vital role as signalmen; or, in the case of the Federal army, served in the Veteran Reserve Corps. It is true that in every service there were those who failed to fulfill their duties due to incompetence, intemperance, or dishonesty. It is a sad fact that these few men were often the ones who received the most attention in postwar writing. Confederate general Thomas Neville Waul, in an undated wartime report on the organization and administration of the special branches within the Confederate Army, summarized the service of the vast majority of these soldiers in a tribute that could apply as well to their counterparts in the Federal army. "The labors of these Departments penetrate the entire military establishment, breathe life into the army, nurture its growth, give it strength and efficiency in the field, maintaining its health, and facilitating its movements; vigilant, prepared and present, it moves unnoticed amid the stirring events of the field, and obscured by the dust and smoke of combat it remains unobserved even while collecting the fruits of victory."[1]

The uniforms of the special branches, both officers and enlisted men, were the same as those worn by the combat soldiers they supported. As a general rule, only the color of the trim and/or insignia set them apart. The exception was the Federal Veteran Reserve Corps, whose enlisted men wore a jacket made of the same sky blue material as the standard-issue trousers. Some members of the Veteran Reserves also received black cavalry greatcoats.[2] Rarely seen is the prescribed uniform for officers of the Veteran Reserves. Regulations called for them to wear a sky blue frock coat, with dark blue velvet collar and cuffs, and sky blue trousers with two

*Embroidered officer's hat badge of the Signal Corps, worn by Pvt. Henry R. Congdon. With no regulation enlisted man's device authorized, Private Congdon obtained an officer's badge to wear on his cap.* TROIANI COLLECTION.

*Regulation U.S. red morocco belt with three embossed gilt stripes, worn by Maj. Gen. Amos B. Eaton, commander of the Subsistence Department during the war.* TROIANI COLLECTION.

*An unusual Louisiana red morocco leather officer's belt with interlocking state seal buckle. Of particularly high quality, this belt features a snake device sword hook to carry the sword against the hip when walking on foot.* MUSEUM OF CONNECTICUT HISTORY.

$^1/_2$-inch dark blue stripes.[3] It is evident from the lack of surviving examples and contemporary photographs that this regulation was not at all popular and was often ignored in favor of the standard dark blue frock coat.

The organization of the U.S. Army in 1861 made allowance for enlisted men in only the Medical Department, the Corps of Engineers, the Corps of Topographical Engineers, and the Ordnance Department. The other special branches were composed of officers only.[4] These officers wore the same regulation uniforms as officers of the other branches of the army, with the exception of appropriate insignia on the hat and a dark blue background on the shoulder strap. For full dress occasions, they wore epaulets that included, along with the insignia of rank, an additional device that indicated the corps or department in which they served.[5]

Confederate regulations of 1861 dictated that the uniforms of general officers, as well as officers of the Adjutant General's, Quartermaster, and Commissary General's Departments, and corps of engineers, have buff facings on the collars and cuffs, and that medical officers' uniforms be trimmed with black.[6] All of these officers were to wear dark blue trousers and caps.[7] As with most Confederate officers' uniforms, these regulations were not always strictly adhered to. Confederate enlisted men assigned to the various staff departments were generally detached from various combat regiments and always continued to wear the uniform of their original service. With Confederate uniforms, particularly those worn by persons in high command, while regulations set a standard, reality was often something quite different. The dictates of availability and of personal taste often superseded everything else.

Within both the Union and Confederate armies, the expanded duties brought on by the war meant a rapid expansion of all special branches. The need for rapid communications in the field brought hundreds of officers and enlisted men into the Signal Corps. Although not strictly a separate branch, the development of organized pioneers at various levels of command served to set these men apart from their comrades in the infantry or cavalry. Both signalmen and pioneers were usually detached from line combat regiments and wore regulation army uniforms distinguished only by sleeve insignia indicative of their special skills. The 1864 quartermaster's manual described the pioneer insignia as two crossed hatchets of cloth the same color as the trim of the uniform, to be worn on each arm above the elbow. Each hatchet was 5$^1/_2$ inches long, with the blade 2 inches long. A corporal was to wear the crossed hatchets above and resting on the chevron. By 1864, signalmen had been authorized to wear embroidered signal flags on each sleeve in a manner similar to the hatchets of the pioneers. Hospital stewards also wore distinctive sleeve insignia: a 1$^3/_4$-inch-wide half chevron of emerald green cloth, to be worn on the sleeve angled down, with an embroidered caduceus of yellow silk 2 inches long in the center.

Within the special branches of both the Union and Confederate armies, a multitude of civilian employees served in the offices in the capital cities and at the various depots. These men and women dealt with the mountains of paperwork necessary to keep armies in the field, although the men constituted a reserve pool of potential combat soldiers that could be used in an emergency. On May 30, 1863, Maj.

*Pair of embroidered shoulder straps owned by Col. John Wilson of the 43rd New York Volunteers at the time of his death in the battle of the Wilderness on May 6, 1864. This set is still with the original pasteboard box bearing the label of Tiffany & Co., one of the ultimate military outfitters of the day.* COLLECTION OF NEW YORK STATE DIVISION OF MILITARY AND NAVAL AFFAIRS.

William S. Downer, superintendent of armories in Richmond, received an order from the office of the chief of ordnance to organize "all able bodied men under [his] charge, including the clerks, into companies of not less than 60 or more than 80 men. . . . Uniforms to consist of pantaloons and shirt, will be made of blue serge—shirt trimmed with red."[8] The following year, the clerks in the Quartermaster Department in Washington and the major U.S. supply depot of Nashville were organized into battalions called Quartermaster Volunteers. These men received standard Federal uniforms of fatigue blouses, forage caps, and trousers. In both cases, the services of these civilian soldiers would be required. Those in Washington manned the city's defenses in July during Confederate general Jubal Early's advance to the northern defenses of the capital. In December 1864, at the battle of Nashville, the Quartermaster Volunteers were called on to aid in the repulse of the Confederate attack.

General officers in both the Union and Confederate armies wore uniforms that were intended to make them readily recognizable by those who would have a need to approach them or to receive direct commands from them. These marks of superior rank at times also made their position of authority apparent from a distance to enemy sharpshooters or even individual soldiers during close combat. The result is apparent from the number of generals on both sides killed and

*Federal officer's regulation "cloak coat" worn by Col. Ezra Carmen of the 13th New Jersey Volunteers. This opulent, French-inspired overcoat for officers featured a detachable cape that could be used with the overcoat or independently. The wearer's rank was indicated by a varying number of flat, black silk braided knots at the cuff.* TROIANI COLLECTION.

wounded during the war. At the battle of Spotsylvania on May 9, 1864, Gen. John Sedgwick, commanding the Union VI Army Corps, was killed by a Confederate sharpshooter. Two days later, the renowned Confederate cavalry commander J. E. B. Stuart was mortally wounded by a dismounted Federal cavalryman in the fight at Yellow Tavern, Virginia. It is likely that those who fired the fatal shots knew only that the uniforms of their targets were those of enemy commanders.

## UNITED STATES

U.S. Army regulations of 1861were specific in describing the uniform of general officers. Nevertheless, generals were prone to embellish and alter their uniforms. For every rule set down, there is at least one exception.[9]

### *Headgear*

The regulations of 1861 refer to both a hat and cap for generals. The new hat was of a pattern commonly referred to as the Hardee hat. The shape was identical to that prescribed for enlisted men, but the officer's hat was of a finer quality, and rather than a wool hat cord, it had a gold cord with acorn-shaped ends. The insignia on the front of both the hat and cap was a gold embroidered "US" surrounded by a wreath of like material. Several variations of the 1858 forage cap were favored by officers. Generals' caps were embellished with a band of dark blue velvet toward the lower edge. All of this aside, photographic evidence shows that most generals, and indeed most officers, preferred the slouch hat for wear in the field.

### *Coats*

All officers of the U.S. Army were mandated to wear dark blue frock coats. Those ranking above captain were to have a double-breasted coat with two rows of buttons. It was possible to determine at a glance that the wearer was a general by a quick look at the placement of the buttons. A major general was to have nine in each row, placed by threes, while a brigadier general was to have two rows of eight, placed by twos. For generals, the collars and cuffs of the coats were to be of dark blue velvet.

As the war progressed, so did the popularity of the looser-fitting sack coat for undress. Numerous examples of this coat can be found in photographs and museum collections. It was normal for those worn by generals to maintain the style of the frock coat with regard to button placement, with the coat being of a much more relaxed, and therefore more comfortable, cut.

### *Trousers*

Trousers of generals and staff officers were to be dark blue. Generals had no stripe, welt, or cord down the outer seam. Staff officers by regulation had a seam welt of gold color.

### *Insignia of Rank*

Shoulder straps indicated rank with silver stars placed on a dark blue background. A major general commanding an army was allowed to wear straps with three stars, while the normal straps for a man of that rank would have two stars. A brigadier general's straps would have a single star.

### *Sash*

Generals were allowed to wear a buff-colored silk sash, while all other officers wore a sash of crimson silk. When a general was on duty in the field, his sash was often stored with his baggage.

### *Sword Belt*

The belt from which an officer's sword was suspended was worn over the sash. For officers other than generals, the belt and slings were of black leather. Generals were authorized a belt of Russian leather, with three stripes of gold embroidery around the belt and similar embroidery on the slings.

### *Boots*

Although the regulations called only for an ankle, or Jefferson, boot for all officers, most generals, particularly those with the army in the field, wore boots that extended well up the leg. The style and cut of these varied with the taste of the wearer.

## CONFEDERATE STATES

The uniform for Confederate general officers was set down in the regulations established for the Confederate army June 6, 1861, in War Department General Order No. 9. It is inter-

*General's regulation kepi with dark blue velvet band and embroidered staff wreath on the front. This cap belonged to Maj. Gen. Amos B. Eaton, commissary general of the U.S. Army.* TROIANI COLLECTION.

*Regulation Confederate general's coat worn by Thomas Lafayette Rosser. It was captured from his headquarters wagon in the Shenandoah Valley by his West Point classmate and old friend George Armstrong Custer. Custer, ever the prankster, left a note for Rosser saying that in the future, the coats would fit better if made "a trifle shorter in the tails."* WEST POINT MUSEUM.

MARGUERITE MERINGTON, *THE CUSTER STORY* (NEW YORK: DEVIN-ADAIR, 1950), 128.

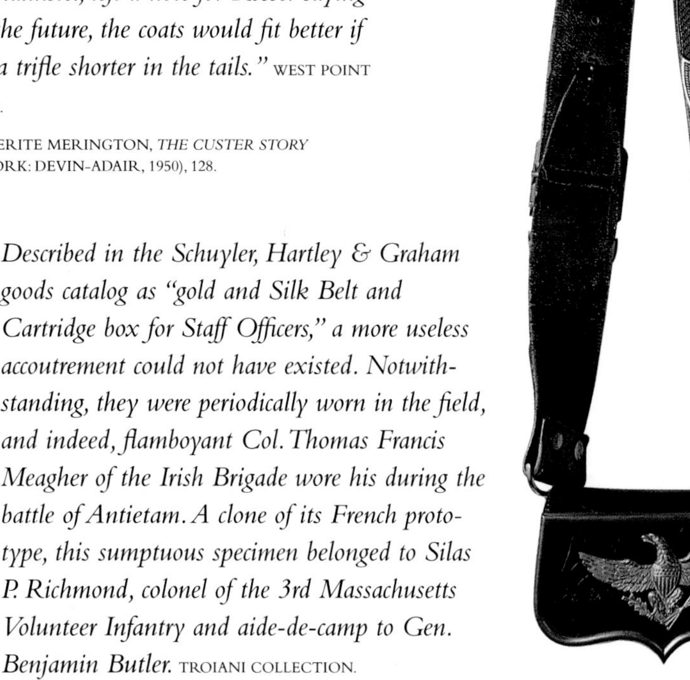

*Described in the Schuyler, Hartley & Graham goods catalog as "gold and Silk Belt and Cartridge box for Staff Officers," a more useless accoutrement could not have existed. Notwithstanding, they were periodically worn in the field, and indeed, flamboyant Col. Thomas Francis Meagher of the Irish Brigade wore his during the battle of Antietam. A clone of its French prototype, this sumptuous specimen belonged to Silas P. Richmond, colonel of the 3rd Massachusetts Volunteer Infantry and aide-de-camp to Gen. Benjamin Butler.* TROIANI COLLECTION.

*Coat worn by Gen. Franklin Gardner, who commanded the Confederate garrison at the siege of Port Hudson in 1863. Aside from the four simple gold chevrons on the sleeves, this coat complies with the regulations for generals. Branch color for general staff often ran the gamut from yellowish buff to pure white.* CONFEDERATE MEMORIAL HALL, CLAUDE LEVET PHOTOGRAPH.

*Confederate officer's belt with interlocking tongue and wreath "CS" brass buckle, worn by Brig. Gen. James Holt Clanton. Elected colonel of the 1st Alabama Cavalry in 1861, Clanton served through the war until wounded at Bluff Spring, Florida, in 1865.*

COLLECTION OF NEW YORK STATE DIVISION OF MILITARY & NAVAL AFFAIRS.

# GENERALS ROBERT E. LEE AND A. P. HILL, GETTYSBURG CAMPAIGN, 1863

The Confederate army that marched north into Pennsylvania in June 1863 was full of confidence and hope. At their head rode a man who, for many, had become a living legend—Robert E. Lee. With him was one of his most trusted lieutenants, Ambrose Powell Hill, commanding the Army of Northern Virginia's newly formed III Corps.

The uniforms worn by these men during the fateful days of this campaign were in a measure indicative of the self-confidence earned by two years of war. Those who saw General Lee invariably commented on his well-groomed, neat appearance. As he had his personal baggage with him, many daily clothing options were at his disposal. One staff officer, G. Moxley Sorrell, observed that Lee rarely carried a sword but always had his binoculars by his side. On the march during the Gettysburg campaign, a soldier of the 17th Mississippi remembered that "he wore a long linen duster which so enveloped his uniform as to make it invisible." The image was further enhanced by a "broad brimmed straw hat, evidently the art of his many lady admirers." An account in the *Harrisburg Daily Patriot* described him as wearing "a heavy overcoat with a large cape and a black felt hat." Another witness quoted in *Gettysburg Sources,* commented that on July 1 he was "plain and neat in his uniform of gray. Hat of gray felt with medium brim and boots fitted neatly coming to his knee with a border of fair leather an inch wide." Lee's unadorned style was perhaps more of a surprise to those who were not close to him, or even in the same army. Hospital Steward Henry F. Miller, Company D, 142nd Pennsylvania Volunteers, while attending wounded behind Confederate lines at Gettysburg on July 3, 1863, wrote in his diary that "General Lee and several of his Staff Officers were in the Hospital this morning. Lee was dressed like a citizen without any side arms." Lt. Col. Arthur J. L. Fremantle commented of Lee at Gettysburg, "he generally wears a long grey jacket, a high black felt hat, and blue trousers tucked into his Wellington boots. I never saw him carry arms; and the only mark of his military rank are the three stars on his collar." Contradicting others about the sword, Gen. John Bell Hood reminisced about Lee on the morning of July 2, "General Lee with his coat buttoned to throat, sabre belt around his waist and field glasses pending at his side walked up and down in the shade of large trees near us." Lt. J. Winder Laird who saw the great commander nearly a year later, remarked in his diary on the general's plain dress and noted that while mounted, "he carried a bush in his

DICK AND M. E. CLOW

*Confederate staff officer's kepi worn by Maj. Hugh Mortimer Nelson while serving on the staff of Gen. Richard Ewell in 1862. Rather than the more customary quatrefoil configuration of gold lace on the crown, three concentric rings of gold tape were used.* TROIANI COLLECTION.

*Staff officer's frock coat worn by Capt. Edward C. Wharton as quartermaster general in Houston, Texas, from 1861 to 1865. As per Confederate States regulations, the coat is faced in buff, the designating color for a staff officer.* GARY HENDERSHOTT.

*Straw cap worn by Confederate general Pierre Gustave Toutant Beauregard during the war. With a black velvet band and stars proclaiming his rank, such a lightweight cap would have proved most acceptable in the heat of the South. Beauregard is recorded as having worn a straw hat at the battle of First Manassas.*
CONFEDERATE MEMORIAL HALL, CLAUDE LEVET PHOTOGRAPH.

hand with which he brushed flies from his horse."

One of Lee's most able subordinates, Gen. Ambrose Powell Hill, has been inaccurately characterized by modern writers as invariably wearing a bright red battle shirt throughout the entire war. It has been noted that General Hill, in the heat of the summer during the 1862 Peninsula campaign, sometimes wore a red and black striped shirt, and when on the march, an unadorned "hunting shirt" without insignia of rank. However, the uniform he wore more often on campaign, "a Fatigue jacket of gray flannel, his felt hat slouched over his noble brow" and hip-length boots, must certainly have seemed more appropriate attire. In the battle that surely lay ahead, the officer's sack coat, with general's rank plainly visible, would forestall any question of authority. This could be particularly important when commanding troops in the newly formed corps—troops who may not yet know him on sight. In addition, unlike General Lee, and perhaps some other Army of Northern Virginia officers, according to British military observer Lt. Col. Arthur J. L. Fremantle, General Hill most always wore his sword.

# BERDAN'S SHARPSHOOTERS

STEVEN ROGERS

In the fall of 1861, a unique regiment of men was being raised throughout several Northern states, from New England to Wisconsin. Those members encamped at Weehawken, New Jersey, were described as having the "complete outfit of the Sharpshooters, which consists of a regulation undress blue jacket and Austrian gray pants, a frock coat and fatigue cap of green cloth, an extra felt hat with leather visor and cape, blankets, shoes underclothes, etc." Col. Hiram Berdan ultimately recruited eighteen companies of proven riflemen for the defense of the Union, and two regiments were formed from them: the 1st and 2nd Regiments of U.S. Sharpshooters. Berdan was a mechanical engineer from New York City who was also one of the top amateur marksmen in the United States prior to the war. He hoped to prove the value of such men in war and to promote his ideas and inventions in the process

It was Berdan's idea to clothe his men in distinctive uniforms. Originally he had even proposed a fringed blue sack

The Confederate States Marine Corps was, in almost all respects, a duplicate of the United States Marine Corps, and its functions were similar. Confederate States marines saw action in nearly every major engagement on the South Atlantic and Gulf coasts. Most of the ironclad rams carried marine detachments, as did all but one of the Confederate commerce raiders. Battle honors included the engagement at Ship Island, Mississippi, July 9, 1861; raid on Santa Rosa Island, Florida, October 8–9, 1861; engagement at Head of the Passes, Louisiana, October 12, 1861; battle of Port Royal, South Carolina, November 7, 1861; bombardment of Fort Pickens, Florida, November 22–24, 1861; battle of Hampton Roads, Virginia, March 8–9, 1862; battle of New Orleans, April 24, 1862; battle of First Drewry's Bluff, May 15, 1862; battle of Fort Sumter, South Carolina, September 8–9, 1863; destruction of USS *Underwriter* off New Berne, North Carolina, February 1, 1864; battle of Second Drewry's Bluff, May 9–16, 1864; capture of USS *Water Witch* in Ossabaw Sound, Georgia, June 3, 1864; battle of Mobile Bay and Fort Gaines, Alabama, August 5–8, 1864; siege of Savannah, December 10–21, 1864; battles of Fort Fisher, North Carolina, December 23–25, 1864, and January 13–15, 1865; battle of Sayler's Creek, Virginia, April 6, 1865; and the siege and battle of Fort Blakely, Alabama, April 2–9, 1865. The last Marines to lay down their arms did so just north of Mobile, Alabama, May 10, 1865.

The arms and accoutrements of Confederate States marines varied from post to post. Long arms included the .69-caliber M1822 musket, altered from flintlock to percussion; the M1861 Springfield .58-caliber rifle musket; the Austrian Lorenz .58-caliber rifle musket; and the prized .577-caliber Enfield rifle musket and rifle.

The field or sea service kit was patterned on those worn in the British service. The cartridge box, cap pouch, and bayonet were intended to be worn on the waist belt, but cartridge boxes were also attached to a separate leather shoulder belt. The knapsack was attached to the waist belt by means of metal slides. A haversack and canteen were slung over the shoulder. All leather components of the kit were black. Plates of undetermined design for the waist belt and cartridge box were a regular issue.

No uniform regulations for the Confederate States Marine Corps have ever been located, and given the many changes that occurred during the course of the war, it is likely that none were ever officially ordered.

In 1861, marine officers lately resigned from the U.S. Marine Corps wore the uniforms from the old service. Newly commissioned officers were obliged to purchase their uniforms. In late 1861, marine officers were wearing gray uniform coats with navy blue collars and cuffs. It appears that the buttons were not standardized. Some officers wore state seal buttons. Army-style rank devices were worn on the collars. Navy blue trousers and kepis rounded out the uniforms. Sidearms were privately purchased or bought from government stores. Later, the sleeve braid worn by army officers was attached to the sleeves of the marine officers' uniform coats, which still had the navy blue collars and cuffs. The navy blue of the trousers was changed to gray, with a navy blue stripe attached to the outside seam. In 1863, Russian-style shoulder knots, identical to those worn by officers of the U.S. Marine Corps, became part of the officers' uniforms.

Uniforms for enlisted Confederate marines initially came from Federal stores captured at Pensacola, Florida. The first regular issue of uniforms, in September and October 1861, consisted of navy blue satinette frock coats and jean trousers. Later, gray uniforms from the C.S. Army Quartermaster Department were issued, adapted to marine usage by the addition of navy blue trim on the cuffs, front, and collar. Gray kepis with a navy blue branch band completed the assemblage.

White linen trousers and overalls were summer issue for the enlisted men, tweed greatcoats were issued during the winter months, and blue fatigue jackets were worn year-round. The uniform button initially had a Roman "M" later replaced by the button of the artillery, with a Roman "A." Evidence exists that a distinguishing mark was worn on the kepi—the hunting horn and Old English "M" of the U.S. Marine Corps.

*Ambulance Corps forage cap with designating green band 1 1/4 inches wide, as authorized in August 1863, superseding the previously 2-inch-wide band.*

TROIANI COLLECTION.

GENERAL ORDER NO. 85, ARMY OF THE POTOMAC.

# UNITED STATES MARINES, 1861–65

In January 1861, the officers and rank and file of the United States Marine Corps numbered less than 2,000, more than half of those attached to warships of the U.S. Navy. Four years later, there were twice that number, serving ashore and afloat in approximately the same proportions.

At the battle of Bull Run on July 21, 1861, a battalion of some 350 marines, most in the service less than six weeks, engaged the Confederates three times in the seesaw fighting on Henry Hill. It was they who made the penetration of Rebel lines while supporting the attack of the 14th Brooklyn.

Aboard ship, marines, manning main or secondary batteries, won praise for their gallantry in action at the battles of New Orleans, April 24, 1861; Hampton Roads, March 8–9, 1862; First Drewry's Bluff, May 15, 1862; Mobile Bay, August 5, 1864; and First Fort Fisher, December 23–25, 1864.

The uniform worn by the U.S. Marines during the Civil War was ordained by the regulations approved by the Navy Department on January 24, 1859. It was not until the middle of 1861, however, that all marines then in service were outfitted with the new uniform.

PRIVATE COLLECTION

The full dress uniform of the marine officer consisted of a dark blue, double-breasted frock coat with a high standing collar with two loops of gold lace on each side. Sky blue trousers were worn during the winter months and white linen during the summer months. (Staff officers and officers serving at sea could wear dark blue trousers.) Rank was indicated by loops of gold lace on the cuff and by army-style devices mounted on gold epaulets. A scarlet welt was sewn into the outer seam of the trousers. Headgear for staff and field-grade officers was a French chapeau with red feather adornment; for company-grade officers, it was a stiff black uniform cap with a gold net pom-pom (later changed to red feathers) at the front top and a gilt U.S. shield with the marine hunting horn emblem and half wreath in the front center.

The undress uniform worn by marine officers consisted of a dark blue, double-breasted frock coat with a short stand-up collar, and the same trousers worn with the full dress uniform. During the summer months, a uniform of white linen, cut in the same fashion, was worn. Rank was indicated by army rank devices mounted on gold Russian shoulder knots with a scarlet underlining. In 1863, an order did away with shoulder knots for field-grade and staff officers, authorizing them to wear army-style shoulder straps. A dark blue cloth fatigue hat (French kepi style) with a band of black silk at the base of the crown was worn with the undress uniform. Slim bands of black ribbed silk were sewn vertically into the sides of the kepi and looped to a quatrefoil knot in the crown. The cap ornament was a gold embroidered bugle on a scarlet background, with a silver, Old English "M" in the center of the ring of the bugle. In summer months, a flat-crowned straw hat with a black band at its base was worn.

Marine officers wore a dark blue fatigue jacket cut short at the waist, with sixteen small marine buttons aligned in the center. The collar was edged with gold lace, and a six-inch inverted V made from this same gold lace adorned each sleeve. Shoulder knots were worn with the fatigue jacket. The overcoat for marine officers was of dark blue cloth, fastened by four frog buttons, with rank indicated by the number of braids in the knot at the cuff of the sleeves.

The 1859 regulations replaced the M1827 Mameluke sword with the M1850 army foot officer's sword. The sword belt was white glazed leather and fastened by the M1851 eagle-wreath sword belt plate. A sash of crimson silk net was worn under the sword belt.

The full dress uniform for enlisted marines consisted of a dark blue, double-breasted frock coat with a high standing collar adorned with a horizontal double row of yellow worsted lace. Brass epaulets were worn on the shoulders, with yellow worsted bullion of varying widths according to rank. Sky blue woolen trousers were worn during the winter months, and white linen during the summer months. The sergeant major, quartermaster sergeant, and all musicians had a scarlet cord sewn into the outer seam of the trouser legs. The dress hat was a dark blue shako, with a brass U.S. shield with the marine ornament in the center, and a half wreath identical to that worn by marine officers. A red pom-pom was worn on the front center of the hat. Noncommissioned officers wore red worsted sashes. Stripes made of yellow lace on a red background were attached, points up, above the elbow on the sleeves of their coats to denote rank. Noncommissioned officers were authorized to wear the M1850 foot officer's sword, but on a sliding frog attached to the waist belt.

The enlisted undress uniform consisted of a fitted frock coat with a scarlet welt sewn into the lower seam of the short standing collar, the same trousers worn with the dress uniform, and a fatigue hat in the style of the French kepi. The marine ornament was worn on the front center of the fatigue hat. In summer months, a white linen cover was worn over the crown of the hat. Rank chevrons in the same style and color as on the dress uniform were worn on the frock coat in the same position.

Dark-blue flannel fatigue sacks, actually shirts that opened halfway down the front, were also issued to enlisted marines. These were later replaced by flannel frock coats with fold-down collars. Rank stripes were worn on both the fatigue shirts and coats.

Enlisted marines wore white cross belts—a cartridge box belt running from the left shoulder to the right hip, and a bayonet belt in opposition. An unadorned oval-shaped plate was worn on the bayonet belt at the intersection of the two belts. A white waist belt with an unadorned belt plate completed the ensemble.

For the winter months, marine enlisted men were issued overcoats of blue-gray wool with stand-up collars, buttons down the front, and detachable capes. Rank stripes were worn on the cuffs rather than in the usual place above the elbow.

One uniform item for both officers and enlisted men, basically unchanged since 1775, was the leather stock worn around the neck.

*Wool felt and leather uniform cap of the U.S. Marines as specified in the regulations of 1859, made by the firm of Bent & Bush in Boston. This cap was seldom, if ever, used in active service, the fatigue cap, or kepi, being preferred.* RAY DARIDA COLLECTION.

# CEMETERY HILL, GETTYSBURG, JULY 1, 1863

Since early morning on July 1, 1863, a fierce and bloody battle had raged in the fields north and west of Gettysburg, Pennsylvania. For the Union army, the brunt of the fighting had fallen on the shoulders of the I and XI Corps of infantry. Now, as the tide of battle turned against them, they fell back through the town to the high ground marked by a towering brick gate that served as the entrance to the community cemetery. During the retreat through the town's streets, regiments became mixed. Now I Corps troops—the 14th Brooklyn Zouaves, wearing the distinctive jackets and red chasseur trousers, 142nd Pennsylvania Bucktails with deer tails adorning their forage caps, as well as other regiments—mingled with XI Corps soldiers, some, in regiments such as the 45th New York, in state-issue jackets. Many from both corps had chosen to fight in the four-button fatigue blouse that had become the favored campaign dress of most of the Federal army. Were it not for the newly issued corps badges—a crescent for the XI Corps and a sphere for the I Corps—there would have been little except the brass regimental numbers on their caps to tell them apart. These men would re-form under the guidance of Gen. Winfield Scott Hancock, commander of the II Corps, who had temporarily taken overall command of the field, as well as Gen. Abner Doubleday in command of the I Corps and Gen. Oliver O. Howard leading the XI Corps. Along with their comrades of the Army of the Potomac, they would emerge the victors in the battle that many believe sealed the fate of the Confederacy.

*Lt. Green Smith, son of famed abolitionist Gerritt Smith, wore this black braided kepi with a staff insignia during the Petersburg campaign of 1864. The crown is emblazoned with a red anchor and cannon badge of the 1st Division, IX Army Corps.* TROIANI COLLECTION.

BOOTH MUSEUM OF WESTERN ART, CARTERSVILLE, GEORGIA

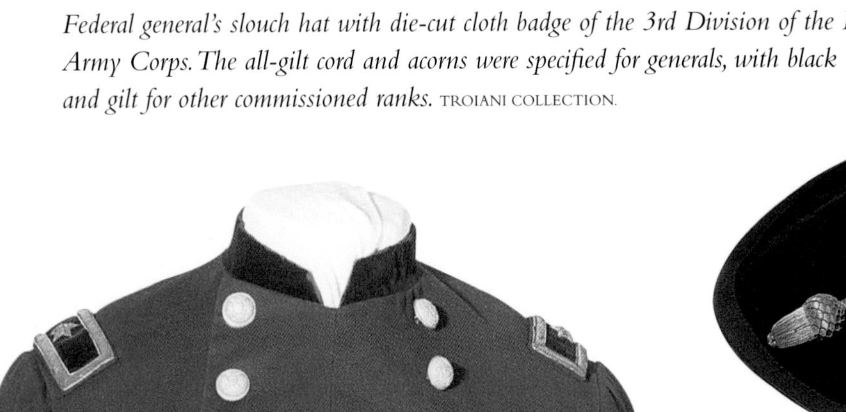

*Federal general's slouch hat with die-cut cloth badge of the 3rd Division of the III Army Corps. The all-gilt cord and acorns were specified for generals, with black and gilt for other commissioned ranks.* TROIANI COLLECTION.

*Regulation Federal brigadier general's coat with dark blue velvet collar and cuffs, and the buttons spaced by pairs. This coat was worn by William S. Tilton, who commanded a brigade in the Wheatfield at Gettysburg and was appointed brevet brigadier general on September 9, 1864.* TROIANI COLLECTION.

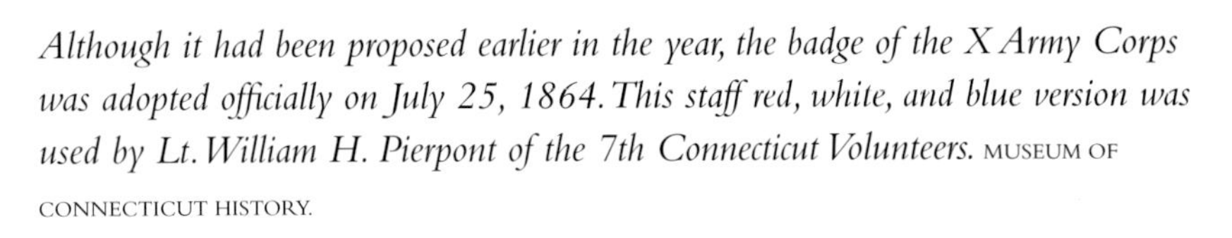

*Although it had been proposed earlier in the year, the badge of the X Army Corps was adopted officially on July 25, 1864. This staff red, white, and blue version was used by Lt. William H. Pierpont of the 7th Connecticut Volunteers.* MUSEUM OF CONNECTICUT HISTORY.

# VETERAN RESERVE CORPS, CORPORAL, 8TH REGIMENT, MARCH 1864

The Veteran Reserve Corps was instituted in April 1863 under its original designation of the Invalid Corps. The idea was an excellent one, in that it provided an opportunity for disabled U.S. soldiers to continue to serve their country even though they were no longer physically able to serve in fighting regiments. The name was changed a year later after a series of jokes, and even a popular song, alleged that this corps was a safe harbor for able-bodied malingerers to escape the danger of battle.

Eventually the Veteran Reserve Corps consisted of twenty-four regiments and a number of independent companies. They served in hospitals, as guards in prisoner-of-war camps, and in other noncombat capacities. In each case, they took the place of able-bodied soldiers, who could then be sent to the armies in the field. The 8th Regiment, along with the 15th, provided guards for Confederate prisoners being held at Camp Douglas, near Chicago.

The uniform of the Veteran Reserve Corps was identical to that of the soldiers of the Federal army serving in the combat forces, except for the jacket. The jacket was adopted in May 1863 and was described by quartermaster regulations as being "of sky blue kersey, with dark blue trimmings, cut like the jacket for cavalry, to come well down on the loins and abdomen." The jacket was actually varied from that issued to the cavalry, being about an inch longer, with shoulder loops and a slit on either side of the bottom edge. Officers were initially intended to be uniformed in a frock coat of sky blue cloth, but few of these were actually worn.

The arms of this corps initially consisted of obsolete weapons that had been turned in by the regiments serving at the front. The 8th Regiment of the Veteran Reserve Corps was first armed with imported muskets. In late 1864, these were replaced by Enfield rifle muskets.

*Elegant set of cased medical staff officer's gilt epaulets bearing the crest "MS" within a wreath. These belonged to Asst. Surgeon Jeptha R. Boulware of the 177th New York Volunteer Infantry.*

COLLECTION OF NEW YORK STATE DIVISION OF MILITARY AND NAVAL AFFAIRS.

WILLIAM RODEN

# UNION ARMY SURGEON, 1861–65

PRIVATE COLLECTION

Medical officers at any level of service, from regiment to army corps, were considered members of the headquarters staff. As such, the uniform of a surgeon in the U.S. Army had little to distinguish it from that of any other staff officer of equivalent rank. Army regulations called for medical officers to wear a sash of "medium or emerald green." The medical officer was also prescribed a sword of a pattern first adopted in 1840. Unlike the heavy-bladed swords carried by line officers, the medical staff sword was not designed for serious work in combat. The blade was 28 inches long but only 3/4 inch wide at the hilt. A shield, cast as part of the guard, had the letters "MS" applied in Old English script.

*Set of false embroidered Smith's patent shoulder straps for a Federal army surgeon, with the regulation Old English letters "MS" in the center. Medical staff officers used the staff background color of black.* TROIANI COLLECTION.

*Hospital steward's frock coat with distinctive sleeve insignia: "a caduceus two inches long, embroidered with yellow silk on each arm above the elbow, in the place indicated for a chevron, the head toward the outer seam of the sleeve." Although not noted in the regulations, all known examples have a green background. Privately purchased examples often tended to be more elaborate, with metallic embroidery on green velvet. Regulations specified crimson piping, but most existing examples of hospital stewards' frock coats are untrimmed.* UNION DRUMMER BOY.

*UNIFORM AND DRESS OF THE UNITED STATES ARMY, 1861* (WASHINGTON, D.C., 1861), 4, 6, 14.

*Federal officer's black enameled waist belt, used by Surgeon Ambrose Pratt of the 22nd Connecticut Volunteers. Note the green stitching, the branch color of the Medical Service.* TROIANI COLLECTION.

This same sword was also carried by officers of the Pay Department. Many medical officers chose to wear shoulder straps that denoted their rank in the usual manner but had the letters "MS," similar to the design found on the sword affixed to the middle of the strap.

As with the medical staffs of all armies in history, the job of the army surgeon in either the Northern or Southern army during the Civil War was to attempt to save lives. Those who traveled with the armies in the field worked under conditions that favored the Grim Reaper. Disease, infection, and small-arms projectiles that shattered bones beyond any hope of repair were facts of daily life for these men.

# CONFEDERATE STATES MEDICAL SERVICE

GREENSBORO HISTORICAL MUSEUM

The Medical Service of the Confederate army was organized and patterned after the same service in the Federal army. Each regiment of infantry and cavalry had its own surgeon and assistant surgeon, who held the rank of major and captain, respectively. Senior ranking regimental surgeons would be assigned to brigade or division level, with added responsibility. All of these nominally were under the overall supervision of the surgeon general. While on paper this may appear to be ideal, in reality the quality of those surgeons who served the fighting men in the field varied as greatly as did the backgrounds of those whose health and well-being depended on them. Doubtless the majority of those who chose to follow the armies had good intentions. Most were given examinations to assure their expertise in their profession. But few were prepared for the challenge that lay before them. In solitary winter encampments, surgeons often were called upon to cope with disease of epidemic proportions. In a single battle, a regimental surgeon could well face more serious injuries than he might see in a decade or more of ordinary domestic practice.

The uniform of the Confederate surgeon was identical to that of line officers, except that the trim of the coat collar, cuffs, and trouser stripe were black, and the letters "MS" were embroidered in gold on the front of the hat or cap. Enlisted men serving with the Medical Service were usually chosen from the ranks of the various regiments and often were members of the regimental band. No distinctive uniform was issued. The nature of the work performed by those men, though not without danger, was attractive for some, who would fall out of ranks during battle to help wounded to the rear, thereby avoiding combat. To counter this, a more regulated Ambulance Corps was formed, to which men who were unfit for battle were assigned. Although not universally adopted, many enlisted men serving with the Medical Service wore red badges on their hats to set them apart from those who might have less than honorable intentions. Lt. Col. Arthur J. L. Fremantle, a British observer with the Army of Northern Virginia, who described Semmes's and Barksdale's Brigades on the march during the Gettysburg campaign, took particular note of the Ambulance Corps: "In the rear of each regiment were from twenty to thirty negro slaves, and a certain number of unarmed men carrying stretchers and wearing in their hats the red badges of the ambulance corps—this an excellent institution, for it prevents unwounded men from falling out on pretense of taking wounded to the rear."

*Badges for corps staff were required to be in the colors of all the divisions of that corps, usually red, white, and blue. Capt. Elliot C. Pierce of the 13th Massachusetts Volunteers wore this cap with a tricolored sphere while commanding the ambulances of the I Corps at Gettysburg.* TROIANI COLLECTION.

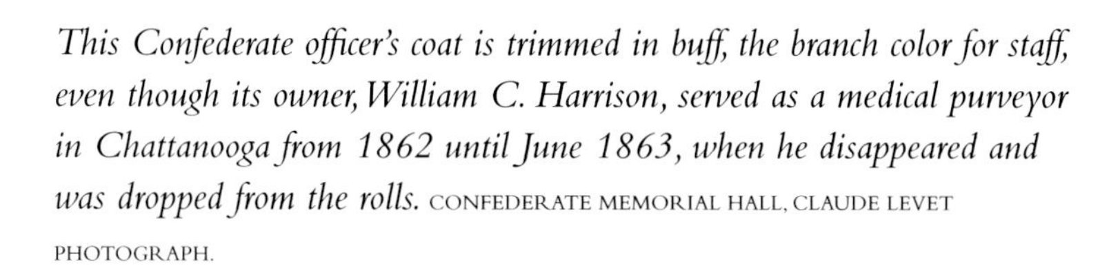

*This Confederate officer's coat is trimmed in buff, the branch color for staff, even though its owner, William C. Harrison, served as a medical purveyor in Chattanooga from 1862 until June 1863, when he disappeared and was dropped from the rolls.* CONFEDERATE MEMORIAL HALL, CLAUDE LEVET PHOTOGRAPH.

*This sober Confederate officer's blue-gray frock coat with Federal eagle staff buttons was worn by Lt. Col. Minor Meriwether, who served as an engineer officer constructing fortifications and railroads throughout the Deep South. Meriwether's wife, Elizabeth, made the coat for him in 1862 by altering a gray civilian coat and had a jeweler cut out the collar stars from silver quarters. He wore it until his surrender with Gen. Richard Taylor in 1865.* M. CUNNINGHAM COLLECTION.

ELIZABETH A. MERIWETHER, *RECOLLECTIONS OF NINETY-TWO YEARS, 1824–1916* (NASHVILLE: TENNESSEE HISTORICAL COMMISSION, 1958).

*The 1858 uniform hat was known by several popular names, including the Hardee hat, the Jeff Davis hat, and even the Fra Diavolo hat, after a character in comic opera. The hat was a modified version of a black felt hat adopted for the two new cavalry regiments in 1855, and it had been authorized for use by all branches in March 1858. This hat was worn by Harlan Page Cobb, who enlisted in the Battalion of U.S. Engineers on November 7, 1861.* WEST POINT MUSEUM.

*Regulation officer's hat insignia of Lt. Charles B. Norton of the 50th New York Engineers, with the prescribed crest of a silver castle encompassed by gold-embroidered palm and laurel leaves.* TROIANI COLLECTION.

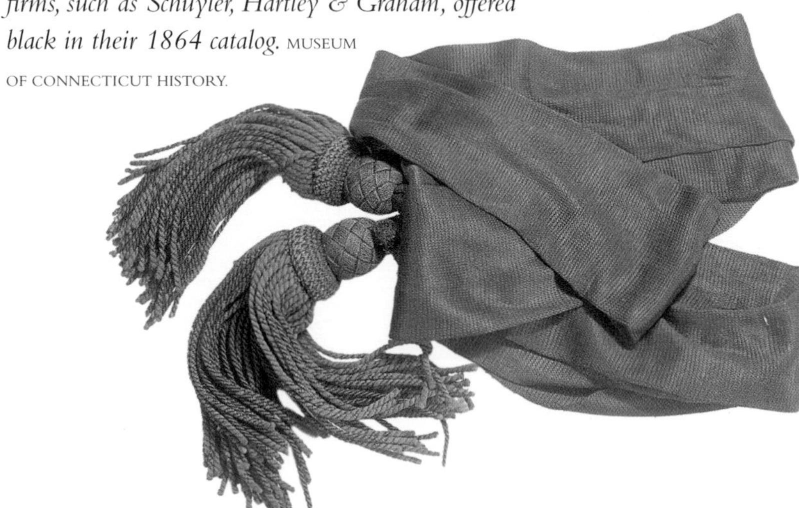

*Black sash for a Federal chaplain. Although regulations specified that all staff officers wear crimson silk net sashes, some private military goods firms, such as Schuyler, Hartley & Graham, offered black in their 1864 catalog.* MUSEUM OF CONNECTICUT HISTORY.

*Fatigue blouse of Maj. Gen. Nathaniel P. Banks, who commanded Union forces at the battles of Cedar Mountain and Port Hudson, and the ill-fated Red River campaign. This is a simplified version of the regulation frock coat, with less chest padding, a lay-down or stand-up collar, exterior breast pocket, and plain cuffs.* TROIANI COLLECTION.

*Painted wooden drum with device of Company C, 1st New York Volunteer Engineers. Like their Regular army counterparts, volunteers often used the traditional castle device.* TROIANI COLLECTION.

# PIONEER, ARMY OF THE CUMBERLAND, 1863

By the spring of 1863, the use of separate detachments of pioneers had been fully established in both the Army of the Potomac in the East and the Army of the Cumberland in the West. These soldiers were selected from the various regiments of a brigade or division and provided with the necessary tools to allow them to clear roads, throw up temporary earthworks, and other like duties. One task that called for quick action and bravery was the rapid throwing up of small breastworks, or lunettes, to protect artillery pieces being placed in position during battle.

As they were detached, and often worked ahead of the moving combat troops, it was necessary for pioneers to wear an identifying insignia that would clearly show that they were officially separated from their various commands. The insignia chosen was one that had been used in the Regular army since its adoption in 1851: crossed axes, each about 3½ inches in height, cut from cloth and sewn to the sleeve of the uniform in the same position as noncommissioned officers' chevrons. These soldiers carried most of their tools—axes, picks, and spades—in leather holders attached to slings. Because these units often were in advance, and thereby exposed, positions, each man was also required to be fully armed and prepared to fight if necessary.

On May 29, 1863, a recently appointed pioneer serving in the 3rd Battalion, Pioneer Brigade, Army of the Cumberland, described his distinctive insignia and what it meant to him: "We wear a badge on our left arm. The badge has two crossed hatchets on it and that badge is the same as a pass. We can go anywhere and the guards don't trouble us any."

The pioneer chevron was worn in the U.S. Army until 1899.

PRIVATE COLLECTION

*Gold-braided kepi worn by Brig. Gen. John Henry Hobart Ward, who commanded a brigade of the III Army Corps at Gettysburg. Though such dress caps were occasionally worn in the field, most officers preferred a less extravagant display and wore unadorned forage caps or slouch hats. Black braid was often preferred over the eye-catching gold.* GARY HENDERSHOTT.

# SERGEANT OF ORDNANCE, 1863

EARL J. COATES

The Ordnance Department was one of the few Special Branches that utilized both officers and enlisted men. This unique department included some of the most highly educated officers and technically competent enlisted men to serve in the U.S. Army. The deference shown to the men of Ordnance was made evident by the fact that throughout the war the enlisted men were allowed to continue to wear the dark blue trousers that by early 1863 had given way to sky blue ones in the rest of the Regular army. A letter dated February 16, 1865, from the Quartermaster General's office notes that "in the last six months . . . 396 pairs [of dark blue trousers ] were for Ordnance soldiers." The same letter mentions the fact that when the change to sky-blue was ordered in 1861, the "large number of dark blue kersey trowsers [*sic*] on hand . . . were by special request, held for issue to Ordnance soldiers."

It should be noted that within the department the rank of sergeant of ordnance differed greatly from that of ordnance sergeant. Army Regulations go to great lengths to explain the unique duties and status of an ordnance sergeant. Those soldiers assigned to duty as ordnance sergeant wore a silk chevron consisting of three stripes surmounted by a large five-pointed star. They were individually posted to every fort and permanent army facility to take charge of any and all ordnance stored there. A sergeant of ordnance worked within and for the Ordnance Department and served at Ordnance facilities, such as Frankfort Arsenal, often in highly skilled positions. The rank of sergeant was usually attained within this department only after long service and proven ability.

Frankfort Arsenal was one of the main facilities for the manufacture and distribution of munitions to the army and also handled the transshipment of some arms received from major manufacturers such as Colt. Located in a northern suburb of Philadelphia the arsenal had been in existence since 1816. Senior enlisted men stationed here and at other Ordnance facilities not only supervised lower ranking enlisted workers but also filled such important positions as machinest and armorer.

Army Regulations provided a diagonal half chevron to be worn on both sleeves of the uniform coat for each five years of faithful service. Service during war was indicated by a light blue narrow stripe on each side of the chevron for artillery, and a red stripe for all other corps. With service stripes indicating over twenty years service, along with the crimson trim on his uniform and flaming bomb insignia on his hat this sergeant of ordnance would command respect on any post occupied by the U.S. Army.

*One of a pair of regulation red silk tape Federal ordnance sergeant's chevrons. Although ordnance sergeants' uniforms were trimmed with crimson, regulations specified that they were "to wear the uniform of the ordnance department with the distinctive badge prescribed for the non-commissioned staff of regiments of artillery."* C. PAUL LOANE COLLECTION.

*REVISED UNITED STATES ARMY REGULATIONS OF 1861* (WASHINGTON, D.C.: GOVERNMENT PRINTING OFFICE, 1863), 27.

# CHAPTER 7: SPECIAL BRANCHES AND GENERAL OFFICERS


**INTRODUCTION**

1. National Archives, Record Group 109, M-331, Compiled Service Records of Confederate General and Staff Officers, file of Gen. Thomas N. Waul.
2. Ibid., Record Group 92, entry 62, vol. 22, 629; "Quartermaster's Manual of 1864" (never published, but planned for publication by Thomas Publications of Gettysburg, Pa.).
3. National Archives, Record Group 94, entry 44, 1863, General Order 158.
4. Francis B. Heitman, *Historical Register and Dictionary of the United States Army,* vol. 2 (Washington, D.C.: Government Printing Office, 1903).
5. *Regulations for the Army of the United States, 1861* (New York: Harper & Brothers, 1861); Frederick P. Todd, *American Military Equipage,* vol. 1, (Providence, R.I.: *Company of Military Historians,* 1974).
6. *Regulations for the Army of the Confederate States* (Richmond, 1861).
7. Ibid.
8. National Archives, Record Group 109, M-331, Compiled Service Records of Confederate General and Staff Officers, file of William S. Downer.
9. *Regulations for the Army of the United States, 1861* (New York: Harper & Brothers, 1861); Editors of Time-Life Books, *Echoes of Glory* (Alexandria, Va.: Time-Life, 1991), Union vol., 98–102, Confederate vol., 104–7.
10. Leslie D. Jensen, *Johnny Reb: The Uniform of the Confederate Army, 1861–1865* (London: Greenhill Books, 1996).
11. Judge C. C. Cummings, "Chancellorsville, May 2, 1863," *Confederate Veteran* 23 (September 1915 ): 405.
12. *Echoes of Glory* Confederate vol.: 160–61.
13. Ibid., 102–7.
14. Ibid.
15. Ibid., 189.
16. William A. Turner, *Even More Confederate Faces* (Orange, Va.: Moss Publications, 1983), 150.

**CONFEDERATE GENERAL BRAXTON BRAGG**

Grady McWhiney, *Braxton Bragg and Confederate Defeat,* vol. 1 (New York: Columbia University Press, 1969), 269–71.

Judith Lee Hallock, *Braxton Bragg and Confederate Defeat,* vol. 2 (Tuscaloosa: University of Alabama Press, 1991), introduction.

Don C. Seitz, *Braxton Bragg: General of the Confederacy* (Columbia, S.C.: The State Company, 1924), 3, 111–12.

Grady McWhiney, "Braxton Bragg: Misplaced General," Cincinatti Civil War Rountable Presentation, n.d.

William Miller, *In Camp and Battle with the Washington Artillery of New Orleans* (Baton Rouge: Louisiana State University Press, 1966), 279.

*Uniform and Dress of the Army of The Confederate States* (Richmond, 1861).

**GENERALS ROBERT E. LEE AND A. P. HILL, GETTYSBURG CAMPAIGN, 1863**

G. Moxley Sorrell, *Recollections of a Confederate Staff Officer,* Wilmington, N.C.: Broadfoot Publishing Co., 1987), 68.

Judge C. C. Cummings, "Chancellorsville, May 2, 1863," *Confederate Veteran* 23 (September 1915): 405.

*Harrisburg Daily Patriot,* July 18, 1863, 1.

James Power Smith, "General Lee at Gettysburg," in *Gettysburg Sources,* compiled by James L. McLean, Jr., and Judy W. McLean (Baltimore: Butternut and Blue, 1986), 36.

Arthur J. L. Fremantle, *Three Months in the Southern States* (Edinburgh: W. Blackwood, 1863), 253–54.

I. Scheibert, "Causes of Lee's Defeat at Gettysburg," *Southern Historical Society Papers,* vol. 5 (Richmond, Va.: Southern Historical Society, 1878), 79.

Unpublished diary of Lt. J. Winder Laird, 2nd Maryland Infantry.

Lt. Gen. A. P. Hill, *Southern Historical Society Papers,* vol. 19 (Richmond, Va.: Southern Historical Society, 1891), 178.

Dr. J. William Jones, "Gen. A. P. Hill," *Confederate Veteran* 1 (August 1893): 234.

Fremantle, *Three Months in the Southern States,* 254.

**BERDAN'S SHARPSHOOTERS**

Charles A. Stevens, *Berdan's United States Sharpshooters in the Army of the Potomac, 1861–1865* (Dayton, Ohio: Morningside Bookshop, 1984).

*New York Tribune,* October 15, 1861, p. 8.

National Archives, Record Group 92, Quartermaster Letters Sent and Received, 629, 472.

**CONFEDERATE STATES MARINE CORPS**

Muster Rolls and Pay Rolls of Marine Detachments of the C.S. Navy, Record Group 45, entry 426, Naval Records Collection of the Office of Naval Records and Library, National Archives, Washington, D.C.

Ralph W. Donnelly, "Battle Honors and Services of Confederate Marines," *United Daughters of the Confederacy Magazine* (March 1960): 31–32.

Quarterly Returns of Ordnance and Ordnance Stores for Companies A, B, C, and E, C.S. Marine Corps, 1862–1864, Subject file of the C.S. Navy, Subject file O, "Operations of Naval Ships and Fleet Units," file OV, "Miscellaneous," Record Group 45, Naval Records Collection of the Office of Naval Records and Library, National Archives, Washington, D.C.

*Official Records of the Union and Confederate Navies in the War of the Rebellion* (Washington, D.C.: U.S. Navy Department, 1894–1922), series 2, vol. 2, 86.

David M. Sullivan, "Robert M. Ramsey, C.S.M.C.," *Military Images* 11, no. 6 (May–June 1981): 3; David M. Sullivan, "Confederate States Marine Corps Officers' Uniforms: Mobile Naval Station, 1863," *Military Collector & Historian* 50, no. 4 (winter 1998): 175–76.

Ralph W. Donnelly, *The Confederate States Marine Corps: The Rebel Leathernecks* (Shippensburg, Pa.: White Mane Publishing Co., 1989), 241.

Quarterly Returns of Clothing, Camp and Garrison Equipage Issued and Received by Companies A, B, C, and E, C.S. Marine Corps, 1861–1864, Subject file of the C.S. Navy, Subject file O, "Operations of Naval Ships and Fleet Units," file OV, "Miscellaneous," Record Group 45, Naval Records Collection of the Office of Naval Records and Library, National Archives, Washington, D.C.

Ralph W. Donnelly, "More on Confederate Marine Uniforms," *Military Collector & Historian* 31, no. 4 (winter 1979): 170–71; verbal description of the uniform worn by Pvt. Samuel Curtis, CSMC, preserved by his family since 1865, and now in the hands of a descendant.

**UNITED STATES MARINES, 1861–65**

David M. Sullivan, "The Marine Battalion at Bull Run: Emending the Record," *Leatherneck* (February 2002): 42–49.

Orders issued by John Harris, colonel, commandant, Headquarters, Marine Corps, Washington, D.C., April 27, 1861: "Regulations for the Field Officers of the Corps," Washington, D.C., July 15, 1863, entry 4, "Letters Sent: August 1798–June 1801; March 1804–February 1884," Record Group 127, *Records of the U.S. Marine Corps,* National Archives, Washington, D.C.

Maj. C. G. McCawley, USMC, Maj. George R. Graham, USMC, and 1st Lt. Norval L. Nokes, USMC (members of a Board of Survey) to Col. Jacob Zeilen, Commandant, U.S. Marine Corps, Marine Barracks, Washington, July 20, 1864, entry 42, " Letters Received: 1818–1915," Record Group 127, National Archives.

*Regulations for the Uniform and Dress of the Marine Corps of the United States, October 1859, from the Original Text and Drawings in the Quarter Master's Department* (Philadelphia: Charles Desilver, 1859).

**VETERAN RESERVE CORPS, CORPORAL, 8TH REGIMENT, MARCH 1864**

Frederick H. Dyer, *A Compendium of the War of the Rebellion* (New York: Thomas Yoseloff, 1959), 3:1741.

"Quartermaster's Manual of 1864" (never published, but planned for publication by Thomas Publications of Gettysburg, Pa.).

**UNION ARMY SURGEON, 1861-65**

*Regulations for the Army of the United States, 1861* (New York: Harper & Brothers, 1861).

Harold L. Peterson, *The American Sword, 1775–1945* (Philadelphia: Ray Riling Arms Books, 1970).

**CONFEDERATE STATES MEDICAL SERVICE**

Deering J. Roberts, M.D., C.S. Army surgeon, *Confederate Medical Department,* www. Civilwarhome.com.

Frederick P. Todd, *American Military Equipage* (Providence, R.I.: Company of Military Historians, 1977), 2:493.

Lt. Col. Arthur J. L. Fremantle, *Three Months in the Southern States* (Edinburgh: W. Blackwood, 1863).

**PIONEER, ARMY OF THE CUMBERLAND, 1863**

National Archives, Record Group 94, entry 12, Letters Received, Adjutant General's Office, 1851.

Letter written by Isaac Raub, copy in Troiani Collection.

William K. Emerson, *Chevrons: An Illustrated History* (Washington, D.C.: Smithsonian Institution Press, 1983).

**SERGEANT OF ORDNANCE, 1863**

National Archives, Record Group 92, entry 2177, Letters Received by the Philadelphia Depot Quartermaster.

*Regulations for the Army of the United States* (New York: Harper & Brothers, 1861), article XIV, paragraphs 127–39.

James J. Farley, *Making Arms in the Machine Age: Philadelphia's Frankfort Arsenal, 1816–1870* (University Park, Pa.: Pennsylvania State University Press, 1994).

# APPENDIX

## Institutions Holding Significant Collections of Civil War Uniforms and Relics

**CONFEDERATE MUSEUM OF NEW ORLEANS**
Second largest collection of Confederate relics extant. Only a block from the D-Day Museum, a must-visit when in New Orleans. Very helpful and dedicated volunteer staff.

929 Camp Street
New Orleans, LA 70130
504-523-4522
*www.confederatemuseum.com*

**BOOTH WESTERN ART MUSEUM**
Under construction in downtown Cartersville, Georgia. Scheduled to open in late 2002. Will contain world's largest collection of Don Troiani battle paintings.

*www.boothmuseum.org*

**WEST POINT MUSEUM**
Superb collection of Civil War and other uniforms and artifacts especially related to West Point graduates. Expert and helpful staff.

U.S. Military Academy
West Point, NY 10996
845-938-3671
*www.usma.edu/museum*

**CHARLESTON MUSEUM**
Interesting collection of South Carolina–related Confederate uniforms and other items.

360 Meeting Street
Charleston, SC 29403
843-722-2996
*www.charlestonmuseum.com*

**PAMPLIN HISTORICAL PARK AND MUSEUM OF THE CIVIL WAR SOLDIER**
Well-displayed collection of Civil War artifacts and original earthworks on the Petersburg battlefield.

6125 Boydton Plank Road
Petersburg, VA 23803
877-PAMPLIN (toll free)
804-861-2408
*www.pamplinpark.org*

**NATIONAL CIVIL WAR MUSEUM**
Large Civil War collection in an expansive, state-of-the-art museum. Several original Don Troiani battle paintings.

1 Lincoln Circle at Reservoir Park
Harrisburg, PA 17103
717-260-1861
*www.nationalcivilwarmuseum.com*

**GETTYSBURG MUSEUM OF THE CIVIL WAR**
One of the greatest Civil War collections, especially strong on firearms, uniforms, artillery, and Gettysburg-related relics.

Gettysburg National Military Park Visitor Center
97 Taneytown Road
Gettysburg, PA 17325
717-334-1124
*www.nps.gov/gett*

**GREENSBORO HISTORICAL MUSEUM**
Dr. John Murphy collection of Confederate firearms and several original Troiani paintings.

130 Summit Avenue
Greensboro, NC 27401
336-373-2043
*www.greensborohistory.org*

**UNITED DAUGHTERS OF THE CONFEDERACY MUSEUM**

Excellent collection of Confederate uniforms, flags, and other memorabilia.

328 North Boulevard
Richmond, VA 23220-4057
804-355-1636
*www.hqudc.org*

**MUSEUM OF THE CONFEDERACY**

Largest collection of Confederate memorabilia in the world.

1201 East Clay Street
Richmond, VA 23219
804-649-1861
*www.moc.org*

**SMITHSONIAN MUSEUM OF AMERICAN HISTORY**

The best collection of Federal (and many Confederate) Civil War uniforms extant. Unfortunately, little to none is on display, and access for researchers can be frustrating.

14th Street and Constitution Avenue, N.W.
SI Building, Room 153
Washington, DC 20560-0010
202-357-2700
*www.americanhistory.si.edu*

**VIRGINIA HISTORICAL SOCIETY**

Large collection of Virginia Confederate military items.

428 North Boulevard
Richmond, VA 23220
804-358-4901
*www.vahistorical.org*

**WHITE OAK MUSEUM**

Astonishing hoard of excavated Civil War relics displayed with reconstructed soldiers' winter huts.

985 White Oak Road
Falmouth, VA 22405
540-371-4234
*http://mywebpage.netscape.com/whiteoakmuseum*

**CIVIL WAR LIBRARY AND MUSEUM**

Outstanding collection of Union Civil War memorabilia particularly relating to members of the Military Order of the Loyal Legion of the United States.

1805 Pine Street
Philadelphia, PA 19103
215-735-8196
*www.netreach.net/~cwlm/*

# RECOMMENDED READING


Bazelon, Bruce S., and William F. McGuinn. *Directory of American Military Goods Dealers and Makers, 1785–1915.* Manassass, Va.: privately printed, 1990.

Coates, Earl J., and James L. Kochan. *Don Troiani's Soldiers in America.* Mechanicsburg, Pa.: Stackpole Books, 1998.

Editors of Time-Life Books. *Echoes of Glory.* 3 vols. Alexandria, Va.: Time-Life, 1991.

Field, Ron. *American Civil War Confederate Army.* London: Brassey's, 1996.

Garofalo, Robert, and Mark Elrod. *A Pictorial History of Civil War Era Musical Instruments and Military Bands.* Charleston, W.V.: Pictorial Histories Publishing Company, 1985.

Gladstone, William A. *United States Colored Troops.* Gettysburg, Pa.: Thomas Publications, 1990.

Howell, Edgar M. *United States Army Headgear.* Washington, D.C.: Government Printing Office, n.d.

Jensen, Les. *A Catalogue of Uniforms in the Museum of the Confederacy.* Richmond, Va.: Museum of the Confederacy, 2000.

Knopp, Ken R. *Confederate Saddles and Horse Equipment.* Orange, Va.: Moss Publications, 2000.

Langellier, John P. *Army Blue: The Uniform of Uncle Sam's Regulars, 1848–1873.* Atglen, Pa.: Schiffer Military Books, 1998.

Langellier, John P., and C. Paul Loane. *U.S. Army Headgear, 1812–1872.* Atglen, Pa.: Schiffer Publishing, 2002.

McAfee, Michael J. *Zouaves: The First and the Bravest.* Gettysburg, Pa.: Thomas Publications, 1991.

McAfee, Michael J., and John P. Langellier. *Billy Yank: The Uniform of the Union Army, 1861–1865.* London: Greenhill Books, 1996.

Mullinax, Steve E. *Confederate Belt Buckles and Plates.* Expanded edition. Alexandria, Va.: O'Donnell Publications, 1999.

O'Donnell, Michael J., and J. Duncan Campbell. *American Military Beltplates.* Alexandria, Va.: O'Donnell Publications, 1996.

Pohanka, Brian. *Don Troiani's Civil War.* Mechanicsburg, Pa.: Stackpole Books, 1995.

*Revised Regulations for the Army of the United States, 1861.* (Philadelphia: George W. Childs, 1862.)

*Schuyler, Hartley, and Graham Illustrated Catalog of Civil War Military Goods.* Mineola, N.Y.: Dover Publications, 1985. (Reprint of original 1864 catalog.)

Sylvia, Stephen W., and Michael J. O'Donnell. *Civil War Canteens.* Orange, Va.: Moss Publications, 1990.

Tice, Warren K. *Uniform Buttons of the United States, 1776–1865.* Gettysburg, Pa.: Thomas Publications, 1997.

Todd, Frederick P. *American Military Equipage.* Providence, R.I.: Company of Military Historians, 1974.

Winey, Michael J. *Union Army Uniforms at Gettysburg.* Gettysburg, Pa.: Thomas Publications, 1998.

Woshner, Mike. *India Rubber and Gutta-Percha in the Civil War Era.* Alexandria, Va.: O'Donnell Publications, 1999.

CALDWELL COUNTY PUBLIC LIBRARY
5 0669 01084433 1

WITHDRAWN